BETWEEN WYOMINGS

A TNP Production

Written And Survived By
Ken Mansfield

Marshall Terrill Creative Director

Joel Miller Executive Producer

Kristen Parrish & Heather Skelton Content Editors

Kristen Vasgaard Cover Art

Curt Harding Publicist

David Schroeder Best Boy/Gaffer/Key Grip

Gabe Wicks Light & Sound

Bucky Rosenbaum Stunts & High Wire Maneuvers

THOMAS NELSON
Since 1798

NASHVILLE   DALLAS   MEXICO CITY   RIO DE JANEIRO   BEIJING

Ali,

I edited this beautiful book and I think it will resonate with you.

Enjoy!

Starring

Andy Williams	Ken Mansfield
Bill Gaither	Linda Ronstadt
Bobbie Gentry	Mrs. Elva Miller
Brian Wilson	Neil Young
Captain Midnight	Paul Mc Cartney
Chief Joseph	Phil Spector
Connie Mansfield	Quicksilver Messenger Service
Cowboy Clements	Ray Charles
David Cassidy	Ringo Starr
David Geffen	Robin Leach
Dolly Parton	Ron Kass
Don Ho	Roy Orbison
Four Freshmen	The Band
Gene Clark	The Deep Six
George Harrison	The Godfather
Geronimo	The Holy Spirit
Glen Campbell	The Seekers
God	Tompall Glaser
Graham Nash	Town Criers
Guru Raj Ananda Yogi	Waylon Jennings
Jessi Colter	Whitney Houston
Jesus	Willie Nelson
John Lennon	Yoko Ono

And Introducing—Moses The Van

Published in Nashville, Tennessee, by Thomas Nelson. Thomas Nelson is a registered trademark of Thomas Nelson, Inc.

Published in association with Rosenbaum & Associates Literary Agency, Brentwood, Tennessee

Thomas Nelson, Inc., titles may be purchased in bulk for educational, business, fund-raising, or sales promotional use. For information, please e-mail SpecialMarkets@ThomasNelson.com.

ISBN: 978-1-59555-165-8

Printed in the United States of America

09 10 11 12 13 QW 5 4 3 2 1

to Connie...

...now I am found

THREE CHORDS AND
AN ATTITUDE

B etween Wyomings is factual invention—metaphorical musings about real-life occurrences. Only the decadence has been changed to protect my innocence.

After thirty years in the entertainment business, I sometimes confuse or countercreate times and places—some say it has to do with rock and roll and remaining brain cells. As the old saying goes, "If you remember the '60s, then there's a real good chance you weren't there!"

I admit that I write like a Christian on acid, but to be honest, the whole entertainment industry is built on induced fantasy and even less certainty. Long periods of being submerged within its abstraction does leave a person with the mind-bends when finally floating up from its depths. Those of us who survive this immersion find our salvation even more precious than some believers— because we have paid for it so dearly. It's not because we are more saved or more loved; it just might be because once we emerge from that degenerate mire, we are startled by the purity we experience through His unconditional love, mercy, and grace. The contrast is rather extreme.

Because I have indulged the whimsical aspect of my character in telling my story, I feel I have an obligation to carefully preserve the integrity of the actual events described herein. The happenings and people are authentic, but the settings and side trips have sometimes been rearranged to make room for my imagination.

Between Wyomings is about searching the geography of my life and homeland—my past and my passions—the events, tragedies, blessings, discouragements, gifts, and betrayals that befell me along the way. The fact that the setting is the entertainment industry tends to magnify the perceptions. Knowing that a real search needs momentum, I decided to go back down the physical roads of my past so that I could catch up with the mystery of what I have become today. But by going *there*, I found that *where* was never the question, and that the *why* things turn out the way they do was forever a question that couldn't be answered in my present state of understanding.

It was the *Who* that it all fell down around, was raised up to, and leveled out on. Not the who of self, which had become the attraction all those years, but *the* Who—the Who that always has been, is now, and ever shall be.

As an old Jewish friend would say, "So who knew?"

How right he was—*Who* knew!

Grab your Guccis and hang on. Together we shall roll out onto the open road as I retrace in mind and milestones the hard-rock stirrings of the soul and classic events of my time in the most fascinating "biz" on earth.

KEN MANSFIELD
Author
Hopeless Romantic
Three Chords and an Attitude
Humble Servant of the Living Lord

The revelation of GOD is whole
and pulls our lives together.
The signposts of GOD are clear
and point out the right road
The life-maps of GOD are right,
showing the way to joy.
The directions of GOD are plain
and easy on the eyes.

PSALM 19:7–8
THE MESSAGE

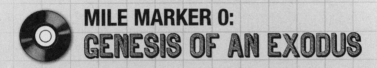

MILE MARKER 0:
GENESIS OF AN EXODUS

Between Dawn and Dusk

I seem to be working
and thinking.
But I am really running
through a meadow.

I seem to be a canyon with love
and happiness filling me.
But I am really a mountain
reaching up for more.

I seem to be a sparkling smooth running brook
cool and refreshing.
But I'm really dawn and dusk joined together
to make the stars come out.

I seem to be like the moon
floating along lazy like.
But really I am a cricket
trying not to be eaten tonight.

It's California, and it's 2009.

I have carried this poem with me since I was nine years old. The author, a twelve-year-old Navajo Indian lad, remains anonymous.

I never knew why, but I've always had a deep sense that someday I would be required to penetrate its meaning.

I examine the piece of paper, noticing for the first time that I have never trimmed its edges. As a young boy I had simply torn it out of a magazine and put it in my first official billfold. This sensitive essay has been wadded, stuffed, and beaten up over the years to the point that it is on the verge of disintegrating. As I hold it in my cupped hands, I raise it to my eyes almost in reverence and realize it is the single touchable constant in my life. It also looks a lot like how I feel at this moment—ragged around the edges.

As I read it I am once again taken back in time to the feeling I would get in my youth when a Camas prairie rainstorm appeared on the distant Idaho horizon. I remember a certain smell that preceded its moving reality into my life. I hadn't felt the drops yet, and didn't know whether I was going to be drenched or refreshed, but that was never the point. Something was coming my way both familiar and mysterious, and it possessed the sweet dichotomy of being both welcome and threatening in its unknown offering.

This native poem is a long-ago kind of thing, but it now tells me that the ending time of my life is crowding the beginnings of my days, and I am left with a long space in between that needs definition. I now realize that I have spent my whole life peering over a hazy edge, an ethereal inch away from understanding what was happening, what had just happened, what was going to happen next, and now—most important—what the sum of it all had been about.

In looking back I have this sense I stumbled through my life with the music of my circumstances blaring so loudly that I missed the meaning of the lyrics. The years flew by at such a cacophonic clip that a lot of incredible things happened where I didn't take the time to perceive the enchantment. It was like I had gone from conception to coda with no verse, chorus, or bridge in between. When I say this I am not talking about the people, places, and performances I experienced during those fascinating decades in the guts and glee of the entertainment industry—they are what they were, and there is a definitive edge that I can recapture.

The part that is less discernible is where I was in all this as it was going down.

Idaho, I Don't Know,
I Think I'll Take
My Bananas and Go

It's Idaho, and it's 1955.

I didn't like where I grew up, that small, smelly town in northern Idaho. I believe this perception had more to do with me than the town. Lewiston wasn't always smelly. In fact, when we first moved there it smelled downright nice. When I was thirteen years old, a pulp mill joined the saw-mill on the river. The sweet scent of fresh-cut white pine was replaced by a yellow, rotten, eggish aromatic mist that filled the sky and eventually found refuge inside our cars, clothes, homes, and senses.

It is strange to write something that would appear unfavorable about my hometown because all that I am today seems to have come out of that place. Growing up, I hated school, and my hormones hurt. I didn't seem to belong, and yet it was my world and nothing was more important. Don't get me wrong—I had everything that goes with the freedom of youth and was in the heat of the fray at all times. It's just that those teen years are tough years for anyone at any time and in any place. It was especially confusing to me because I had this feeling that I belonged somewhere else. Somehow I made it work, growing up there in the Northwest, but mentally I felt like nothing fit—I couldn't get up to speed without something always flapping in the breeze.

I would be walking down a dusty Nez Perce county road, looking for Hollywood and Vine. I had the sound of cowboys and dirt in my ears, and what I really wanted was to rock out with the Tinseltown sun in my star-glazed eyes. I ate taters three times a day, and I longed for vichyssoise even though I had no idea it was just cold potato soup. I liked the departure counter at the railway station better than I liked the local gas station. I liked the paved road out of town better than I liked the dirt lane that led to my house. I liked the music on the radio station from far away much better than I liked the songs of my church choir. I liked what I wanted . . . I liked what I didn't have . . . I liked elsewhere.

They called that remote area in the Idaho panhandle the "Banana Belt"—supposedly because of the reasonably moderate weather we experienced, considering we were only 220 miles south of the Canadian border. I find it ironic that anyplace that could have 10-degree-below weather in the winter could be called anything suggesting bananas. I guess it was a matter of comparison at best. I didn't like the cold, I didn't think the food was that great, and I wanted to talk like the people I would listen to on the radio programs that emanated from romantic sounding places like Van Nuys, California. I was petrified at the possibility that I would someday find myself old and still living far away from these exciting locations.

I turned seventeen, graduated from high school, and joined the navy just so I could get out of town. I heard their boot camp was in San Diego, California, and that meant I was going to be living only a hundred or so miles from LA and Hollywood.

I now realize it has always been about the miles—about the spaces, the dreams, the people, and the distances in between.

Therefore here's my decision (kind of a cowboy way of going about things): I need a long period of separation from the stuff around me. I need a relative quiet space to reflect and gather some sense of order. Because I spent most of my life "on the road," as is the case with most people in the entertainment business, I have decided that in order to be comfortable in sorting things out, I need a sense of movement beneath me.

So, like the Lone Ranger, I, too, shall become a contradiction in terms and go about my travels not alone. My Tonto will be my wife, Connie, who for over two decades has been my faithful companion in life and adventure.

The main difference between us and the cowboy and his Indian sidekick is that we shall sleep together.

For some odd reason I am avoiding thinking through this too clearly. Thinking is what you have to do to deal with the "man things." This is a "God thing." As I find my success with man lessening, I find my faith in God increasing. I find I am being separated from fun things and becoming immersed in joyful things—His goodness, mercy, and unfailing love. With these soul goodies, plus a mixed bag of T-shirts, reversible sweats, two pairs of blue jeans, a white shirt, my favorite tie, and an all-purpose suit for the churches on the way, I am prepared to head out onto the back roads in search of something. Connie and I have spent weeks loading up our personal iPods with our favorite music, anticipating that they will provide needed separation from each other in the months ahead. Hers is green to match her eyes—mine is black.

I am expecting nothing and looking forward to everything in between.

I am becoming an emotional martini—stirred but not shaken.

Join me at that midpoint between the mind and the heart, and wear heavy shoes, because we are going to have to step over a lot of junk.

Let's not define things too clearly or they will lose their mystery and magic. When I was a child, they turned the lights up in the theater after the movie, and the fantasy was blown away when my eyes adjusted to the light and I saw the sticky floor, torn seatbacks, and scuffed walls. Let's not do that. Let's keep the lights down low and the music cranked up.

Poetically and romantically I know I need to give my van an identity. (I don't want to go "through the desert on a van with no name.") I think about it for a while and decide that maybe Moses would be a good name. Yeah, I like that. Moses is the perfect name because together in faith we will head out across this beautiful land of promise I was blessed to be born in, and hopefully I'll end up in a better place.

It's time to go.

If it looks like I am getting smaller, it's because I'm leavin'!

MILE MARKER # 1
THE JOURNEY BEGINS

Toward Tomales

I drive out of our little town of Bodega Bay on the northern California coast to the cliffs at Bodega Head and say good-bye to memories of the shattering sunsets and visions of the migrating whales. I then direct my faltering momentum up the coast a couple of miles and climb the steep Coleman Valley Road to a favorite prayer spot on the hillside.

Once there, I sit on an ancient Pomo Indian rock outcropping. From that magnificent vantage point, I gaze out at the miles of rugged coastline that holds tight to the turbulent shores of the Pacific Ocean. After a long look, a relentless wind drives me away from this familiar perch and I head back to town. As I drive through this odd fishing village, I can't look at the handful of stores and shops that line Coast Highway One. I don't want to see the people who have filled my life for almost a decade outlined in the windows. I drive to the south end of town where I take one last walk on Doran Beach. I want one final kneel on my knees into the timeless sand that has cradled my hurt, confessions, and jubilation for a million amazing moments of silent meditation. After telling the sea, the seals, and the sea-birds that I'm leaving, I make my way to the van that will carry me away from where I thought God had placed me for good.

As I pull away from the dunes, I have that same sense of leaving home that I did when I was seventeen. Once again I find myself excited and filled with rapturous anticipation. Back then I was going away—now I have a feeling that not only am I going away, but that in some odd way I am com-ing back. To what, I don't know.

I sense this unexpected euphoria may have something to do with the half century that has passed between these two events. Back then I didn't know any better, which had an inherent freedom in its naiveté. Now it is better that I don't know what lies ahead so I won't become imprisoned by the disenchantment of past misadventures. If I didn't trust God with all my being, I think the uncertainty of what lies ahead would have me freaking out right now. But this is a heart tug, not a mind-set. The feeling of adventure is stirring inside so loud I can't hear myself think. I know it may sound like I am being forced from these vibrant shores, but that's not what it is—this feeling I have borders on being a "now or never" situation. It was Christmas 1996 when I was diagnosed with a rare, incurable cancer and given the news that I had one to three years to live. I was also informed that because it was so rare, there was currently no research on it, leaving me with little room for hope. I figure now, because it is over a decade later, I have used up more than most of those years, so maybe I will just cop out to that old news as my current reason for this journey.

As I drive back toward town, I look out the window and realize deep down that the distance between the ocean-hugging Highway One and the pounding surf yards away is honestly about as far away from that coastline as I ever want to be. But at the same time there is an adventure blowing in the wind that rushes by the window on the inland side of Moses. Trusting in the long friendship I have with this incredible place, I feel a sense of security in knowing that it will always be right here for me when I come back. To put an honorable handshake to the commitment I am making to this puzzling excursion, I stick my arm out the window and clasp the wind in my palm, holding on to it all the way into town.

Suddenly the pieces of this inner juggling fall to the ground, and it is at this moment I truly understand what is happening. My reason for leaving all this serenity *is* very much like leaving home for the first time. I remember how easy it would have been to stay there, but I remember even more clearly the desire to explore other worlds. I believe that man has three stages in life: (1) boy, (2) man, and (3) boy. I have the same feeling I did as a young man, drinking wildly from a strange maniacal brew of trepidation and anticipation. I need to leave another safe harbor because I know something is out there to discover. It has been many years since I was "out there," and I have forgotten what the allure was. As I get older I have a hard time remembering all those exciting things I discovered in my early ramblings. Now I am being called forth not for discovery, but for rediscovery.

I pull up to the local grocery store, get out, and gallantly hold the door open for my wife, Connie. She has just gathered some last-minute supplies for the maiden portion of our journey. I shut her door, run around to my side, and jump in. We turn away from the bay, heading south toward the tiny town of Tomales and Tomales Bay beyond. Connie has dropped her seat back a bit and is resting her head on the headrest with her eyes closed. She could be sleeping by the way she is sitting there, but I get the sense she is simply hanging on. I believe leaving is different for a woman who has that inborn sense of nesting.

We leave the ocean behind for a while and head south, retracing a favorite, familiar trail. Suddenly the reality of this move sets in for both of us in the silence. We have just committed to spending the next year roaming the highways and back roads of our homeland. I can see our entire dwelling in the rearview mirror—it is an odd sensation, knowing we have committed the next few months to living in a van in a space smaller than the bathroom of the house we just left. I retreat inside my thoughts for these first few miles. Connie knows me well enough by now to instinctively understand when I have mentally left the planet. Although I can't imagine two people being any closer than we already are, I have a premonition that we are really going to get to know each other over the next few months and miles.

It's not long before we are skirting the edges of Tomales Bay. Everything gets incredibly serene in this place that was created by monstrous upheaval and the thunderous watery intrusion that opened the land into a bay. You can see it on the California map just north of San Francisco. It looks like God fashioned the bay by pulling a piece of the Pacific Coast away from the continent to make a crack where the waters could come in. Out of habit we roll down the windows when we glide through the eucalyptus groves that gather at sheltered spots along the water's edge. Sea air and tree scents intermingle, and for the moment, everything is OK.

After barely an hour we are driving down the main street in a "stuck in the '60s" town called Point Reyes Station. Beads and crystals fill the shop windows, while faded tie-dyed T-shirts and bell-bottom trousers cling to the perpetually long-hair hippydom inhabitants who hang about the comfortable streets. We both came out of this era, so we venture ahead without stopping, for fear we may forget our quest if we get too involved in what we see. Simultaneously we look over at each other, place our thumb and index finger against our lips, and make a loud sucking sound like we were taking a hit from a joint. We do this the full length of the main street, rolling our eyes back at each other and leaning out the window with our long exhales.

From Point Reyes Station we continue south and come to the turnoff that leads to the time-challenged, coastal "love in" town of Bolinas. Bolinas makes Point Reyes look like *Futurama*. I'll bet they even put sprouts in their martinis. There is no sign on Highway One to mark the turnoff to Bolinas because the locals drive out to the road and tear every new one down. They really don't care if outsiders visit their little hamlet where the road and advancing civilization dead-ends at the edge of the Pacific. We pull into Stinson Beach less than two hours into our yearlong journey. Our plan is to sleep in the van most of the time and to spend occasional nights in cheap motels for showers and sanity breaks.

Even though we had only driven a few miles, there was little question we had traveled beyond our emotional limits. Exhausted and drained, we decided it was time to make camp before the sun left the day.

EIGHT MILES HIGH

I admit that part of the plan was to get back to the basics, sleep in the van, steam some veggies on our single burner camp stove, and grill local offerings outside the van's passenger side sliding door. I now confess that our first official meal was taken last night on the patio of a trendy coastal grille. For overnight accommodations, we found an ocean-side condo where the sunset seemed stuck to the edge of the horizon.

It will get rougher as we go, I am sure.

The next morning, after croissants and coffees, we head out of Stinson Beach through a light, silver-toned fog onto Shoreline Highway One. The narrow two lanes quickly climb up the coastal bluffs. They hug the edge of dramatic cliffs on their way into the backside of Marin County, Mill Valley, and the eventual 101 South onto the Golden Gate Bridge into San Francisco. Eight miles out of town we find ourselves clinging to the cliffs and as high up as I want to get in a moving vehicle. Our iPods plug into the dash, and I am already dominating our soundspace with mine set in "shuffle" mode—bouncing between Erik Satie and J.J. Cale. Suddenly, the Byrds' "Eight Miles High" comes wafting out of the state-of-the-art sound system in the van. A bit cosmic, wouldn't you say?

While Connie cringes against the locked door, refusing to look out and down at the sheer drop into the ocean far below, I get lost in the song and the memory of one of my dearest friends from the rock-and-roll days, Gene Clark. Not only was Gene a founding member of the Byrds, he was the author and lead singer on the song now filling my mind. I begin drifting back.

▨ ▨ ▨

In 1975, I had just finished a marathon recording stint in Nashville. Upon returning to LA, I was so burned out that I couldn't sleep in what was becoming a very unfamiliar bed at home. I left LA the very next morning and headed north into the comforting countryside of rural California. In those days there were no cell phones, text messages, iPhones, or wireless laptops, so the best place to get away was in your car and the open road. I was spaced-out from the sessions and the doings that surrounded them, and I simply needed some open space.

After two days of intentional wandering, I crash-landed in Booneville (population 280). The town is located in central Mendocino County, 500 miles from home and about 120 miles north of San Francisco. I didn't want to see anyone, hear music, make friends, or be any part of society for a few days. I checked into the dilapidated, old, historic Booneville Hotel, which wasn't necessarily nice, but it was convenient and seemed to fit my battered bones and mangy mood. It was the perfect launching point from where I could walk, drive, or get purposely lost in the beautiful Anderson Valley hills. Booneville was also nicknamed "Moonville" because Reverend Sun Myung Moon and his followers had set up shop in the nearby hills. They essentially made the little town and its surroundings their own special agrarian ashram.

It was imperative I cleanse my mind and body of the madness and excesses that were part and parcel of spending too much time with "Waylon, Willie and the Boys." I probably slept for two days without turning over. I finally awoke to the crisp, fresh air of a Mendocino mountain morning. Choosing not to eat at the tofu and sprouts restaurant the Moonies had established in Booneville, I drove down the road a few miles to a much smaller Yorkville. Past jaunts had brought me here to a great little roadside café and cowboy bar. I wanted a real breakfast. Halfway through my buttered biscuits, farm sausages, and hard-fried, broken-yoked eggs, a long-haired, snaggle-tooth dude sat down beside me, and with a certain lack of hesitancy, he began talking to me like kinfolk.

"Hi, I'm Tommy Kaye, and I can tell you're in the music business. Who are you?" I didn't know whether to bite or bolt, but this was exactly what I had driven ten hours to get away from. I looked up into a much traveled though very kind face and knew that my intended loneliness had come to the end.

Some individuals surpass all logic and can get away with belching at the opera house during the "Prelude to Parsifal" and still make friends with the people in the seats around him. It turned out that Thomas Jefferson Kaye was not only one of those types but also one of the music industry's legendary producers, musicians, and songwriters. Tommy produced the super session album *Triumvirate* (with Mike Bloomfield, Dr. John, and John Hammond) and was responsible for hits such as Question Mark(?) and the Mysterians' "96 Tears," the Shirelles' "Soldier Boy," Loudon Wainwright III's "Dead Skunk," as well as artists Gene Clark, Three Dog Night, Jay and the Americans, and Link Wray, among others.

※　　※　　※

Tommy and Gene Clark had put together a new group, simply called, for the time being, the Gene Clark Band. They were breaking in the band at this cowboy bar/night club out in the middle of nowhere.

An odd ceremony exists between people in the entertainment business. For whatever reason, exchanging credentials immediately upon meeting someone is somewhat akin to the generic ritual of a dog raising his leg to mark his spots. Once Tommy and I had established that we were fans of each other's work, he called the reclusive Gene over from the pool table that was half-hidden toward the back of the darkened bar/club/cafe.

Gene Clark and I formed an immediate bond that, like with Mal Evans* from my Beatle days, would go right up to his untimely death at a way too young age. Gene was all heart, fists, and musical madness. He vacillated between pure melodic genius and going completely stomp crazy from being on the road. It always came down to his inability to successfully

---

* Mal Evans was the Beatles' road manager and the first person I met the first day I worked with the Fab Four. He was a giant of a man in all respects and had been with them from the beginning. To this day I consider him one of the best friends I ever had. I tell our story in The White Book.

deal with the concept of success and the infrastructure of the music business machinery.

When we met that morning, he was at the stage of simply making music and at his happiest point in a repeated sequence of ups and downs. Gene was in some sort of lyrical limbo—that rhythmical suspension where he was writing and creating—that sweet dulcet fragment of time he could enjoy before the managers, lawyers, agents, and record execs started fostering his eventual and predictable mental blowouts. If Gene liked you, he hugged you to death. If he wasn't quite sure how he felt about you, he would most likely get drunk and maybe beat you up at some point in your relationship until he made up his mind.

We spent the rest of the day together becoming friends, and I even joined in the rehearsal. As is consistent with most record producers, I offered my wisdom and unsolicited two cents' worth throughout the sound check. The band was incredible that night—a quixotic blend of blues, folk, rock, country, and heartland funk. The Gene Clark Band never went much further than the Yorkville Café confines, but I can still hear its beat and bravado in my personal rock chamber.

Later that night, Gene and I went to his house up on the Navarro Ridge. An historical gem, this romantic structure had been a stagecoach stop in the old days and was the layover spot in the run between the towns of Elk and Mendocino on the north coast. We drank longneck beers and ate red-hot cowboy chili until the firewood ran out. I knew a very special friendship was forming here, a bond, a tie that with men is a rare thing because our machismo tends to get in the way most of the time. We sat by the fire until dawn, talking about the inherent tragedies that seem to stalk the fame and fortune of our career paths (a phrase that neither of us ever dreamed of using). After an evening's worth of dialogue, we decided the obtuse reality of our successes actually fenced us in instead of setting us free, as we thought it would. We both grew up hard country and knew deep inside we needed the pines, the oaks, and wild winter wheat grass around us just to settle us down.

We detoured into Hollywood simply because of our love for music. But as we became more publicly apparent through our accomplishments, we were drawn back into the woods, hillsides, and meadows that sheltered the very soul of our heritage. We both discovered the rugged northern California edge and coastal ranges. We agreed it was a beautiful compromise and reasonably accessible to LA, if you didn't mind driving all day to get there. Nevertheless, it was close enough to where we could run into its wooded and convenient arms when the mayhem and the music got too frenetic. I knew we were going to be long-time friends when we stopped talking. As the sun came up, we found we could just sit together at the end of the first day of our friendship and stare quietly into the fading coals. The lack of heat and a form of sweet exhaustion decreed a one-word good-bye. That being said, Gene headed up the worn wooden stairs to bed, and I headed out into the crisp morning air back to the hotel.

From there, Gene, Tommy, and I combined forces in the LA scene— always taking advantage of our renegade status. We were crazy cowboys who would bounce in and out of momentary suspension between fame and the ideals of dirt-common upbringing. People expected us to be wild, accepted us that way, and actually needed us to feed their own fantasies. We faithfully obliged and had one heck of a good time, unfettered by convention. After blowing it out on the Sunset Strip and Hollywood Hills haunts for long stretches, we would often find ourselves sharing uncoordinated escapes into the northern California wilderness. I joined Gene as a landowner on the north coast, and we bounced back and forth between these two actualities in a rhythmic pattern that only made sense to us.

In those heady days of building bands and artists, one of the notches of potential success on your recording rifle was to play the Whisky A Go-Go on the Sunset Strip. If you were the headliner at the Whisky, it was a good sign you were on your way to a record deal and had a valid shot at rock notoriety. About a year after meeting Gene, I had accomplished this feat with one of my bands, Hothead. This was during a time when Gene was in the middle of one of his more dizzying spinouts. At times it was all Tommy and I could do to just keep him away from disasters. Of course, having Tommy and me as guardians didn't help matters any.

Opening night came, and in Gene's loving mind, he decided to bolster the credibility of my band's career-breaking, headlining night with his presence—yes, we were to be graciously blessed with one of the famous and legendary Byrds. (Part of this little "making it" melodrama on an artist's climb to the top was the number of important people who came out for your opening night at the Whisky).

Gene had polished his cowboy boots and put on his favorite Nudies shirt so he could support the band and me on this exciting occasion. As luck would have it, the evening's outcome was dictated by the fact we somehow neglected to put Gene's name on the guest list at the front of the club or at the stage door. Even though we thought it was an oversight, I wonder if in fact we were subconsciously counting on his crazed condition to cause him to forget about the event.

Gene did arrive, slicked up, shining bright, smiling wide, and with a nice little buzz on. After being rejected at the ticket window, he good-naturedly assumed his privileged position, which meant that he was to be secreted into the club via the stage door to save him from the crush of fans who would naturally want his autograph. The stage door to the Whisky was in an alley behind the club and opened into a small landing with a stairway that led up to the dressing rooms in one direction and a short pathway to backstage and the stage in the other direction.

After quietly but unsuccessfully assuring the sentries at the backstage door there must be a mistake, Gene stoically moved on to his next most successful, *or should I say typical*, means of persuasion. He proceeded to punch out three security guards, two roadies working for the opening band, and a few other toughs who mistakenly joined in the fray. As the number of bodies involved in the skirmish grew, momentum eventually took this act public as the brawl started spilling out of the stairwell and on to the edge of the stage. While the stage manager was frantically trying to save the club's expensive microphones and electronics, the owner was out on the curb, waving down the police who patrolled The Strip. He ushered them past the waiting patrons in order to bring the burgeoning melee to an expeditious end. Gene's performance replaced our spot on the program that night, and my band never made it on stage. The only thing we did get was an invitation to never return. We closed before we had opened.

I don't get much madder than I did at Gene that night. A lot of hard work and a lot of peoples' hopes had just gone down the drain. He sought me out later that evening at a friend's house. With bowed head and proverbial white cowboy hat in hand, Gene "aww shucksed" me, hard-hugged me, and tearfully hoped he hadn't done anything wrong. I think I choose to remember him that way—it is crazy, but I don't think I ever loved him more than I did at that very moment. Gene had a lot of hurt inside, and he just had to come out swinging sometimes to make the noise and pain go away. The only thing bigger than the agony this unique human lived with inside was the heart that eventually let him down. He died in 1991 of a heart attack at age forty-nine.

Many years later, I met the young lady who was with him the night he passed on. She told me he must have sensed something that night because a few hours before he died, he became very reflective and began reminiscing about a handful of people who were special in his life. She said it was nice to meet me because I was one of the people he mentioned. She also said that Gene had included Ringo Starr in that small group. The irony in this is that I had just placed Ringo with Private Music/BMG, the record company where the young lady was the head of publicity. Sometimes I wonder if it was the music we were drawn to or if the point of it all was that in life we were destined to be drawn to each other.

❧ ❧ ❧

The song and these thoughts end as if on cue. We have left the ocean and are now heading into the Muir redwoods. Once we get through the redwoods and Mill Valley, I need to plan a route where I can cross 101 and head eastward, avoiding San Francisco. That means traversing the Champagne famous Carneros District that hugs the northern edges of San Pablo Bay and the southern tip of the Napa-Sonoma Valley wine regions.

It may take awhile to cover these few familiar miles. For almost a decade this has been the fringe area of my stomping grounds, and once I leave them

I am letting go. I feel like I am hooked to a large rubber band, stretched to its max, and if I break away, I will be snap-slung into the purpose of my journey beyond the reaches of all my safety nets. Life is like a shaky slingshot at times—but I know in my heart the Hand that holds it is steady.

I finally let go and drive on, hanging on to Moses with all my might.

OUTWARD BOUND

Wine country has its own special allure. There is something both biblical and romantic about the culture and crops that thrive there. The food is finer, the weather typically pleasant, and the whole smell and feel of the place is sweeter than almost anywhere I have ever been.

The wine makers are like humble rock stars (contradiction of terms?) in that they are worshiped by hordes of followers for their expertise and craftsmanship. Like proud musicians who will play their latest song for you at the drop of the hat at late-night gatherings (after they have been on stage all night), wine makers are always ready (after a long day of blending and tasting) to share their latest offering. Like music, the whole existence is mesmerizing, and a person's job becomes their joy. The delineation between work and play becomes easily diffused. But I have already danced to a tune in that key, and the song is over, so I hold a tight rein on Moses, keeping our noses aimed eastward. Leaving the ambiance of the wine country terrain is always a letdown no matter where you are headed. Eventually, my observations shift away from the scenery and focus on the journey that lies ahead. Clueless of the actual direction we are headed, I become lost in thought.

I always thought of a pilgrimage as something outward bound, but the farther I travel away from my point of departure, the deeper I seem to journey inside—inside my past, inside my dreams, inside my disappointments and expectations. The longer the road, the more extended and convoluted my memory trail becomes. The harder I try not to get caught up in these thoughts, the more I seem to be drawn into the past. Movement becomes ethereal, and current reality becomes meaningless. All that remains are my impressions, and that is vaguely lovely in itself because there is no gradation in the recall.

There are no clear markers when your mind leaves the street journey and your thoughts take over the steering wheel. There are just the darkened exits and dimly lit entrances of your migration. Only cold, hard signposts remain, barely reflecting the once-wide turns and sudden stops. Left behind are the bumps, oil slicks, and roadside attractions where you were refused, refueled, or reformed.

I should probably entitle this sojourn "A Pilgrim's Certain Lack of Progress." First, this particular journey I have set out upon is one that I wasn't totally sure I should take. Second, in direct contradiction, I couldn't wait to get on the road. I feel like the Israelites, being impelled toward some distant land that I have a hard time even imagining. Like them, I had become comfortable in my discomfort, and moving in any direction felt like a bad move to me. I, too, have spent over forty years of senseless meandering. What more does God expect of me? My pastor in Nashville used to say that when God unleashes the hounds of heaven after you, they will eventually corner you. Well, He did, and they did, and I did finally accept Him as God Almighty. For a time I found it very cozy, resting in a corner I thought He had put me in. Now He has flushed me out—tearing down the walls that protect me, tearing up the floor that supports me, and tearing away the roof that covers me. Having entertained these thoughts, I can only imagine how Connie feels about our trip.

The terrain and the weather seem to dictate the exploration of this drifter's tangled interior. I've known all along I had no idea where I was heading, but now I am beginning to wonder if I can even get where I didn't know I was going. An unexpected rain against the windshield recalls tears shed from eyes glassed over with disappointments desiring to be forgotten and childish joys buried deep inside like time-tempered treasures. The steady sweep and beat of the wipers are the rhythm section of the band of rocking rogues I thundered through life with. The rolling rhythm of the tires represents the continuous things of my life, the seamless things; the things without end or interruption. These are the precious things like the memory of a loving mother, round and full without beginning or end. The roadside is cluttered with discards of too many pointless quests, and the bordering weeds represent the corroded crops of the reckless seeds carelessly planted along the way. My eyes keep checking the gas gauge as it nears empty, and once again I begin debating the efficacy of this excursion. There comes a time when we will either run out of fuel or decide to pull over and let God crawl in and take over.

So I do just that—I pull over at a gas station in Rio Vista, a small town in the back delta of the San Francisco bay area. Connie announces she also has a calling at this point of the ride and heads for the snack bar and restrooms. I need filling up in more ways than one. The gas pump becomes my altar, and I kneel beside the rear tire in prayer. The pump whirs, my lips stir, and the guy in the Winnebago thinks I am checking the air pressure.

I weep for the wandering souls who have fatal crashes before the realization that Jesus is the only way to go in life's travels. I shudder in sincere regret that they must encounter an unexpected inheritance—an unplanned journey into an unfortunate eternity.

Traveling to this point in life seems like it has taken forever, but then I am reminded of eternity—that's going to be the real long part of our existence.

A Slathering of Angels

The service at the Church of the Chevron lets out, and I return to my communion with Moses and the open road.

Connie has been quiet for a very long time. It could be days since she said anything as far as I would have known, having excused myself from any sense of involvement with reality. She has been distant as we've made our way from the coastal mountains and wine country valley into the flats of the back delta. She becomes even more detached as she closes her eyes for the next part of our excursion.

We head out from Rio Vista across bland vistas onto the tedious trail that will eventually lead us into the Sierra Nevada foothills on the eastern edge of California. We traverse Highway 12 without conversation, eventually crossing both Interstate 5 and Highway 99 as we ebb our way eastward. Finally skirting north of Manteca, we break loose. With Stockton in the rearview mirror, we can finally see the foundations of beautiful mountains ahead. We awake from the travel trance that has set in during these last few hours on the road.

Our destination is the gold rush town of Angels Camp. We chose this town for our first real evening in the van because we saw its name on the map. We thought if we were going to start camping in Moses' bosom, we should start where the "angels' camp"—just to be safe. We spend half an hour meandering in the van around the little town, looking for an inconspicuous place to park and sleep for the night. Being new at this, we are acting like a dog that keeps going around in circles in one spot before he finally drops. Nothing felt right, so we abandoned our angle about the angels and ambled out of town on Highway 4, driving deeper into the Sierra Nevada foothills.

We move into the mountains, passing through Murphys, a quaint little town known as "The Queen of the Sierras." In less than an hour we arrive at Big Trees State Park where we find a legitimate spot to spend the night. After paying our fee, we snuggle in for the night with other campers of all shapes and sizes. We are in a van, not a travel trailer, so there is no leveling or hooking up to do. We just turn off the engine, finish a bag of Fritos with some bean dip, and try to be inconspicuous as we make our beds in the van for the first time. We laugh like kids on a scout camping trip, trying to figure out how the bunks work. We are in nature's sweet-smelling woods, and we find if we don't leave a window open, we smell vinyl, leather, plastic, and other car smells emanating from Moses' interior.

We awake in the morning to the aromas of several varieties of fresh coffee filling the air. Within moments we, too, enter into the reverential morning ritual of the veteran nomads as they sit quietly by their trailers and tents. The serenity of the dawn left no other recourse but to listen to the forest sounds and to watch with curiosity the deferential deer watching us from the trees. All this is a bit alien to us, but there is something in the air that hints of muted adventure.

As the deer blend into the foliage, I have this sense I am sticking out like a sore thumb—not physically, but as if I am mystically separated from the hands of time. I am troubled but oddly focused. I decide the deck I have been dealing with my whole life has had too few aces and too many jokers. I reach for Connie to touch upon actuality and find she has crawled back into the van and pulled the covers over her head. I look back into the forest and want to explore its enchanted offerings. I want to run into it and glide and weave with the buck and the doe between the pines until we melt into the buttery shadows of the glade.

This is almost too much confusion so early in our trip. Right now I could be in the woods that border the open fields of the Indian reservation lands of my youth, wishing I could run away to where I have just left. I am aimed at more romantic places on this journey, and visiting my roots is not in my immediate plans either physically or mentally. Why do I feel like I am running instead of riding? I would like to at least be moving in some assured direction when my wheels fall off.

I thought I was taking a road trip. It is beginning to suspiciously feel more like a head-trip.

Monterey Pop Festival

Talk about head-trips and flashbacks—I suddenly become aware of a certain similarity in the perched suspension I find myself in at this precise moment.

Here I am, sitting in the woods next to a van that I sleep in. I am trying to live in the moment, eating organic yogurt while searching for new meaning in my life, when Connie swaps out iPods and cranks up Jimi Hendrix's 1967 masterpiece, *Are You Experienced?* This soaring, acid-inspired opus—this fiery flash from the past—was her first officially purchased album and became the soundtrack that delivered her into her teen rebellion years. Is it any wonder my thoughts grow young and vibrant as I remember the free-love, peace-and-pleasure, hippy times of Volkswagen vans, love-ins, Electric Kool-Aid, Ken Kesey, and his band of Merry Pranksters days of yore?

※ ※ ※

The Monterey Pop Festival in June 1967 changed everything for all of us in the record industry. It was not only the first major rock festival in the world, but it also became the model for future festivals, Woodstock in particular.

If you can picture this in today's terms—over two hundred thousand flower children, hippies, peaceniks, free lovers, and freer spirits attended this festival over a three-day period. I'm talking close to fifty thousand mostly stoned people occupying a small space at one time. In those seventy-two hours there was nothing but music and good "vibes" filling the confines of the festival grounds. Everybody was blissed out and enjoying the tranquility of the weekend. There were no fights, no one overdosed or died, and nobody was hurt. I learned later that this makeshift mini-city had no arrests during the three-day festivities. In fact, the Monterey deputy chief of police was quoted in a local paper as having said, "We've had more trouble at PTA conventions."

Connie's first musical selection of the trip takes me back to my early years as an executive at Capitol Records. We had a reputation for being a fairly "straight" company those days when it came to our artist roster. Much of the time I felt like a lonely voice in the wilderness when I would try to turn their attention to some of the bands that were playing the Sunset Strip clubs and other hole-in-the-wall rock joints around LA. In all honesty, as a company we were vaguely aware of the Monterey Pop Festival that was coming up. It was almost happenstance that at the last minute it was decided that a group of us would attend the festival. One of the great things about being with Capitol is having major clout in everything you set out to do. Even though we made last-minute plans, we ended up with good accommodations at a nearby hotel and fifth-row center seats at the festival for the entire three days.

We were definitely "suits," and our business attire for the trip consisted mainly of slacks and white shirts with sport coats. Once we arrived on scene, we were stunned at what we saw. It was truly peace and love with flower children all around the fairgrounds. They were getting high, dancing, singing, and basically just loving on each other. We stood out like nuns in a mosh pit. At the end of the first day—when we got back to the hotel—everyone who had jeans changed into them. Those of us who didn't wore our shirts untucked with collars turned up and no coats or ties. I remember washing my hair and combing it straight down in a sorry attempt at creating a "long hair" look. None of us had ever done drugs before and were not ready to even consider it at that point. But during the course of the three days, I think we emotionally got with the program—and the sweet scent that permeated the air aided in our experiencing some degree of contact high.

What we saw on stage is something we could never have prepared for. This was the turn of the musical century. The old way was definitely tossed out the window that weekend. I think the five of us sat in our seats with our mouths open the entire time. It was one amazing performance after

another. We had heard about some of these bands, but we weren't hip to
the underlying swell that accompanied this new era of music and counter-
culture. Picture sitting fifty feet away from pumped-up performances by
Janis Joplin and Big Brother and the Holding Company, Jimi Hendrix, the
Who, the Byrds, Simon and Garfunkel, the Mamas and the Papas, Canned
Heat, Jefferson Airplane, Country Joe and the Fish, Otis Redding, the
Grateful Dead, Buffalo Springfield, Eric Burdon & the Animals, Quicksilver
Messenger Service, and more.

It was a mind-boggling array of cutting-edge, fresh new talent. We
walked back into the "Tower" with a whole new attitude about what was
going on in the business. Capitol's only artist on the bill that weekend was
Lou Rawls, which reflected where our roster was culturally at the time.
Oddly enough, though, we did have the two biggest bands in the business
that did not perform that weekend but had a lot to do with putting the festival together—the Beatles and the Beach Boys. I believe that fact was the
impetus for us going there. We did take note of what was happening and
signed the Steve Miller Band shortly after Monterey and eventually were
able to bring the Quicksilver Messenger Service on board as Capitol artists.
Around the time of the Quicksilver signing, we added a real feather to the
Capitol cap with the addition of The Band.

The Band was a rare phenomenon in the business. I remember being
called up to the twelfth-floor conference room at Capitol for a meeting.
Sitting in the room were Karl Engemann, the head of A&R (Artists &
Repertoire—a fancy term for staff record producers); general manager
Bob York; Brown Meggs, VP marketing and merchandising; and the
Band's legendary personal manager, Albert Grossman. Also present was a
young fellow who was there as a spokesman for the act we were about to
sign—Robbie Robertson. I didn't know who he was, but I did know who
Grossman was, and his presence in the meeting meant something big was
going down. Grossman wanted to meet with the person who would be
heading up the mechanics of launching his new group and their newly
recorded album entitled *Music from Big Pink*. My position as national
promotion manager with artist relations responsibilities under my juris-

diction sorted me out as one of the people Grossman wanted to scope out before signing final contracts. This was an important meeting in Capitol's evolution into the current pop scene that had been kicked off in Monterey the year before.

Albert Grossman was an intimidating man accented by the fact that he knew he was holding all the winning cards with this project. His appearance was imposing, very New Yorkish in manner, long gray hair pulled back into a pony tail, and he chain-smoked with the cigarette held in a most unusual manner. As my knowledge of this "scene" advanced, I learned later that it was a customary way of holding a marijuana joint to take in more air as it was smoked. In his cupped hand he would hold the cigarette (a Camel cigarette, I believe), sticking straight up from between his ring and little fingers. Grossman would take a drag from the hole made by his curled forefinger at the other end of his hand, with the smoke coming down the air tube created from where the cigarette was placed. The deeper puffs that this method required gathered in more oxygen and outside air as it traveled the length of the inside of his closed hand. Something about this had the effect of him establishing his difference from the rest of us and, for some reason, augmented his power position as he spoke slowly and precisely. This, coupled with heavy eye contact as he made his inquiries one by one to the executives seated around the table, gave the impression all the chips were going to stay at his end of the table. Robbie was polite, and when entering the conversation, he gave the impression of being well educated and very comfortable in his dealings with the "suits."

Things must have gone well that day, as I believe it was the final look at the label before actually signing with us. I imagine Robbie was there to give band approval to Grossman. Now when I said The Band and *Music from Big Pink* was a rare occurrence, here is what I mean—something happened at the label that we had never experienced before. As soon as it was announced to the public that the Band had signed with Capitol, we had immediate pre-orders in excess of 100,000 records for their debut album. This was a first for us with a new group or debut artist. There was such a groundswell of support behind this group that they were one of our bestselling acts before any of us even knew their names or what they looked like. In fact, we hadn't even pressed a record yet!

So here we were with both Quicksilver Messenger Service and The Band on our roster, and one afternoon I found out that they were going to be appearing on the same bill that night in San Francisco. (I believe it was the Fillmore West.) I grabbed Al Coury, who headed up the Artist Relations department, and we immediately left the Tower offices at Hollywood and Vine in order to catch an afternoon flight to San Francisco so we could attend their performances that evening.

We made our flight, caught a cab from SFO to the venue, and grabbed something to eat before the show at a nearby café. That night we once again became witnesses to something very different to our corporate world—the fascinating aura that surrounded the Grateful Dead, Jefferson Airplane, Big Brother and the Holding Company club scene in the city by the bay.

It wasn't like you bought a ticket, went to your seat, and prepared to enjoy a concert that would begin promptly at eight o'clock. Once you walked in the place, it was more like things melted in to each other. There were the flower people, the liquid graphics behind the stage, the black lighting in corners, and the acrid smell of weed in the air. We also spotted people laughing a lot, even though they were alone, as they stared off into space, and others were dancing whether there was music playing or not. The dress code was indescribable, but there was an abundance of tie-dyed shirts, dresses, blouses, scarves, headdresses, and yes, even tie-dyed underwear to be observed. Things were otherworldly when the bands were playing. As I described it in my formalized Capitol Industries trip report, "Everyone seemed to be having a real good time."

Al and I went backstage afterward to say hello to the bands and let them know that their record label was behind them and ready to do anything to be of service. The Band was particularly distant and standoffish, while members of Quicksilver Messenger Service were friendlier, but you could tell nobody was going to ask for our home phone numbers so they could hang out with us when they were in LA. We were still "suits." But they were aware their record label had gone out of its way to come see them, and even though they seemed aloof. I could sense they liked the attention.

In acceptance of their hospitality, Al and I drank some of their Kool-Aid, ate a couple of their brownies, and left to catch one of the last late-night flights back to LA.

Then the strangest thing happened when Al and I got on the plane. As we were getting situated, both of us became hilariously funny no matter what we said. I had never been so happy in my life, but I have to tell you—all the other passengers looked real odd. We looked down the aisle toward the front of the plane and could not believe how long it was—that small commuter airliner must have been a mile long. We thought maybe we were supposed to get up and walk to the front, and when we got off we would be LA. No need to fly—just "be there!"

When we got back to Hollywood, it was very late, but we decided we would get something to eat. Besides, we were having so much fun and couldn't stop laughing about everything. Neither of us had ever been so hungry at that time in the morning. I don't know who drove or how we ended up below the Los Feliz area around Western Avenue, sitting on a curb outside a Falafel stand, eating stuff wrapped in other stuff and talking a mile a minute at three thirty in the morning. We were in our nice suits, sitting on this dirty curb with cars zooming by and just having the best time.

I can't figure out why we were so hungry; after all, we had just had some Kool-Aid and brownies in Quicksilver's dressing room not too long ago.

Between the Rock and My Heart Place

To be brutally honest, there are times when I actually don't like being a Christian. It's that peculiar place I find myself when I am really up against a stone wall that blocks me from my walk. It should be no surprise that there is a direct relationship to the fact that this usually happens when I am setting my own rocky course.

I get stuck in an emotion, and I know I am out of line with God's will during these times—yet my hardened heart can't seem to change its offbeat ways. I know I am in the wrong, but no matter how hard I beg Him to reveal the answer, He gives me no relief. It's that time when I need Him the most, and in my heart of hearts know I really do want to change my direction. It's that time when I know I wouldn't feel so awful if I was not clearly out of His will. I find that I draw in to Him most earnestly when I am experiencing great blessings or, conversely, when I am in the deepest of turmoil.

My perplexity lies firmly between the Rock of my salvation and the reoccurring times when my very gut is hurting from a situation I can't understand. I become frozen in place, unable to move toward Him and away from myself. I find I have become a partial apostle Peter. Sometimes I am like the part where he denies Jesus just so he can get away from a bad situation. The other part is that like Peter, I, too, end up weeping when I realize what I have done.

I stand up, turn around, and reach through the open window in the van and grab my Bible from its chosen position between the cup holders. I open the Word, looking for solace, but I can't seem to concentrate. My own solutions and desires are whirling so wildly inside my brain that my natural desires exclude all godly reasoning. Righteous gems are just waiting to pour forth from these precious pages into my heart if only I would take heed of His promises. I grow tired of leaning on Moses, and so I decide instead to go into the woods and forage for forgiveness. I need to be broken, and I know it, but I can't bring myself to ask Him to do it. I sometimes feel that when I actually do muster up the courage, my prayer to be broken is the only one He ever answers! I fear the pain more than I relish the joy of deliverance. I slow down in the forest floor of my earthiness. I rage out in the calm of Christ's offered peace.

I can't see the trees for the forest. The forest is the massiveness of the world's confusion that surrounds and overwhelms me with its complexities. The trees are the majestic truths that the Book I hold in my hand offers. As usual, when I get done being myself, God in His mercy waits me out. And then when I am not looking (at my circumstances), His Holy Spirit enters between the cracks of my hardened exterior. Instead of forgetting to remember His promises, I begin remembering that I need to forget the lies of the devil and just take God at His Word.

I stop at a stump and sit in this calm cathedral and begin worship service. I begin ministering to the trees as I read out loud from His holy Word. Once I find the perfect psalm that settles my wondering mind, I then begin my familiar trek—starting in the first chapter of James—that puts me on a holy roll through favorite and comforting verses of love and promises. The subdued shadows lengthen around me as I get lost in the wisdom of His words. I feel embarrassed as His truth overtakes my waywardness. I know He has granted me revelation, because I feel like I need to apologize for my foolishness. I am also amazed I can smell a plain old tuna fish sandwich being made for an early lunch by Connie quite some distance away from the shadowed glen.

I return to Moses, Charley Tuna, and Connie and take my place beside them on a blanket on the ground. She doesn't ask where I have been for the last hour. She recognized that dazed look on my face as I ran off into the woods. The law of repetition assures her I would find what I was looking for once I thrashed through the thoughts that tormented me. I have a tendency to get tangled in the underbrush of self-inflicted stoicism but always emerge with a narrow victory when I finally let go of it all and rest in the mercy of my loving Savior. Safe at home, which is any place within the sound of Connie's voice, I come to rest before the blessings of a feast. She looks at me like I am crazy as I enter into the longest grace ever given over a tuna sandwich in the history of Calaveras County campsites.

Why did I feel so confused and lost just a while ago? The whole idea of this trip was to have no destination in the first place. Even though I don't have a clue where we are going, at least I now am assured that we are back on track.

We spend the rest of the day walking among the giant redwoods, exploring the banks of the pristine Stanislaus River, and finding quiet spots to just sit and meld into the unknown. Last night was a little disconcerting as we spent our first evening sleeping in the van—even though the bunks across the back were fairly comfortable. Up until now, Connie's idea of roughing it or camping out was accepting one of the smaller cabins at a church retreat. When evening beckons, we return to our bunks in the bosom of the van and turn in for a second evening.

We don't actually wake up in the morning but more or less morph out of a semi-state of dozing into the new day. In some ways, I think we actually advanced the dawn in order to move out of this phase and get back into the "on the road again" aspect of our journey.

The morning is fresh and vibrant on the western slopes of the Sierra Nevada foothills. We have now officially completed two days of migration with Moses. We get up and both have this strange look in our eyes as we realize this is not a dream. We have actually packed it all in, headed out on this bizarre bivouac, and much to our surprise, we are more excited than we are anxious about what lies ahead. It is not as surreal as it was in the beginning—sunup begins as planned, with coffee, granola, and fresh fruit. Refreshed and ready to go, we pack up and head out to new horizons.

We leave Big Trees State Park and turn eastward on Highway 4 toward Ebbetts Pass, one of the few seasonal passes that traverse this mountain range. We head for the top where we will find ourselves in the thin, crisp air that rests at an elevation close to nine thousand feet. Our plan is to decide our next destination when we come down the other side and hook up with Highway 395. I don't know if it was the combination of the Columbian coffee we just drank along with some fermented baklava, but in two short days we have vibed into one of the most important aspects of taking an undefined journey—learning the art of accepting mini goals. When we reach Highway 395 (a mini goal), we will proceed as the mood dictates from there. The sudden freedom of this loose form of realization opens up a whole new slant on how to go about our travels.

Day trippin', yeah!

Catch a Stone Poney

Moses gets tired of the steep, continuous climb and begins to overheat, so we turn off the road at a viewpoint and climb out of the van to shake out our legs and look out at a diffused horizon that appears to be a thousand miles away. After a long stretch of breathing in the sweet, rarified air of the high Sierras, we crawl back into the van. I replace Connie's iPod with mine and once again put it on "shuffle"—the first song that plays catches me off guard. As we drive back out onto the narrow highway, it fills the inside of the van as if on cue—almost as if I had programmed it for this moment.

I have always thought of my life as a soundtrack, and there have been times when, trudging through my personal little episodes, it was as if I could hear a voice-over playing in the background. I feel like this new movie that Connie and I have starring roles in is still in the "coming attractions" stage, but the credits are rolling and a mood song is engulfing the journey. This is a little creepy, because the musical accompaniment to our trek I am now hearing is "Different Drum," a song by the Stone Poneys. For some odd reason, the song, the singer, the sound, and the era soar Wagner-like into my head as both a leitmotiv and a present summary of my past as it prepares its way into my future.

※　※　※

We were a different breed in the '60s, those of us who came out of the folk era into the rock years. We were a bit like the beat and bohemian jazz rebels from the old days because it was their music we heard growing up. But it wasn't the music we emulated; it had more to do with attitude. It is interesting

36

because we were mainly country-bred-kins following, the sweet melodic scent of the pied piper's call into the places where music was made. We loved mixing our roots with the current blend of what was beginning to happen at the small clubs, along the back streets, and in the cutting-edge recording studios on the peripherals of Hollywood. Whether anyone agreed with what we did with our voices and instruments was immaterial. Our defiance of tradition and free expression made everything seem so daring and romantic.

Linda Ronstadt was the lead singer in the Stone Poneys, a trio signed to Capitol Records in 1966. A year later, they scored their first hit with "Different Drum." It was a fresh sound. It had to do with not being stationery. It was about being different and marching to your own beat and guidelines. That's what we did then, and hearing this song now gives me that same sense of letting go and following my dreams. The Stone Poneys struggled after the success of "Different Drum," and Linda eventually left to embark on a solo career. The band was one of my promotional projects, and I had come up with the slogan "Catch a Stone Poney and give your mind a ride." I thought my slogan was pure genius, in addition to being right on the money for the times. As it turned out, my slogan had an even shorter lifespan than the band, but that didn't matter because I was on my way to the top, and they were just another ride along the way.

I remember shortly after leaving Capitol I returned one day to pick up a former workmate for lunch. When I pulled up in front of the Tower, Linda was just coming out of the front of the building after a meeting with her producer, Nick Venet. She spotted me in my new Mercedes sports car (top down, of course) and walked over to the curb to say hello. To this day I can see her leaning into the car with both hands on the passenger door, scanning the new leather interior and saying to me, "Someday I'm gonna have one of these."

I leave this recollection to join the song in its last chorus, wondering how many of "these" she has parked in her garage today as Connie and I tool along in our van—the only wheels we own.

Wafting on Water

The roads are narrow and softly curving. Our daybreak drive brings us to a special place on the central Sierra Nevada mountain range—tiny Mosquito Lake.

I love our position because as we approach this sweet body of water, we have the sensation of almost being above the clouds. The outer edges of the little lake introduce the trees, then the sky beyond, while the eastern rising sun paints a shiny gold sliver across the molten mirror that is the lake itself. I am stunned into silent reverence as His glory overtakes our motion, and my heart levels to the surface of the quiet shimmering waters before me. As His presence consumes more and more of my being, I have this sensation that He is beckoning me to come to Him across the waters.

I leave my earthly essence in times like these and experience this subtle sensation that I could emerge out of Moses, onto the lake's surface, and actually walk on the waters before me into His waiting countenance. It was an invitation of peace, a fluid appeal to enter into an eternal softness and calm. It is these moments where the words don't get in the way that I am able to understand Him and His promises. There *is* a peace that passes all understanding, and I am lulled into the majesty of the moment. But the instant I try to analyze what lies before me, I start sinking. The reverie suddenly disappears into unwelcome reality, and my imaginary walk on celestial waters gets lost in the waves of wondering—wondering if it is at all possible.

I remember one time conjuring up this picture of God while sitting on a hillside on a warm, Indian summer morning. He has one of His arms lovingly stretched out across my shoulder and is pointing out over the landscape with the other hand. I imagine Him explaining, just to me and no one else, all the orbital things I could never understand in my fallen state as a human being. Then an old, horn-honking, faded-yellow Volvo station wagon roars out of the horizon, and once again a dream divine drops and shatters into the wet earth. Naturally, I am awakened before He has a chance to finish explaining the best part.

I sense Moses' seatbelt tight against my chest and once again return to real life— a seeker traveling along a narrow path. The road ahead comes into vision as if a blurry travelogue has been brought into focus. It is at this moment of emergence I am thankful that Connie was driving when I decided to take my liquid space walk.

I remain quiet and rest in the reflection of what didn't just happen.

Is it possible to wander off if you are already lost?

His wonder and my wondering keep us in touch.

I am refreshed by the encounter.

PHOTOGRAPHIC MEMORIES

It is shortly before noon when we roll up to the intersection of Highway 4 and Interstate 395, which runs north and south along the eastern edge of the Sierra Nevada mountain range. We are literally at a crossroads and have no idea which way to go.

Taking the northern route would suggest heading for the northwest and possibly a return to Idaho. If we proceed eastward, we would be committing to a rather monotonous crossing of the dusty breadth of Nevada, followed by a scenic trek over the Rocky Mountains and then on into Utah and Colorado. Turning right would send us on a southbound journey that would eventually drop us into Southern California. At this precise moment of idling suspension, Ringo Starr's 1973 hit "Photograph" begins playing. I begin to wonder if my iPod has turned into "HAL" and is starting to dictate our moves.

Hearing Ringo brings back a surge of memories from our times together in LA. I turn right and become Baja-bound toward familiar stomping grounds. It seems that someone is having a little problem making a clean break from California, doesn't it? It is my recollections that have determined our course.

Moving forward with Moses, I drift back to Babylon . . .

* * *

We have actually determined a specific destination point for the first time in our undefined journey. We are going to LA—actually, Hollywood and the "Hangover House" as it was affectionately called. This legendary Laurel Canyon estate was one of the Hollywood Hills homes I occupied during the most riotous of my years as an independent producer and president of my wholly owned Hometown Productions Inc. It is my recollections of Ringo that made this decision because of his many visits there and the times we spent in this magical place. I told many Ringo stories in *The White Book*—stories that covered our years together in the big "L's"—London, Las Vegas, and LA. This is one I had almost forgotten about.

It's a story that defines Ringo to me, and it took place in the warmest room at the Hangover House—the room where we took our meals. The dining room was special, with its restored, antique wooden floors, hanging tables, Moorish fireplace, and large windows that looked down through the canyon. It was a large room and a perfect place for one of the antique pianos gathered from the back roads of my travels. This is not a musical memory but one with gentle overtones.

It was November 1977, and several of us from our select group had invited Ringo over to our respective homes for Thanksgiving dinner. Caught in a diplomatic dilemma, he came up with a kindly solution, one that would appease everyone and offend no one. His way of handling this was somewhere between brilliance and down-home benevolence. What led him to his plan of action had to do with the fact that he had recently received a magnificent English bone-handled carving set as a holiday gift. In response to our many invitations, he asked each of us what time we were serving our turkey. He then had us formalize and in some cases adjust the time slightly. He said he would come to each of our homes and carve our turkeys for our guests at that precise time.

It was a family affair at our house and definitely not a Hollywood gathering of the hip and cool. It consisted of relatives who had driven, in some cases, from far away to join us in our heightened universe. Most of them looked at my lifestyle with feelings that lay somewhere between total fascination and utter disgust because of the fantastical decadence of it all. But they were family, and it was the season. All things divisional were simply set aside.

At my house that Thanksgiving Day, we had a table of about a dozen chilled-out kinfolk enjoying the moment, when the doorbell rang. (I had purposely not told anyone about Ringo's surprise visit.) Our San Salvadorian cook, Berta, was in on the plan, and I gave her a heads-up when I went to answer the front door. I quietly let Ringo in, and as he entered the dining room from the foyer, Berta brought the turkey in from the kitchen and placed it in the center of the table. I introduced Ringo to a stunned group of people. He graciously bid everyone at the table a personal hello and then proceeded to carve the turkey and serve each guest individually. I loved watching him in his kind intent, as his head, hands, and heart were totally dedicated to the meaning of the moment. He bent his very being softly into the occasion and served each person in the most humble way. I honestly don't believe that there was anything of equal import on his mind at that time outside of the gentle task at hand. For me, I was watching an old friend, an associate, a neighbor, and—the least important category of my observant reflection—for a fleeting moment, a Beatle. The person sitting behind the drum kit at the Beatles' last concert that historic day we shared on the Apple roof and the person carving off the drumstick at my dinner table were uniquely one in the same, and at the same time were as different as if they were from separate planets.

After everyone was served, he took a ceremonial bite for himself, lifted a perfunctory toast to all in good cheer, and disappeared out the door. The kind of thing you would expect from a rock star of this stature? No. Typical of Ringo? Yes!

• • •

I tell Connie this story as we drive by Mono Lake, which is mesmerizing at this time of day as the slanted sun reflects off its glassy surface. In her role as a card-carrying member of the Directors Guild of America and an associate director in television, Connie had worked with superstars on several occasions in the past. She was totally tuned in to the fact that the turkey carving is exactly the kind of thing some of the superstars would do. They are like everyone else in certain ways—some will give you the shirt off their back no matter who you are, while others won't give you the time of day unless you are in their "league."

Connie had lived in LA for a while when she migrated from Nashville years ago to take her brief shot at making it in "Hollyweird." Our destination has now become formalized as a dual revisit and not a solo return flight on my part. Our first stopover would be the Hangover House, where the "birds of different feathers got carved together" many times.

GOD IN AB MINOR

O ne thing I have noticed when you are on an expedition without a predetermined physical goal: the mind-set is quite different than when you are simply en route from specific point A to definite point B.

Although we don't have an actual *final* destination, spiritually we are purposing to end up in a specific place. Any place we are headed, such as the upcoming Hangover House, is merely a stopover. This does take the edge off in some ways, and with each new location a certain sense of mystery and wonderment develops. I begin to see a rhythm emerging in my thought processes as the miles click by. We are admittedly new at this but are becoming quick learners as to how we will operate during different phases of our little adventure.

We talk more and get real elemental when we are driving through scenic places. The visual seems to stir up the visceral, and we tend to relate what is coming into our eyes with things that need to come out of our hearts. This trip is meant to be cathartic, so as we roll along, sharing our insides, we have coined the word "car-thoughtic." *Car-thoughtic*: the thought process involved in getting things off your chest while driving in a car.

We have left the eastern foothills of the mountains and are now passing through the slightly less picturesque Owens Valley, which is tucked between the small Inyo Mountain range and the tail end of the Sierra Nevada range. It is times like these when one tends to turn inward. There is not much stimulation coming in through the windows and into our senses. Conversations cease and we become alone together. I am headed for the place where I made music for decades, and reflections and recollections become a mixture of geography, melody, and spirituality. Connie keeps the van on track while I mentally drift off to the side of my long and winding road.

Learning to know God, to be able to hear from Him and think more like Him, is analogous to learning to play a musical instrument. At first it takes effort and repetition. To get the feel for your God instrument, you need to pray every morning, read the Bible, go to church, do devotionals, meditate on His Word, and then talk to Him about things on a daily basis. It is so awkward in the beginning, but not at all unlike learning to master the intricacies of the guitar. Initially you find that it is hard to play the notes, and the resultant sound you make is stiff and cumbersome. Your hands hurt from the effort, and you wonder if it will ever be worth the trouble, while the beckoning promise of harmonic success keeps you going. But if you keep at it long enough, you discover one day the process moves from your mind and your fingers and goes somewhere else. Eventually, something new occupies a place deep down inside. You don't think about playing the notes—they are a part of you, and you are a part of them. The hard work and perseverance turns into joy. Good things start coming out of you, and the freedom lets good things come into you.

A person experiences the same sensation after an extended period of pressing in to the heart of God through His Holy Word, fellowship with the saints, and a working relationship with His presence. What at first takes great effort, in time becomes not only effortless but a natural component of your everyday makeup. Years of struggle and an eternity of looking for answers, one day suddenly and mystically turns into a sweet encounter, and you find yourself playing the song that is you before the very throne of God. The rewards from dedication to His Word flow naturally in and out of your soul. You become aware that God is always talking to you.

As a non-Christian I couldn't hear God's voice because I had no desire to hear what He had to say. Decades of decadence took place in the city where we are headed, but like a dog returning to its vomit, we aren't thinking through things—just going with them. I *am* marching to a different drummer now and singing a whole different tune. What I feel beating inside of me now is the heart of God; and the song I sing is in praise of His Holy nature. In retrospect, I have been able to see God's pull on my life and have developed an understanding of that occurrence. I sense that same pull now, and I trust Him that this will be a trip of obedience.

Blessings follow obedience.

Connie and I are both country-raised and backwoods-bred. Once again we find ourselves, like the Clampetts, heading for the hills—Hollywood Hills, that is!

MILE MARKER # 2
LOS ANGELES TIMES

VALLEY OF THE DULLS

It is time to leave the simplicity of the interstate. If we don't make a strategic sideways jog, we'll hit the Mojave Desert. If you have ever been there—you've been there! At the junction of Interstate 395 and State Highway 14, we turn southwest and aim ourselves toward Palmdale, the San Gabriel Mountains, and the municipal madness beyond. This move buys us another hour or so of relative monotony until we finally see Palmdale in our rearview mirror and the mountains ahead.

Although the hills bring some relief from the parched panorama, I find myself clinging to Moses for support as we draw near to the backside of the San Fernando Valley. I remember when this valley was a valley, but then that is another story—*for sure*. The knowledge that LA lies just beyond the Mulholland spine that separates the San Fernando Valley from the city enters my spirit like the smog that is about to enter our lungs. That old feeling I used to get when I would return from one of my escapes to my place in Mendocino County grabs my gut.

The scenario was always the same in those days. No matter how exciting and glamorous things would be, I would still routinely find myself being suffocated in the heat of that familiar fray during my heyday in "Hollyweird." This feeling was followed by the country-boy thing boiling up from deep inside, and that is when the outward journey began. The simplicity and sweet smells of the open fields and riverbanks of my youth would overpower my senses, prompting me to bolt out of the city, headed north. As I fled LA, a sense of lightness would come over me, and I would slowly begin to shed the weight of things I didn't understand. My Mercedes and me making a break for it—man and metal taking it to the limit in a ravenous rush to get out of town and hit the north coast.

It was a ten-hour drive to Mendocino County in northern California, so I would typically leave around ten p.m. and drive Highway 5 north during the evening hours because there was absolutely nothing to see along the way. In fact, outside the wunderkind windows of my mind was a visual vacuum I didn't want to see. I would be able to cross over south of Sacramento from this inland route to the Oakland Bay area and navigate through that mangled mess on my way to Highway 101 and Coast Highway One before the morning rush-hour traffic began. The best part of this time-table was when I would finally hit the coast at Bodega Bay, it would be right around sunrise. I would drive the last three hours during the soft first light of the day, along the western water's edge.

My drive through the dawn always ended at the historic old Gualala Hotel where the best breakfast in the world preceded landing at my final destination—Anchor Bay. My home there was perched on the edge of a 150-foot cliff in the middle of ten oceanfront acres I had carefully named "Sonata." The place had been built before the California Coastal Commission established strict rules concerning their proximity to the cliffs, and Sonata was one of the few homes in the area that had such a dramatic view. It was the perfect place for solitude. If my life was a sheet of music, then the inter-lude that followed this one point landing at Sonata would be musically annotated as plenteous pages of rests and adagios.

I liked Anchor Bay because: (a) it had a scenic name; (b) the whole town was for sale for $750,000 at one time; and (c) I could have thrown a baseball from one end to the other in about one and a half tries. It is amazing how time flies when you are doing nothing to aggravate its movement. These visits would usually end abruptly with a phone call from my attorney asking me when I was coming back, as I did have contractual obligations to fulfill and recording projects to complete. I was always surprised by these calls to return because I felt that I had just arrived home. Once when I mentioned this, he gently reminded me that I had been gone for over three weeks.

Jolted back to unavoidable reality, I would reluctantly close up the house and head southward. I usually left mid-afternoon in order to enjoy the smells and views of the Mendocino and Sonoma coastline before I found myself back on Interstate 5 during the darkness once again. I know it may be confusing to some that I would dread returning to a life that was about as exciting as anyone could imagine, but that deep-down, country-boy thing was always there. There was a call from the wide-open-spaces side of my childhood that kept pulling me back to the quiet honesty of distant surroundings. This nurtured pull was most apparent when I was driving north, away from the city toward Sonata, and my speed could best be described as breakneck. I find it interesting that as I headed southward, away from the north coast, and the closer I got to LA, the slower I drove—the dawdling way a kid walks into his dentist appointment.

I find that old feeling returning as Connie and I cross Mulholland Drive and head down into Laurel Canyon. After decades of inhabiting and in some ways haunting these familiar hills and canyons, my inner dial turns to automatic pilot. I begin absorbing the memories, both good and bad, that float by the windshield.

We make a right turn at the old Canyon Country Store onto Kirkwood Drive, then another right, followed soon by a third right. We continue climbing to the top, deeper into the heart of the canyon and higher up on its hillsides.

We make a left turn, and Moses stops.

I look up at the Hangover House.

It looks down on me.

I look away.

THE HANGOVER HOUSE

The Hangover House looms over me as I stand staring up at it from the narrow gutted street below. I am trying real hard not to remember things too well, but the seventy-seven carefully carved stone steps that lead up to its incredible stance on the Laurel Canyon slopes of Hollywood cry out for recollection. Memories like reverse echoes begin rolling down upon me from the hillside like a "rock" slide as I turn back into the twisted trek that drove me up and down those stairs in the days of my crazed years in the music business.

The Hangover House had been the symbol of my success and the point of my eventual downfall. The fancy and the famous as well as ragged rebels of equal notoriety had climbed those stairs. We all wandered in and out of the dream that the successes and excesses of the rock-and-roll world had created.

A struggling movie director named Tay Garnett built the house in the early '20s. His success and partying became legendary, and the house grew like "Topsy" as each addition represented some new film milestone in his career. In the beginning, he and his also-struggling actor pal, Marion Morrison (who later took on the stage name of John Wayne), built the staggered path that took the houseguests up and far away from the street and the real world.

In the early days of career struggles, Tay and his cohorts would venture out in the dark evenings and steal tiles and supplies from building sites in ritzy Beverly Hills. With their stolen treasure and gathered gems, they began piecing this "hunting lodge" together. The guest bathroom downstairs boasted imported sky-blue tiles from legendary film mogul King Vidor's mansion—the result of one such successful late-night raid.

As Tay's success blossomed by directing movie classics such as *The*

Postman Always Rings Twice (1934: Lana Turner, John Garfield), *China Seas* (1935: Clark Gable, Jean Harlow), and *A Connecticut Yankee in King Arthur's Court* (1949: Bing Crosby, Rhonda Fleming) the property eventually grew to a rambling abode that flowed into the very nature of the Laurel Canyon hills. Tay had copied the exterior look from a pictorial heading that publishers typically placed at the beginnings of chapters in turn-of-the-century, Austrian fairy tale books.

In time, within this overgrown Hansel and Gretel house, there evolved a forty-foot living room, a projection booth, a bar room sunk deep into the heart of the house, back stairways, built-in phone booths, fireplaces everywhere, and three guest houses spread over thirteen lots of Hollywood Hills real estate. At the time it was built it was one of four hunting lodges in Laurel Canyon. The other getaways were owned by cohort legendaries Ty Cobb, Tom Mix, and Harry Houdini.

The edifice became known as the "Hangover House" because of the wild parties and the fabulous stars that entertained and reveled in its romantic interior. The signatures of Tyrone Power, Hedy Lamar, Clark Gable, Spencer Tracy, Bing Crosby, Dorothy Lamour, and dozens more movie stars who were equally as famous can still be seen on the bar room wall. (Our era and a different wall in that room offered a few of our contributions, which included Dolly Parton, Ringo Starr, Leonard Nimoy, Duane Eddy, Diane Keaton, Roy Orbison, David Cassidy, Waylon Jennings, the Byrds' Gene Clark, and Roger McGuinn.) I have been told that if there was some way we could pull those foot thick cement and plaster walls out of the deep of the house, they would be worth more than the house and the land itself.

Tay's life eventually fell apart in that place. He spent his last years in a rented upstairs room of a small, suburban LA house owned by an aging film buff who was a big fan of the director's work. He died alone in the county hospital with his only daughter and myself being among his last visitors. He and rival movie director King Vidor had been bitter enemies for many years, yet when he was dying, Vidor was the first to give blood in an effort to prolong Tay's fading life. From the hallway as I approached his sickbed, I could hear him screaming. He had just found out about Vidor's contribution, and he was making it very clear that he did not want to die with King Vidor's blood in his veins.

The house eventually became famous as the Lash LaRue estate. The famous cowboy film star's escapades in this same locale made Tay Garnett's ramblings look like he and his hot-shot Hollywood despots were a bunch of choirboys with training wheels. The inevitable demise of Lash's pack of desperadoes was obvious, and his life also fell apart in this house.

Knowing that Lash LaRue once lived in my house was so fascinating for me, because as a kid, I would go to the local two-bit Westerns with my allowance each Saturday; as two of my favorite cowboy stars were Whip Wilson and Lash LaRue. I was intrigued by the fact these two cowboys used bullwhips instead of guns to defeat the bad guys. I would go home afterward and tie a piece of clothesline to a stick and try to make it snap like they did in the movies. Of course, I liked Lash best because Whip was the guy in the white hat, and Lash was always decked out in all-black duds.

I remember one day looking out of the dining room windows down to the parking area in front of the property and seeing an old guy dressed in black, standing outside a rental car alongside a young man who appeared to be his driver. They lingered for quite a while, looking up at the place, so I went down the seventy-seven stairs to the street below and introduced myself as the owner. I was blown away when the man in black responded that he was Lash LaRue. Now, my life at that time was filled with the most famous people in the world; yet when he told me who he was, I was absolutely starstruck!

I immediately invited him up to the house so he could see it again and also to check out what we had done to it over the years. I was surprised when he declined without hesitation and headed for the passenger door of the car. Turning his face to me as he sat down in the front seat, he simply stated that he wanted to see the place one last time but didn't want to go inside and relive what had gone down there. He reached over and tapped the young driver and closed the door with no further explanation. I felt like a kid as I stood in the street and watched the car head back down the narrow canyon road. Years later, a friend mentioned they had read about him in a Florida newspaper. After a stint as an evangelist, he had been picked up as a derelict in some backwater town. The story was that they found him passed out in the trunk of his car with a black bullwhip and a Bible at his side. My kind of cowboy . . .

After brief occupations by Jimi Hendrix, Neil Young, and about a hundred rock bands, the house then chose me to host its next enigmatic episode. It became my home for well over a decade. While I was there, if the notoriety of the visitors and my orchestrated events did not totally measure up to the tempo set by my predecessors, I am sure we made more noise—as the rockin' would roll on sometimes for days, with limos outside and loonies inside. In time, my life fell apart there too. Sometimes I wonder if Lash, Tay, and I were all predestined to some ethereal script we had to reluctantly follow to the bloody end in this hero-hexed place.

▨ ▨ ▨

I now find myself standing in the same place that I observed Lash LaRue standing and am somewhat amused when I realize I am sporting black jeans and a black (Pink Floyd) T-shirt. I, too, am staring up at the house with no desire to go back inside. Connie puts her arms around my waist and rests her head on the back of my neck. She holds me almost as if to keep the pieces intact that are getting ready to fall apart.

No Sharp Edges

Admittedly, I have my own severed reality, and the truth I see is sometimes more amplified than others may perceive. For example, I may write about sitting on the water's edge, talking to Jesus. It is true that I am sitting. It is true that I am looking out across the ocean. It is true that I am talking to Jesus. But to me there is much more to it than that. The simple sky above appears cerulean blue with alabaster clouds that circle my position in perfect quadraphonic accompaniment to Mahler's fourth movement, the "Adagietto" from his First Symphony. Maxfield Parrish stands off to one side with his paintbrush, capturing the moment on canvas. And Jesus, the man sitting next to me, is real, and He is really sitting there.

I can describe Him to you in great detail. His hair is long and soft and always in a state of slight uplift from broad shoulders that act as the speculum that reflects the wind up His bronzed neck. The effect of this ascendant motion causes the ends to stand out and catch the sunlight on its edges. His beard is light and very short and follows the strong lines of His kind face without changing its shape. His eyes are deep and without definable color—just deep and rich. When they are looking straight at you, it is as if they are also looking past some great distance that only He can gather in. His teeth are startling white, in contrast to the copper-tinted tan gracing His holy visage.

When we talk it is timeless, and the sounds and surroundings become accented in a muted form. Everything takes on a sense of beauty and calm—no sharp edges. I like the feeling I get when I say things to Him, because no matter what I say, it is never wrong. His grace and mercy are so all-encompassing that even if I were to speak blasphemy into the moment, it would be neutralized and cast into the waiting sea of forgiveness that lies before us. Our time together has a casual cadence. It melds into carefree camaraderie, gentle gesturing, and a lot of touching for emphasis of point while the laughter comes often from heads thrown back with chins jutting out into the vibrant air that surrounds us.

We don't walk up and sit down together, have a chat, and then after a while get up and leave together—it is more like we are there and then we are not. The conversation has this quiet quintessence that flows over both the beginning and the ending of our encounter. The whole experience is one thing, not made up of many things—more of a feeling than an occasion.

I get so absorbed in my exchange that I have a feeling the people who may chance by us in our moment don't quite see it in the same way I do. That is probably why the general walking path of passersby has more of an elliptical bulge away from where I am sitting as opposed to a straight line, which would bring them too close as they walk past me.

I only pass on to you what is real to me. An observer standing a few feet away may describe a much simpler event and even suggest I may have embellished what just happened. So if they describe a lonely man, smiling as he stares out into the open sea—then they are the ones who have left things out.

TALE OF TWO SPACE
INDUSTRIES

There were two parts to my LA life—one was the way up and the other was the way down. Actually, there was a long part in between, but it seemed to go by so fast that it almost doesn't count—the part where I was on top of the world.

I was twenty-seven years old when I went to work at Capitol Records in Hollywood. It was January 5, the first working day of 1965. The job at the most prestigious record company in the universe was the result of a series of chance events, or so I thought at the time. They were spawned by my years singing in a popular Southern California folk group and owning a folk music nightclub in San Diego. After I quit performing and touring with my band, I kept bumping into a guy named Bill Wagner as I made the rounds of the LA hot spots, looking for acts to book into my club. Bill was the head of Artist Relations for Capitol Records—a cool, older guy who made sure the label's new acts were supported at their club dates. He also kept on top of the current music scene by immersing himself in its guts—these out-of-the-way local clubs where bands and artists "made their bones."

Bill and I hit it off immediately and spent a lot of time sitting together during the dimly lit shows and hanging about the dressing rooms and lobbies in between sets. One night he casually mentioned he was also the manager of the Four Freshmen, who were on Capitol Records. Growing up in the early '50s, jazz was my rebellion music, and those musicians and singers were the stars of that era. Music was always the "it" in my life, and the Four Freshmen were the Beatles of that period as far as I was concerned. I was such a giant fan that I could have sung every one of their songs right along with them—word for word and note for note. As soon as Bill let the cool cat out of the bag that he was their manager, he became something very special to me. I became so enamored with his stories that you would think he glowed when he talked about *his* fabulous four lads.

Bill took a liking to me because he saw something—a very ambitious young man with an unusually mature sense about the music business. I had already experienced the rigors of the road and also a small taste of success in the process. These lessons were followed by taking on the toughest gig in the business—a real down-in-the-trenches nightclub owner.

While I was draining stories and information out of him during our evenings at the clubs, he had been scoping me out. It turned out that an opening was coming up at Capitol, and it was one of the most sought-out gigs in the music industry at the time. The job's official title was District Promotion Manager—West Coast. The work entailed spending days and nights with the most famous people in the recording scene, hosting tony cocktail parties, hanging out at clubs, attending premiers, going to concerts, taking influential people out to eat at the most expensive "in" restaurants in Hollywood and Beverly Hills. Other perks included getting the best seats in the house no matter what the occasion, traveling to all the hot spots on the West Coast and bordering states, getting up when you wanted, staying out and partying all night on a no-holds-barred expense account—just to name a few.

One night over our beers in between one of Steve Martin's early gigs at the Ice House in Pasadena, Bill asked if I ever thought about getting into the record business. He knew that not only did I have street experience in the industry, but I also had the unheard of attribute of possessing a Bachelor of Science degree in marketing. He felt that gave me definite edge over other applicants for the job. I was stunned at the possibility. At that very moment, I knew I wanted to make the music industry my life whether I got that particular job or not. I admit that I had always dreamed about being a "record producer," but it was such a vague fantasy that I never imagined I would ever make a living in the heart of the entertainment industry. The fact that I had no idea what a record producer did made my dream seem even more whimsical. Now the real-life, tangible prospect of working at Capitol Records absolutely floored me.

There were about forty guys with prior experience applying for this "cherry" job. I had zero formal experience in "the business." In fact, I thought everyone who signed to a record label automatically became famous, and the radio stations played their records because they were stars, and all records were hits. (One of the contenders for the job was Sammy Laine, who was singer Frankie Laine's brother. Frankie had just signed a recording contract with Capitol, which gave Sammy the inside track. To top it off, Sammy was a well-respected veteran in the business and therefore the obvious front-runner in getting the gig). When I said I would love to apply for the position, Bill moved swiftly in getting me in the door. Looking back, I now realize he was my sponsor for the job and in time became my mentor in the business.

I interviewed for the job in borrowed clothes because my wardrobe was definitely not showbiz caliber. They must have been OK, because I got called back for a second interview. They had narrowed it down to me and one or two other candidates. Because of this particular job's visibility, Capitol wanted to ensure they made the right choice. I began driving back and forth from San Diego for a series of final interviews. This "back-and-forthness" was a bit wearing, because in addition to running my nightclub, I was working full-time in the aeronautics and space industry during the day so I could afford to keep the club running. (This explains the borrowed duds situation. During the day I wore nerd clothes—polyester slacks with short-sleeve white dress shirts, and yes, the plastic penholder in the shirt pocket like all the egghead scientists I worked with. At night the dress "du noir" was funky bohemian. It was a functional but limited wardrobe.)

I had my final interview on a Wednesday and was told that Capitol would let me know its decision before the weekend. Friday came and went and I heard nothing. The weekend passed and I spent Monday spaced out in my space office. I was bummed because of the obvious and ticked off because I was letting it get to me. Late that afternoon, the phone rang, and it was Bill Wagner, who was especially cheerful. He congratulated me on getting the Capitol job. I told him I was surprised because I had not received a call from the company notifying me I had the position. He was equally surprised—he said on Friday he had lunch with Wayne Tappen, my future boss at the label, who told him I was their man. Bill said Wayne stated he was returning to his office after their lunch to call and invite me aboard. I told Bill this was all news to me. He was as confused as I was, so he said he would check out the situation and get right back to me.

An anxious hour passed before Bill finally called me back. He told me when Wayne Tappen got back to his office, he had an appendicitis attack and was carted off to the hospital in an ambulance before he had a chance to call me. Over the weekend his boss, Earl Horowitz, came to the hospital to visit Wayne. When Horowitz found out the call to the new hire had not been made, he expressed his doubts about their decision. Since I hadn't been notified, Horowitz wanted to open up the interview process for one more round to ensure they were making the right decision. Once again I had to don borrowed clothes, beg for time off from my legit job, and drive back and forth between LA and San Diego.

Well, I did finally get the job, and that was the beginning of a party that lasted for over thirty years.

I left my job in the space industry to go to Hollywood and join the music business—the real space industry.

DANCING BETWEEN
THE RAINDROPS

As I dance between the raindrops of the dilemmas that fall down into my life, there is an inadvertent evasion and childlike closeness that nourishes the excitement I feel. It is a warm, close, sensorial thing, and yet there lurks within the moment a sense of soft danger, an uncertain something mysterious that baffles and excites me. I seem to know that a vision of what is important in the heavenlies is poised on the edge of time, just waiting to invade my being. In spite of this spiritual sensibility, I find myself trying very hard to both defy and deny God's presence, especially when it starts entering my circle of defenses and cool center of calm. Over time I have carefully carved out a safe spot far down inside my own determination and stand in defiance of His eventual and expected intrusion.

Oddly enough, I think the big reason I love Him so much is because He doesn't always knock before He enters. He loves to just storm into my deepest parts and start turning over tables, clearing spaces, and setting things free. I struggle with my indifferences and objections to His leadings, but He is always there, like the patient coach who is just trying to show me how to run the ball. He gently explains that life is like a football—it doesn't always bounce the way we would like it to. The cool thing is that He is the only one who keeps score, and we already have the victory.

Why would I want to reject this glorious disruption? He just wants to get in there and sort me out. I become like a baffled bullfighter with no beast to stick my stuff into. I want the world to be moved by my movements and to amaze them with the twirls and twists that I do amongst the surrounding colors. I want to let them see the bravado of my moments and to thrill in my contortions with the same pleasure that I award myself. But when I turn aside and face into the sunlight of the Son's righteousness, all my courage melts away into another place. The searing reminders of His Word, His promises, and His Spirit replace the cheering crowd. I admit there is a lot of bull in the center ring of my hardened heart, and I soon become impaled on the horns of my thoughts about my personal self-worth. I become the one mesmerized by the red flag of His warnings and finally lay down my sorry sword and fall to my knees in the churned earth beneath my faltering feet and weep into the dirt from whence I came.

I stare into the grandstands, and they are empty. I look around and see only myself in a lonely arena. I look up and He is beside me. He takes the mud of my making and gently places a salve into my eyes so that I may see. The remaining tears are placed in bottles labeled with His promises. He lifts me up and stands face-to-face with me in my circle of despair. I can see the deep scar on the hand He places on my shoulder. His voice is like a soft wind that doesn't use sound to enter my ears; instead, it extends exquisite essence as it enters my presence. He explains the dichotomy of my uniqueness in that He did not create anyone else like me. He carefully selected millions of pieces and assembled them in a time and manner only He can understand. He defines me and then describes me as He sees me—not how I see myself. He puts an unexpected luster on this discourse as He finally explains that the beauty of all this is just how simple and alike we all are in His sight. He tells me all the blessings and special love He bestows on me are no different than those He grants and feels about every one of His children. His gifts are uniquely mine and available to everyone.

And when we cry out to Him—and yes, there will be tears—we can be sure that He never runs out of bottles and balm. Although our wounds are self-inflicted in a useless struggle with our vanity, victory comes when we let go and hold the hands that heal . . . hands that love to help and hold us . . . loving hands waiting to press us deep into the bosom of eternal sweetness that is His fundamental nature.

I leave the arena alone yet serenely surrounded.

A BUILDING WITH NO CORNERS;
A LIFE WITH NO BOUNDARIES

It's Hollywood, and it's January 5, 1965.

W hen I was told to report for work on my first official day in the record business, I was disappointed to learn my office was not going to be in the Capitol Tower. I would be operating out of the distribution center in the San Fernando Valley. As it turned out, those offices were located in an industrial section of the San Fernando Valley. My opulent entertainment-industry mogul office was in reality just a big open room in the warehouse with a shared secretary and devoid of discernible ambiance. This LA outpost was one of several distribution centers for Capitol Records spread around the country that were typically located in less-desirable, cheaper parts of metropolitan areas.

My official title at Capitol was District Promotion Manager—West Coast, and my territory was basically California, with occasional visits to Oregon, Washington, Colorado, Nevada, Arizona, and New Mexico. There were a half dozen of these regional distribution centers nationwide. Operating in satellite formation around these centers were approximately forty of us DPMs strategically placed in major markets. Any DPM whose territory was not located near a distribution center worked out of their homes. My district was the most desirable and the one the other DPMs badly wanted. For a DPM to be moved from the Washington DC/Baltimore market to the Los Angeles market was not a lateral move, because the LA position was very visible to the Capitol Tower executives and the one typically known as the springboard into a national position.

What was especially exciting about the West Coast position was that I spent 90 percent of my time in Hollywood because the artists were always there recording in our studios, appearing on TV shows, or performing in local clubs or concert venues. Most of the successful, big-name artists also lived there because it was the center of the entertainment universe. It was also where all the managers, agents, publicists, etc., were stationed. It was *the* scene and *the* place to be seen and the earmark that an artist's career was flourishing. This was also the indicator of an executive's success path— one was officially "making it" when promoted out of the regional and local markets into "Mecca."

Not that I was confident—but instead of taking an apartment in the San Fernando Valley close to my office, I took a lease on one on Beachwood Drive, which was less than a ten-minute walk from the Capitol Tower in the Hollywood Hills. I had to drive about a half hour to get to my distribution center office each morning, but in all honesty, that is not where I intended to be spending my time in the future.

I was promoted to the Hollywood executive offices into a national position in less than a year. Some of the men in the field had been with the company twenty years. To the man, their eyes were focused on moving up into a national position. Barely there for nine months, I was brought in over all of them. It was about a year later when they all were reporting to me. Within another year, the only person who had more people reporting to him was the president of the company himself. I was brought into the Tower as national single records merchandising manager and then promoted to national promotion manager. I not only had the entire nationwide promotion team under my supervision, but in time was handed the Artist Relations Department, the Radio-TV Department, and the R&B Department. As if that wasn't enough, I was eventually put in charge of the independent labels distributed by Capitol. It was at this point I became the U.S. manager of Apple Records, a position birthed from my time working with the Beatles as a district promotion manager when they came into my market on their early tours. In time I had one of the biggest offices on the floor. One thing I could never quite get used to was having an office with no square corners. The building was round on the inside as well as the outside.

Being a top guy at Capitol, RCA, or Columbia in those days was the business equivalent of being a rock star. Life was one continuous indulgence of parties, luncheons, dinners, concerts, screenings, and hanging out with the rich and famous. My expense account was unlimited, and practically everything was written off to Capitol. These were the days of the Brown Derby, the Cocoanut Grove, the Hollywood Bowl, Ciro's on the Sunset Strip, and Martonis, where all the record and radio people hung out and networked. Martonis was the musical West Coast version of the Algonquin in New York, where during the F. Scott Fitzgerald days, the writers and publishers fraternized. This was the music business as it used to be. In some ways it was an emerging business—one still in the developmental stages. It was a new phenomenon when the dollars got really big with acts like Elvis Presley, the Beatles, and the Rolling Stones. In time some artists were grossing more sales than our entire year's gross revenues at Capitol in the old days.

Back then you could still have a dream and go for it—talent and imaginings could come off the street with heart and a handshake and become famous. Sonny Bono was on the street as a promo man for an independent distributor when he established Sonny and Cher as a duo; Russ Reagan was a local promo man who ended up running major labels and brought Elton John to America. The Turtles' managers were LA promotion men and came up off the streets and into the companies where in time they owned them. The street is where you learned the business. As promotion men we were at the small clubs, getting down with the new and struggling artists and songwriters. We were also at the radio and TV stations, plugging our records and getting constant feedback on what was happening or getting ready to happen. All of us promo guys from the big labels and those who worked with the independent distributors spent a lot of time hanging out and sharing our wares.

We were the street guys, the "down in the trenches where it got dirty" guys. We spent a good amount of our days and nights sitting in the Hollywood coffee shops and bars.

These regular gatherings became unintended seminars. We shared our records, our failures, our successes, our ideas, and our plans to make things happen with our songs and artists. In the evenings we would bring our trophies to Martonis in the form of a famous artist, DJ, studio head, talent promoter, or whoever was key to the success of our adventures. The artists would get a chance to hustle the ones who could make or break their records, and the movers and shakers who wished they were famous entertainers schmoozed with the stars. Everyone got to drink and eat fancy meals all on expense accounts from the record companies. It was amazing how the status order moved around from month to month. We were identified with our companies and our artists and by the successes we had going for us at the time. In those days it did have a lot to do with us because eventual success in most cases started with our efforts.

We developed muscle like an athlete and talent like an actor. We had our contacts and would earn favors with the radio programmers. We would learn their individual tastes and knew which music director would most likely play a new record when it was released. It was always a long process in establishing a new artist or a hit record, and we had to develop that perfect mix of patience and determination. I would bring fresh coffee at five a.m. to the "morning man" at the jazz station. Or I'd visit the underground FM station and sit with the "all-night guy" to help him stay awake as he ministered the latest songs to the lonely people out there in the darkened and lonely halls of La La land. If you could get a handful of smaller local stations on your record and surround that with airplay on even smaller outlying area stations, you could sometimes build some "noise." It wouldn't take too many requests at the major record stores caused by this "noise" before the larger, more important stations would start taking notice. They would do samplings on their late-night shows to see if they would get follow-up requests. Every once in a while you would nail one. After much persuasion you would finally get a station to give your record a shot, and payday came when the program director would call and say those sweet words: "Our phone lines lit up when we played your record, and it will be added into major rotation starting next week."

A Beatles record, be it single or album, would come out, creating bedlam at all levels at the label. Then in the midst of that madness, Brian Wilson would walk in with a "Good Vibrations" or *Pet Sounds*. Buck Owens was the Beatles of country music, and he found a compatriot in me at the executive level in the Tower. Not only did I inherit babysitting his career at the label, but word got out about how down to earth and approachable I was because of my homespun Idaho upbringing. So on top of everything else, I became the go-to guy for the entire country roster.

In addition to my staff at the home office, I supervised about fifty guys in the field. My job required me to travel constantly in order to check on how their relationships were with the local stations, etc. They would also ask me to visit their markets to work with them when they needed a little push from the main office. My job included taking care of everything from planning the various campaigns to monitoring the expense accounts. I had to keep my eye on some of my men. Case in point: My Chicago guy lost an expensive hat to the wind when promoting one of our artists and put the cost of the hat on his expense account the next week. I disapproved it, and for several successive weeks he kept putting the hat on his expense accounts. Each week I would once again disapprove the reimbursement. Finally, I received an expense report without the hat being listed. I thought to myself, *Great, he finally gave up*. My happiness was short-lived. When I went to sign off on the report, he had placed a small asterisk at the bottom that read, "The hat is in there somewhere, you find it, boss!"

In the late 1960s, when the U.S. manager of Apple Records mantle fell on my shoulders, in addition to having to look after seven other labels that we were distributing, things really got crazy. I would head out on the road and the phone calls would keep coming in, which kept me hopping from fire to fire, town to town, preventing me from getting back home for weeks at a time. Try having a successful marriage in all this.

Not only were things getting a little shaky concerning Apple's future, I could also sense that the Beatles were on the verge of breaking up, so I left with several other Apple execs at the end of 1969 and accepted a vice presidency at MGM—a company in real trouble. Talk about jumping out of the frying pan into another frying pan—this once-vibrant record label still had a great roster, but the natives were restless because of bad management. This began the MGM and Mike Curb years. Once again, I was blessed to be associated with great acts—Eric Burdon, War, the Osmonds, Hank Williams Jr., Roy Orbison, Tompall and the Glaser Brothers, and John Sebastian of Lovin' Spoonful fame. MGM also had a movie soundtrack division as well as one of the greatest jazz catalogues and rosters with their Verve subsidiary. In time I was made the head of that division and was instructed to take advantage of the monumental catalogue and to begin building a contemporary roster as well. It was at MGM that my long friendship with Roy Orbison and Tompall developed, which in years to come would foster my role with the Outlaw movement in Nashville.

When I took over the Verve division, I started producing again. This was where my heart really was. I had done some record producing at Capitol and also produced a small hit in 1965 for Liberty Records by the Deep Six entitled "Rising Sun." It was those times in the studio behind the recording console that were the most thrilling to me.

After finishing an album at MGM/Verve with songwriter Larry Murray, I was fortunate to work with some of the great musicians on the LA recording scene. This experience of working with the A-list musicians allowed me to view being a producer on a whole new scale, and it changed everything for me. I had always known but now I knew! I was a producer! I decided to go to Mike Curb and ask him to let me out of my executive contract with MGM corporate. Mike understood where I was coming from because he had visited me in the studio years before when I was producing for Liberty. He knew it was where I belonged. Mike was very gracious and freed me to set up my own company—Hometown Productions Inc.—in 1971.

I had a good start with my new company and put together a couple of lucrative deals right off the bat. However, it was less than a year when Andy Williams made me an offer I couldn't refuse. He invited me to take over the presidency of his Barnaby/CBS label. Andy and former Barnaby president Alan Bernard had parted ways, and he decided he didn't want to replace Alan's position as his manager. He did, however, want somebody with a background like mine to take over his wholly owned record and publishing company. It was another dream job because I was able to be the top guy at the company, and I also had the option to produce the acts on the label. Andy and I were great together as pals, but the label chemistry never quite paid off. After a couple of years I once again resigned to reactivate Hometown Productions. Before I left I was able to return a kindness to Mike Curb by moving our company over to his distribution system, and Barnaby/CBS became Barnaby/MGM. By now the relationship with Waylon and Tompall was in full swing. I was up to speed—prepared, pumped, and primed to become an Outlaw.

I decided that I liked being called "Hoss" more than I did boss.

THE PLANE TRUTH

Have you ever wondered how God sees you? I often imagine myself sitting and talking with Him face-to-face because I am so curious about what He actually thinks of me. I remember the time when I was flying back from some exceptionally heady meetings in Atlanta when I was a young executive at Capitol Records.

I was seated next to Capitol Industries president Stanley Gortikov, which in some ways was a seat of honor at the banquet of my ambitious climb to the top of that corporate ladder. It was obvious to everyone I had virtually come from out of nowhere and shot up through the Capitol ranks. So there I was positioned next to the man himself. I was in my late twenties, and Gortikov was a retired military general and president of one of the biggest companies in the recording industry. Our goal in the record business was to make gold records, and we did this by taking advantage of golden opportunities—I was sitting in the middle of one on this plane.

Basically I asked him how I was doing, knowing that I was the boy wonder within his executive staff. He thought for a minute and replied, "Well, Ken, you seem to have a certain lack of humility!" I have said before that the two people I had learned more from and had the greatest respect for in the industry were Ron Kass, the president of Apple Records, and Stanley Gortikov. Gortikov's clear statement of fact was so pure and on the money that I was neither offended nor crushed, because I could read between the lines. He wasn't condemning me or going to fire me because I was such a hotshot. He was simply admonishing me and giving me guidance because he had a future for me in the company. He knew he had said everything he needed to say to get his message across to me.

Not to compare God with Gortikov, but when I have my imaginary conversations with Him, I feel as if He speaks to me in somewhat the same way—it is more than the words that pour into my head; it is the info that fills my soul. He tells it like it is, and because He is Truth, that is exactly what I get. It's a straight 100-proof shot, directly from the well of knowledge—not a watered-down drink of the day. Because it is so pure, it is strong and sometimes hard to swallow, but you know if you partake of it regularly, it will be the best thing for you in the long run. For example: I can read in the Bible about the walls of the tabernacle being forty cubits high, then in my heart He convicts me about my critical nature or some other displeasing aspect of my spiritual walk. He speaks to me gently without condemnation and gives me guidance and hope. The main thing is that, like Stan Gortikov that day on the airplane, God speaks directly to me and cuts through the chaff.

I was flying high in many ways when this conversation began, and by the time the conversation was over, I found myself grounded by the wisdom that had just been given to me.

Truth is good. God is Truth. God is good.

That's the "plane" Truth.

I WANT MY ABC

The long-running industry practice of paying off broadcasters to play songs—more popularly referred to as "payola"—has been around since the days when recording companies paid cash to DJs. To understand how far back payola originates, consider its roots: the term comes from a contraction of the words "pay" and "Victrola," the brand name of a wind-up record player.

By 1960, Congress enacted a law barring broadcasters from taking cash or valuable items from record companies that want certain songs on the air. But payola never really stopped said Jerry del Colliano, a music professor at the University of Southern California. "When disc jockeys played music, that was a scandal in the '50s so radio companies said, 'We'll let program directors pick the music.' Then the program directors picked the music and they got involved in the next wave of payola in the '60s and '70s."*

The '60s were possibly the most exciting and pivotal decade in the music industry, but there was also an unsettling phenomenon that resurfaced into the public awareness called "payola." I find it interesting that such a melodic word would have such a dark meaning. There were so many shades of what did and did not constitute payola that in the early years the ground rules were vague. When it became rampant and a bit too overt, things started getting out of hand. The big payola scandals emerged in the

* *(Los Angeles Business Journal December 5, 2005)*

late 1950s; politicians in Washington D.C. got involved by forming sub-committees and people started going to jail.

The aftermath of clamping down on payola's participants caused an overreaction throughout the industry, and deep paranoia set in, especially at the major corporation level. The big record companies such as Capitol, RCA, and Columbia had very tight policies pertaining to payola. As head of Capitol's promotion force, I was under strict orders to follow the rules very closely concerning this issue. I also knew that someone "out there" in government land was keeping a close watch on my activities and expenditures.

Payola also extended to television. No one was under more scrutiny at this time than a young man named Dick Howard. Dick was the talent booker for the hot pop show on ABC Television called *Shindig!* If a record company could get one of their new acts on the show, or any act from the label for that matter, it was almost guaranteed both the record featured and the artist performing it would enjoy newfound success. If anyone was a major target to be "bought," it was Dick Howard. The government watchdogs hiding in the shadows kept his activities under a very large microscope. They were waiting for him to succumb to temptation and slip up. In the '60s people in these positions were not typically paid that well, but a job like his was a prestigious one with a lot of perks and a springboard into more lucrative employment in the future. The low pay did increase the lure of the temptations payola had to offer, but Dick was very cautious and made sure that nothing he did would look suspicious when bringing talent on the show.

It was 1965 and my first year at Capitol. Being located in Hollywood, the ABC-TV studios were part of my territory. It was imperative that I establish a good relationship with Mr. Howard and make every effort to place our acts and their records on his show. We hit it off immediately and were well aware we had nailed highly esteemed positions in the music industry at very young ages. Capitol had several acts on the show regularly, and Dick and I had a consistent and healthy working relationship. Dick trusted me, and no one could logically question our business relationship because the acts that he booked from our roster were unquestionably legitimate. There was never any reason to step outside the dictates of the established ethical and legal standards. He was an odd duck in some ways. A lot of people didn't care for him, partly out of their ineffectiveness in being able to get him to put their artists on the show and partly because he did have to be a bit standoffish and protective because so many people approached him for favors.

Shindig! was at its zenith around the time I had just purchased a brand-new little red sports car. It was called a Datsun "Fairlady," and this little roadster was a sharp looker. Because it was new and not very common, people perceived it as being a bit more upscale than it really was. One day I got it all polished up and decided to pull a harmless prank on Dick.

In order to visit the ABC lot, it was necessary for the executive you were scheduled to visit to have your name left at a forbidding gate guarding the entrance to the lot. Once you were allowed access, there was a large circular area right inside the guard gate—a commons area. During lunchtime, it would be filled with employees, visitors, talent, crew, etc., who crisscrossed the area, on their way to lunch or changing locations within the lot. I had made a lunch appointment with Dick that day, and he left my name at the gate so I could enter the studio lot to pick him up. Because his office was close to the entrance, he told me to have the guard call his office when I arrived. He instructed me to pull into the circular area inside the gate and he would come out and jump in my car. That way I wouldn't have to hunt for a parking space.

When lunchtime arrived, I pulled up to the gate in my red sports car. The guard verified my appointment and called Dick's office to let him know I was there. I pulled inside the gate and stopped dead center in the commons area. There was a considerable amount of foot traffic that day, and many people slowed down in order to check out my shiny roadster.

I saw Dick coming my way from the interior lot, so I turned off the motor and got out of the car. When he was about fifteen to twenty feet away, I yelled across the lot so everyone could hear, "Dick, thanks for putting my acts on the show. Here is the car just as I promised." I then threw the car keys in the air to him, and in automatic reflex he reached out to catch them. I turned and started walking toward the guard gate. Dick dropped the set of keys like a hot potato. He exclaimed loudly to the entire crowd who had stopped in their tracks to look at him, "No, no, no—not true, not true, not true!" I waited outside the gate for a minute and then came back in. I walked over to him, smiling, picked up the keys, and asked politely if he was hungry. He was steaming mad, but the joke was funnier than he was angry, and we got a big laugh out of it over lunch.

I put it to him real good one more time, and he suggested very succinctly that he would appreciate it if I ceased being so "damn" funny from that point on.

Capitol had printed up fake one-hundred-dollar bills with an advertisement printed on one side, stating that a certain new record we were promoting had a million-dollar sound. We sent this fake money out along with the record to radio stations across the country as a gimmick to catch their attention. The inference, in jest of course, was we were sending payola along with the record. We made the money look as real as possible while making sure that anyone who saw it would never mistake it for the real thing. A picture of the artist replacing Benjamin Franklin's in the middle of the bill was a dead giveaway the currency was fake.

As I looked down at a pile of this bogus cash sitting on my desk, I came up with an idea specifically aimed at my good friend—Mr. *Shindig!* himself—Dick Howard. I instructed my secretary to make a special trip to the local stationery store and purchase envelopes with the thinnest paper she could find. I wanted that distinctive paper where you could see the contents inside when you pressed on the envelope. I then filled one of these envelopes with a wad of fake money, making sure that the money side faced out on both the front and back in the envelope. I mailed it to Mr. Dick Howard c/o ABC Television Studios 4151 Prospect Avenue, Hollywood, CA 90027. On the lower left-hand corner of the envelope, where it is sometimes customary to print handling instructions, I wrote in big letters: IMPORTANT—PAYOLA FOR RECIPIENT ONLY. I knew that all ABC correspondence went through the central mailroom before it was delivered to the appropriate offices.

I got a call from Dick the day after I mailed the envelope. He asked, not kindly I might add, for me to stop with the funny stuff. The letter was not delivered to his office by the usual kid from the mailroom but by a two-man team of government officials. The bureaucrats made poor Dick open the envelope in front of them so they could arrest him on the spot for receiving payola. When they saw what was actually inside the envelope, they realized it was a joke, but it was not funny to anyone in the room at the time. I had wasted everyone's time and gave Dick a near coronary. Dick admitted he had a few very uncomfortable moments when the envelope was first handed to him.

Almost three decades later, I ran into Dick at a Music Row watering hole in Nashville. Guess what we talked about? According to Dick, it was much funnier in remembering than it was in being there. We agreed the special times we shared as young bucks were magical once we learned our ABCs of the business.

TROUBLED DEER SLIDING

Like a troubled deer
Sensing the hunters' intent
I slide between the trees
Always seeking higher ground

KEN MANSFIELD, 2002

I t's like falling out of a tree—that unique moment between the limb and the earth. You know you're going to land, but you're not sure how the new ground is going to receive you. It's more than just being between things, and it's beyond going from one place to another. During this spatial moment, it is critical to determine whether you are falling or jumping. Did you leap, let go, or lose your grip? One thing is for sure—you are committed.

"There's something happening here. What it is ain't exactly clear."
—BUFFALO SPRINGFIELD, 1967

That's how I felt when I left home at seventeen. My transporting time capsule began with the diesel departing of a rickety 1955 Greyhound bus from the small, insignificant station just off Main Street in Lewiston, Idaho. It was a dank, dark, below-zero day. I didn't bother to look out the window as the "big dog" sputtered me out of my native land.

I know now that I was jumping. I just wanted to get out of there. As I said before, it wasn't so much that I didn't like my hometown; I've always been very glad I grew up there. It was just that I had those far-off cities in my sights, which gave me someplace to go. I knew I was going to end up in LA or somewhere similar. I was also glad I hadn't been there from the beginning.

We lived out of town in an area called the Orchards. Kids from the Orchards were different from the town kids. In those days we were typically poorer and in many cases came from less-educated stock. My dad didn't have a car most of the time I was growing up, and we didn't have indoor plumbing until I was in high school. As a teenager I did talk him into moving the outhouse so it would be hidden behind our small barn. It was a calculated move on my part so that in the evening, when a friend would give me a ride home from a school activity, the headlights would no longer shine on it as we came to the end of the dirt road that became our driveway. The aesthetics of this move were sometimes offset by the discomfort of the distance on those frozen, just-below-the-Canadian-border winter nights, when the frost was more than on the pumpkin.

The backside of the Orchards bordered the Nez Perce Indian reservation lands where Sacajawea was a common word and where the mighty Chief Joseph and his decimated tribe of peaceful people were told to stay. I loved the rolling hills, the beautiful rivers, the smells of the seasons, and the open wheat fields that gave way to the entrance of Hell's Canyon and the rugged Idaho wilderness. The Snake and Clearwater rivers met here and went away to become the Columbia River that ran to the far-off sea. There was a time, before the "damn damming," when ocean vessels came all the way up to Lewiston, which proudly called itself "Idaho's Only Seaport."

※　※　※

I leave my thoughts of Idaho summers and become soft inside, surrounded by the morning glow of Laurel Canyon. I am in the parking lot below the Hangover House, still mesmerized by my thoughts of Lash LaRue. As I lean against Moses' front right fender, I start thinking about another interesting man—the Man of Sorrows. I think about what He did for me and I become ashamed of my confusion. He paid this phenomenal price so it would be perfectly clear to everyone how much He loves us. With the Truth of all truths staring me in the face, I stand, blinking like a frog in a hailstorm.

I am the troubled deer, sliding between the trees of my personal dilemma, and in the process I realize I am hiding from the purity of His message. As if peering out of the fog of some contradictory conquest, the victory of a battle already won eludes me. From the bastion of my resistance, I peer into the mist of His meaning and purpose for my life. I feebly grasp for His nail-scarred hand.

I now understand that the troubled deer represents the scared child within. The hunter's intent is the persistence of a stalking devil, and the slide between the trees is my vain attempt to avoid the scrapes and pain along the way to reaching the sanctuary of higher ground that is God's mercy and grace.

MRS. MILLER'S GREATEST HITS

Raised in Kansas, Elva Connes worked as a housekeeper before marrying John Richardson Miller in 1934. The couple moved to Claremont, California, and Miller's husband, an investor, amassed a modest fortune. Mrs. Miller stayed active with numerous charitable activities, but beginning sometime in the early 1960s, she began indulging her interest in singing by hiring studio time and musicians and recording hymns—"Just for the ducks of it," as she told one interviewer.

At one of these sessions, Fred Bock, a keyboard player and composer of choral works, talked her into recording a current hit, Petula Clark's "Downtown." Bock took a tape of it to Lex de Azevedo, who latched onto the idea of having Miller record a whole album of current rock 'n' roll hits. Bock and de Azevedo brought in some crack session players, including drummer Earl Palmer and bassist Jimmy Bond, and they drilled through eleven numbers while Mrs. Miller warbled, wavered, cracked, gasped, shrilled, and generally sang her heart out. (http://www.spaceage-pop.com/mrsmille.htm)

One of the most memorable artists I worked with over the years was Mrs. Miller. The preceding blurb is part of the story, but here's the inside scoop . . .

The year was 1966. At two p.m. each Wednesday, a handful of department heads would routinely meet in the twelfth-floor conference room and plan the single records to be released on Capitol Records five weeks later. The core group consisted of the heads of sales, marketing, press and publicity, promotion, and A&R. The producers would present their product, play it for us, fill us in on the background of the artist, and explain why their particular recording had hit potential. This was done so that various departments could prepare appropriate strategies for these future releases. It was serious business and it was the heart of the machine—where it all began in the company's bid for success in the industry.

As a little treat, Lex de Azevedo would play us these awful recordings by Mrs. Miller for a bit of comic relief at the end of the meetings. It was explained to us that her affluent husband would humor her singing aspirations by giving the fifty-nine-year-old songbird a recording budget. Once a month she would go into the studio with a keyboard player so she could make her little records. (The term in the industry for recordings made through personal finance without company backing was called making a "vanity record.") Her material was current chart-topping pop records. Keyboardist Fred Bock shared these recordings with his Capitol A&R friend, Lex, and it became a running source of amusement to the singles committee. At the end of one of these meetings, when we heard a butchered version of Petula Clark's "Downtown," we all fell on the floor. (Up to that point, our No. 1 top of the Elva pop charts was her version of the Toys' "A Lover's Concerto.") Once the laughter subsided, someone suggested that if this was so funny to us hardened music guys, then it was quite possible it would be even more amusing to the general public. We decided it was worth a shot, and Lex offered Mrs. Miller a recording contract.

With tongues firmly in cheek, this musical malady grew in its lunacy. You see, Mrs. Miller (Elva) was dead serious about her singing career and actually thought that Capitol was signing her as a legitimate recording artist. She thought the "hook" (the term for a commercial angle different from other artists' approach to making hit records) was that it was so intriguing to hear a singing virtuoso of her caliber performing these little rock-and-roll songs. The title of her first album, *Mrs. Miller's Greatest Hits*, was, in our minds, pure marketing genius.

We released the record, and to this day I will never understand how this thing took off like it did. For some reason it hit everyone's funny bone, young and old alike, and things started going crazy. The album sold

250,000 copies within three weeks, earning her a coveted spot on *The Ed Sullivan Show* and an article in *Life* magazine for openers. We couldn't buy publicity like that for most of our legitimate artists!

My job description put this project squarely in my lap. Record sales were going through the roof; the phones at the Capitol Tower were ringing off the hooks, tying up the switchboards to the point it was interfering with thirteen floors of business. I couldn't keep up with the requests for interviews, photo ops, personal appearances, endorsement solicitations, concert tours, etc. It was sheer pandemonium. Forget Elvis—we had Elva. It was Miller time!

So here was this sweet lady, driving all the way to the Tower from her flower-laden home in Pasadena to spend afternoons with me on daily press junkets. We spent our time together on the phones, meeting with disc jockeys, trade magazine journalists, and newspaper columnists—all the while she worried about watering the petunias in her garden at home. She was so sweet and so sincere and completely clueless that this was all a joke. I was brazened enough already that I thought the whole thing was a hoot and was enjoying every moment of her unrealized embarrassment. I also gathered a little recognition from it all because this was the hottest thing going on at the time. They would ask her questions about her technique, especially how she was able to whistle so well. Mrs. Miller explained in great detail how she held ice cubes in her mouth for an extended period of time before recording her whistling segments—she said it helped tighten up the pucker.

I remember sitting there with her one day, as Elva courteously answered the same questions over and over, noticing what a kind and gentle person she was. She was so unlike the other jaded stars I worked with on a day-to-day basis. I thought to myself that finally here is one person who would never let fame go to her head.

To promote her follow-up album, *Will Success Spoil Mrs. Miller?* the marketing department went into overdrive. They created a full-size cardboard mock-up of Mrs. Miller, standing in her finest garb, holding her first album cover in one hand while holding the new one in the other, with her head tilted coyly to one side and smiling. These were sent out to the major record stores across the nation. Now, this was a very expensive piece of merchandise, and very few artists received this special treatment or expenditure on their behalf, but Mrs. Miller was a proven commodity, and we felt it was well worth the investment.

We placed one of the "stand-ups" in the lobby of the Capitol Tower. The Capitol lobby was by intention very stark, so when visitors entered the building they only saw walls of gold records and this big cardboard cutout of Mrs. Miller. No other artists were promoted in the lobby of that building except our dear, sweet Elva. We had a problem—by this time she had gotten up to speed with the ruse and had a less-than-pleasant reaction. She had already gone on record (the written kind) as to how Capitol had taken her great musical efforts and made them comical.

Elva revealed publicly that during recording sessions she was conducted half a beat ahead or behind time, and the worst of several different recordings of a song would be included on the finished record. Elva said with a straight face she didn't sing off-key or off-rhythm. She also claimed that her producer caused her to sing below her capabilities by making her wait until she was dead tired and having her make the record while she was in that weakened condition. Firing her last salvo, Elva complained that the engineers cut the record before she had a chance to become completely familiar with the songs. Her time lines of logic were bouncing all over the place.

One day she walked into the Capitol lobby and, upon seeing the promotional cardboard stand-up, kicked it over, stomped on it, and then marched upstairs and asked to be dropped from the label. She followed up by starting her own record company, Amaret Records, just off the corner of Hollywood and Vine, to compete with our little recording enterprise. Her vanity album, *Mrs. Miller Does Her Own Thing*, did nothing to dispel the notion that she had no talent. It also did nowhere near the business that our records did.

By 1973, she officially announced her retirement and, save for a few benefit concerts, basically dropped out of sight.

Mrs. Miller had a good run for eighteen months, which goes to prove that it isn't always how good you are but sometimes about how good you make other people feel. As I look back on my role in this melodrama, I am not left with a good feeling about being part of a subtle but cruel deception.

I feel like a child who doesn't realize how much he is hurting the other kids when he makes fun of them.

Elva Connes Miller passed away in 1997 at the age of ninety in Vista, California. She is buried in a mausoleum at Pomona Valley Memorial Park.

When we meet in eternity, I will apologize.

Elva has left the building.

THE WRITHING ON THE WALL

There's this wall when conversations come around to religion. It looms before me when I am asked to give my testimony, to tell my story, to lay it out there for all to see. I become overwhelmed when I consider the magnitude of my salvation and find myself at a loss for words, at least at a loss for a lot of words. But then in this moment of awkward silence, God's still, small voice speaks to my heart, and the thought that comes to mind is . . .

He loved me first!

That realization stops me in my tracks, and I can't get past this astonishing fact . . .

He loved me first!

It all seems to begin and end with that for me. That's all I need to know. I didn't even *like* me, and He *loved* me! I try to wander off from that realization, but like a giant rubber band tied to my heart, I keep getting pulled back to that point in time, an instant of awareness, a gentle explosion of truth that rushed through every fiber of my being when I first realized, wow . . .

He loved me first!

All things seem to come out of that simple fact for me. The deepest emotion, the most important thing in life, the foundation of everything that is inherently valuable is this special godly love I know is mine. It is His point of reference—a font beyond human reference—and it prevails, encompasses, precedes, inhabits, and involves, all that is about Him . . .

He loves first.

When I hit this wonder wall, I find it is not a stopping place: instead, it's a stooping place. It's a place where I fall to my knees and place my face in my hands and weep tears of joy . . .

He loved me first!

I am surrounded by the enormity of His love. This wall is not an obstacle in my way but an observation point from where I can see everything. What stands before me is not something I can't get around; instead, it's a place I am able to crawl into. It rises up from below me, permeates through me, and overtakes me, pushing me up to that beautiful point of being able to simply partake of this gift. It lifts me above and beyond any place I could ever go on my own—simply because I give into it. By letting go I allow its essence inside of me.

I reach down between the cup holders for my Bible and set it on my lap. I place my finger about four-fifths into its pages. I touch upon the place where Jesus talks about the man standing and praying at a wall who can't even look up because of the weight of his sin. I am that man. I skip over that part quickly so I can feel my way to the next part where Jesus says He hears his prayer and forgives him. As my memory reads on it is so sweet to partake of the mercy and grace that flows from the loving words of wisdom I am holding in my hand.

In that moment of sweet communion, my breath is taken away as I ponder the story of the man praying at the wall, which took place long ago. And now, as I travel down lonely stretches of highway, I am warmed by the realization that Jesus hasn't changed a bit.

He loved the man at the wall first too.

LIMO 'N AID

L et's look at a typical Hometown Productions day and some of the regulars who bounced in and out and around and about the edges of our "Hollyworld" in the '70s . . .

My wife (third of four) and I decided to have a no-reason party at the Hangover House. Life was looking good in those days, and we wanted to share the fine times with a few friends. I had just registered a No. 1 record with Waylon Jennings and found myself basking in the limelight as producer of the mushrooming Outlaw movement. We were simply feeling good about life in general, and it was an especially sweet time weather-wise in the canyons. The jasmine, honeysuckle, and bougainvillea were in full bloom around the property, which gave the place a sweet scent and subtle sense of serenity. Because of the uniqueness and historical nature of our secluded estate, we knew people were very curious. We would look out from the house and often see people standing on the street below, looking up at the property. Friends and business associates often hinted to us they wanted to see the place. Our intended soirée would give us a chance to open it up to some of our acquaintances who had never been invited to the house before.

It was Wednesday when we came up with the idea to have a party, and we didn't want to wait. We decided to plan it for the following night. Because it was spur of the moment, we immediately began making calls to a few friends. We told them to go ahead and put out the word and invite anyone in our circle who may want to come. Although this was the '70s, the Hollywood insiders did have their own "high" speed connection. By ten p.m. Thursday night the traffic was backed up all the way down the canyon. Approximately 250 people showed up based on our original half-dozen phone calls.

The reason for the turnout was because we had a very large and diversified group of people to draw from. I had my British friends from the Beatles/Apple days; Nashville and cowboy friends from the Outlaw era; industry friends from the executive years at Capitol, MGM, CBS/Barnaby; as well as musician, arranger, songwriter friends from my many years as a record producer. Throw in the studio people, club owners, restaurant crews, and my wife's movie industry pals, and it was obvious this was not a "few co-workers from the insurance office" type of gathering.

The party roster was absolutely bizarre in its diversity—the rich and the famous, the has-beens and wannabees, directors and drifters, playboys and playmates, cowboys and Indians (yes, real ones from both America and India), and everything in between. The drugs, drinking, and deal making escalated to a fever pitch when the whole thing was forced to shut down around two or three a.m. The police in these various Hollywood enclaves were cool, and their basic approach to matters such as these was one of logic. We were still the peace and love generation, and they knew we never meant any harm. We were instructed to either close it down while they forgot to notice certain illegalities or they would start noticing things, writing them down, and providing free escort service to a place with no bougainvillea or the smell of honeysuckle in the air. We could use our bandwagons to clear the place or they would use their paddy wagons. Our home was cleared by three-thirty, the housekeeping cleaned up, and we were in bed an hour later.

There is always a final act to almost everything you do in Hollywood, and this evening was no exception. It had the perfect climactic ending—a curtain call that in an obtuse way described the parameters of the fantasy world in which we lived. Around five a.m. I heard a loud knock at the front door of the main house. We figured it was someone who had shown up late and was too bombed to notice that the party was over. But the hammering on the door continued with desperate pleas to open up. I eventually recognized the voice.

The Buffalo Springfield, in my estimation, was a wellspring of some of the greatest groups of our time. Out of their lyrical harmonics evolved the people and resonance of bands like Crosby, Stills, Nash & Young; Poco; the Flying Burrito Bros.; and the Eagles to name a few. They were a major catalyst for the country folk rock sound that has been a perpetual sound in our ears and hearts since the late '60s. The first time the Buffaloes came stampeding into my mind I was mesmerized by the uniqueness of their music as well as the almost classical depth of their arrangements and ideas. As the group dispersed into the newer incarnations, I had my moments with some of the original members. I coproduced my first chart record, *Rising Sun* by the Deep Six, with Jim Messina, signed bass player Bruce Palmer to a solo deal at MGM, and got Neil Young to let me change lyrics of his "Are You Ready for the Country" for one of Waylon's historical hits. I also befriended Dewey Martin, Buffalo Springfield's drummer, who, though talented, hadn't fared as well as some of the other original members in sub-sequent years.

Well, it was Dewey at the door. That night he decided my party was an opportunity to reconnect with some of the industry's movers and shakers. To make a favorable impression, he had hired a limo for his grand entrance and exit. As it turned out, when the party was over, he didn't have enough cash to pay for the ride. His dilemma was that in order to let the driver and car go, he had to pay them first. He had driven away from the party in style, but before Dewey could make his exit from the limo, he needed carfare. He set out visiting local hangouts, looking for old pals to borrow some cash. Of course, this rambling about town ran up the bill. The longer it was taking him to score the money, the higher the tab was getting. It was also getting much later and harder to find potential contributors.

The Dewey decibel systematic pounding was getting louder, so I got up and answered the door. I wish you could have seen what was probably the most humble, hat-in-hand, ashamed, in-need-of-a-real-good-friend looks that I had ever seen. The legendary drummer stood there at my door with his head bowed and the saddest eyes, staring up to me with the most forlorn look on his face. I was his last resort.

He explained his situation and it was Gene Clark time all over again. I also choose to remember Dewey that way because the sweetness of our camaraderie and weary miles together all seem to glow at times like these. Almost every one of us in the music business seems to end up in these straits at one time or another—it is simply the nature of the beast. We do become family in some odd way, and there are times when we have to help each other out. It wasn't a loan he needed, and it wasn't a handout either. As far as I was concerned, he was collecting some hard-earned dues to pay the rough road bills that one incurs making their bones in our business.

I went inside and got the cash plus enough for a nice tip for the limo driver. I handed it to Dewey and reminded him how much he had influenced my musical journey. I stuffed the money in his shirt pocket, then softly held both of his drum-stick calloused hands—the outstretched hand and the "hat in hand" hand—and told him straight on it was partial payment for a job well done.

Dewey knew it was OK between us. As he walked away he turned and said to me, "Now you know who to call if you ever . . ."

Leaving the Laurels

I know my lasso doesn't always twirl in a perfect circle, but as John Lennon said in reference to being a dreamer: "But I'm not the only one."

I believe in God as much as I can imagine any man doing. It is in such a deep part of my heart, my being, and my searching soul I know that it can never be separated from me. I breathe in precious life itself in God's sweet air. I bask in His creation where I am warmed by the radiance of the sun and soothed by the mercy of the Son. I paid dearly for my years of resistance to His salvation, and things of such high cost have great value. I believe every word He says is true, and I believe with all of my heart I will spend eternity gazing into His glorious countenance.

So what's my problem? Why am I traveling back up these rugged roads like a gangster returning to the scenes of his crimes? What are these doubts that plague me, and where are they coming from? If I believe so deeply, why am I even remotely troubled? I have an angel on my shoulder and the devil on my back. I have my gaze fixed clearly on the prize according to His perfect promises, while at the same time I seem to have Satan's "hot" hits blaring from an old boom box pressed up against my ears.

I knew when this adventure began that for some odd reason I needed to retrace my tracks. I had to go back to where the world was my home and make withdrawals from my Sunset Stripped memory bank. I was aching to have a Tinseltown showdown with the skirmish that brought me to personal defeat and eternal victory. I needed to take a backward peek and stick my finger into those tinsel-tainted hot spots in order to remember how it feels to be burned beyond recognition but, praise God, not redemption.

In the days of my decadence, I was a reverse hurricane—calm, still, and quiet around the edges, but in the center—pure disaster. Now I am filled with the peace that surpasses all understanding. But I still have days like this where I wonder why I feel like I am one lamb chop short of a mixed grill.

Selfishly I must admit I did enjoy the events that led up into those hills and the estate much more than those that drove me away. As I turn to leave the Hangover House this final time, I am not sure I can find the way out of the canyon of laurels when I am not stoned. I had traveled so far to get to that flashpoint time in my career, but when it all fell apart and was officially over, it is surprising how much faster I traveled backward. I attained much higher speeds falling down than I ever did when I was moving up.

From the day I left the innocent rodeo of my cowboy upbringings, it was always upward to the, as Lennon once said, "toppermost of the poppermost." I did it on my own. No God, no family, no mentor, no coach, no counsel, and no consortium behind me or with me. I just played it by ear, and my potato-bred innocence seemed to pull me through. I was on a collision course the whole time, though. I was blessed with a near genius IQ and cursed with no common sense. This, coupled with zero guidance and less concern, sent me careening down life's highway until I unwittingly encountered the devil's curve that I eventually would fail to negotiate.

I am so glad I found God—Okay, I am so glad He came and saved me. I love being a Christian. I like the people, the ideals, the rulebook, and the goodness that pervades the very existence of this fellowship between God and man. I want perfection; I want to drink from the deepest deep and bathe in the purity of its lucid living waters.

I disengage my mind and put Moses in gear and drive down and out of the canyon. We head into the black heart of Hollywood and wend our way from there via back streets toward the airport. I learned from the several limo drivers who shuttled me about, the shortest, fastest way from Hollywood to LAX. It is amazing I remembered anything at all because not only was I usually stoned the whole time, I typically made sure the driver was likewise mellowed out so I would have someone to converse with on the same wavelength.

I reexamine every building, intersection, billboard, and storefront on this once familiar route—somewhat like taking a time-released inventory.

Everything seemed to be in order on the outside; now it was time to set things in order on the inside.

We have been traveling side streets up to this point. As we approach the San Diego Freeway (Interstate 405), instead of crossing over it on La Tijera Boulevard as we did then, to go in the back way to LAX, I turn Moses onto the freeway and head south toward Orange County and maybe San Diego.

I began my California life in San Diego first as a seaman recruit in the United States Navy and then as graduate of San Diego State University. This was followed by a few years of space industry employment, touring with the Town Criers, and a stint at owning a folk club called the Land of Oden in La Mesa, a quiet suburb of San Diego.

Highway 101 was the main road that connected San Diego to LA, and at that time it was two lanes. Now I am on a fourteen-lane horizontal monolith, making less time with a much faster machine. They call this stretch the world's longest parking lot. As we travel south I nod acceptance to lots of single-fingered peace signs that are offered my way. I guess I am not moving fast enough for my fellow motorists as they speed into their own personal nowhere lands.

Wrapped in the safety of sweet jazz coming from my iPod's turn as musical background to our travelogue, I bend my body into the smog and clamor of it all. I press ahead full speed, not wanting to ever fall behind in this unwelcome race against time and sanity—regardless of whether I had anywhere to go or any idea when I was supposed to get there. In the heat of the challenge, I make up my mind. San Diego it is.

THE FIFTH FRESHMAN

Musical irony continues to pour forth from my shuffling iPod as we head out of LA on Interstate 405 south toward San Diego. Entering this metropolis my thoughts turn to how my decades-long stint began with recollections of meeting Bill Wagner and my fascination with the group he managed, the Four Freshmen.

As we leave town we are treated to the incredible harmonies of the decades-old hit song that made this legendary group famous—"The Day Isn't Long Enough." It is the song that opened my world of musical harmonic possibilities and guided much of the thinking in my group, the Town Criers, as well as the approach I took to many of my vocal arrangements as a producer. I am not the only one who was deeply moved by their unique sound. Brian Wilson has openly admitted that he crafted the Beach Boys' pop surfer sound on the Freshmen's jazz vocal stylings. I heard one of the reasons he wanted to be on Capitol Records was because that was the label the Four Freshmen called home.

Their unique sound was a simple matter of arrangement and parts stacking. Brian, like the Freshmen, put the melody on top of their four-part harmony arrangements, which required the lead vocalist to sing falsetto in order to reach notes that high while leaving enough room for the other parts to be layered below. The surfer groups then emulated this high-pitched falsetto approach, and West Coast surfer music was born. Unlike the Beach Boys, the harmonic stacking of parts by the surfer groups was not as meticulous or creative but leaned more to the falsetto aspect of the male vocal. Like Brian Wilson, my becoming a part of the Capitol team was enhanced by the fact that I would meet and work with the "Fab Freshmen" at some point.

Bill Wagner had the unique ability to be an all business *and* pleasure kind of guy. Doing business with him was always a pleasure. Part of him sponsoring my entrance into the Capitol ranks had a bit to do with business as well as the fact that we connected right away. Bringing me aboard to be in charge of promotional aspects at Capitol in the nation's most influential market, knowing I was a big fan of the group he managed, meant he had a strong ally. That was especially important to him because he was promoting an act whose popularity was waning. Their past success was not enough to keep them on the charts, as the wave of British bands and the new rock sound was taking over. There was still a place for singers like Nat King Cole, Peggy Lee, and Frank Sinatra, but it was farther back in coach; while the first-class seats were being taken by the Beatles, the Stones, and the Beach Boys. Bill wisely promoted my friendship with the Freshmen and made me feel a part of the family. He had told them what a big fan I was and relayed to them my braggadocio of knowing all their songs word for word. My veracity was soon put to the test.

Early on in my stint at Capitol, the Four Freshmen released a new single and were basically fighting to keep themselves on the Capitol roster because their record sales had slumped dramatically. On this new recording they had taken the approach of maintaining their traditional vocal style but updating the band arrangement and lyric content to fit the current market. Bill knew I could be counted on to go to the wire for the group. I did just that by pulling in favors with radio, press, and television, garnering as much exposure as I could for my friends. I even managed to get them booked on Sam Riddle's *9th Street West* TV show, one of the new dance shows based in Hollywood where the artists appeared live and lip-synched the vocals to the instrumental track. It was an important booking because the show was syndicated nationally and was part of a group of "in" pop television shows aimed at the teen record-buying market.

The day of the show I stood off camera at the TV studio with three of the Four Freshmen, waiting for lead singer Don Barbour to show up. We were becoming a bit worried because it was closing in on performance time and there was no Don. A young lady ran over to us and told Bill Wagner there was an important call for him in the production booth on the studio "hot line." It was someone calling from a pay phone. The call was from Don—he had been involved in an accident on the Hollywood Freeway. He wasn't seriously injured but was definitely not going to make it in time for the show. This was an important promotion for the group and a favor I would never be able to hang on to if they were a no-show. I started freaking out when I became aware that Bill and the three "Freshmen" were staring at me.

Bill Wagner broke the silence. "So you know all our songs, huh? Well, here's Don's jacket. (They wore matching outfits.) Put it on and we shall see!" It was a matter of minutes before I was on the set and the group was being introduced. Well, I did know the song and on cue started mouthing the lyrics along with the other guys. I have to tell you, all I could think of during that brief time on camera was that I was one of the Four Freshmen, even if it was only for two and a half minutes! My Town Crier days kicked in and I became immediately comfortable in my role as a member of a singing quartet. I had seen them perform enough times to have a feel for Don Barber's moves. To this day it ranks right up there with the Beatles' January 1969 rooftop performance as one of my all-time favorite moments in showbiz.

I had saved the day for them, but as far as I was concerned, that day definitely was not long enough for me.

▨   ▨   ▨

The song and my thoughts fade away in unison, and I get lost in the momentary silence.

The Dave Brubeck Quartet follows with the strains of "Take Five."

Moses has locked into a middle lane of the San Diego Freeway.

San Diego: 87 miles.

MILE MARKER # 3
SAN DIEGO

LILIES IN THE FIELD

San Diego was pivotal to about everything that happened to me from my twenties forward.

It takes a few days to "do the town," and although Connie and I had been here together before, this time it has an entirely different feel.

I drive her through Mission Valley; we walk the San Diego State University campus, tour Balboa Park, and drive by the various areas where I once lived. We spend an entire day on the shore at Mission Beach and La Jolla, capping it off with a romantic seaside dinner at Shelter Island. It was as if the essence of my youth was still hanging in the air here and I could close my eyes and breathe it all back in. My country boy naiveté had not been overtaken by cruel world realities at that point, and in those early years I was able to bask in the selfishness of youth and enjoy all my victories without concern for anyone else. Life was simple in that way—maybe not nice in a spiritual way but uncomplicated and gratifying. I was classically invincible, emotionally bulletproof; and from this launching pad I headed for the hills—the Beverly and Hollywood kind of Hills.

Connie and I had fun in San Diego because it was possibly the only place on our journey where my life may have not been counterbalanced with trying times. It was an island in the spatial span of my development where the debris had yet failed to wash ashore. The sand was soft and smooth, the nights were tender and warm, and blessings glided smoothly on the gentle breeze that wafted in from exotica into my waiting arms. It was like a dream and such a long way from both the rigors of my growing-up years and the rude awakenings to follow. It was the soft spot in between. I like remembering the happy part of that early sojourn. The "in between" person who existed then was catching, and Connie was able to grab a piece of the old (young) "me" while we were there.

In order to stay longer, I would have had to start repeating side trips and stories, so it was checkout time from both our hotel and my reminisces. We are in the southwest corner of America and have only two of the four directions to choose from as we continue on with Moses. We decide to head east. It is time to depart—we gas up, point Moses at Arizona, and get out of town on Interstate 8. We will hook up with Interstate 10 on our way to our next main stop—Austin, Texas.

It is close to an hour before we have totally broken out into the open, leaving the crush of cars behind. As the last of the San Diego skyline fades away in the rearview mirror, I posit inwardly that something is wrong with all this. I thought when I became a Christian things would sort themselves out automatically. I had figured I would be able to deal head-on with tough situations in a Christlike manner and then just sail on through all the tribulations. But that's not how it's working out. Instead, it seems whenever I place my trust on the Rock, it rolls over me and crushes me beneath its weight. I seek and yet I don't seem to find. I press in and I get pushed out. I pray and bow down and that's where I usually end up—neither my head nor my heart becomes uplifted. I keep the faith, and no one else is faithful. I keep a stiff upper lip and get slammed in the mouth. I reach out a helping hand, and someone steps on my fingers and grinds a burning ciggie into my palm. There are times when I struggle with the pain of trying to deal with it all. Now I know why Van Gogh cut his ear off. He just wanted to close off the noise, to go inside and shut the door to his head—his soul—and to get away from the agitation outside and get lost in the madness inside. Sometimes the familiar inner turmoil feels almost quiet in comparison and becomes a balm that can cover the incessant and bring perplexity to a halt. A roar becomes a sonnet, and the gruesome grind comes to a suspended crawl. Energy becomes lethargy, and the calm prevails through the lunacy.

These disjointed thoughts feel inappropriate at this particular juncture as I have just left a place of fond memories. I am aware this is the usual old earthly stuff coming out of me, and somewhere in the center of all this is a promise. So I grab on to that like a sinking sailor, reaching in desperation for a life preserver. I reach out because it is my only hope—not because I am strong enough to believe on my own but because it is the only way out. It's a way that sometimes gets in the way, but it is more than a way—it is His Way. It is *the* Way.

When this whole inner dialogue has whipped itself up to a fever pitch, I find that as I look down at the speedometer, my inner tensions have made their way down my leg and made my foot heavy. I know Moses and the Israelites took a long time to cross the desert, but at this rate we will get there before we left. (The wilderness route to the Promised Land was 240 miles, and Moses the van will cover that distance in less than three hours if I don't slow down.) I ease back and give God thanks for His many blessings. I also mention that I am thankful that He kept "the fuzz" off my back. I look up and the sand dunes are alive with beautiful flowers that cover the landscape like a carpet as far as the eye can see. My dampening doubts hit the heat outside and evaporate into His mercy and grace. The desert bloom reminds me of Scripture and the lilies and His care and provision.

I am thankful I have kept my thoughts to myself, so I don't have to apologize out loud. I do that now in prayer, and before my words are complete, He has already let the sweetness of His forgiveness flow over me. Peace prevails in the tumult and gale.

I become light and free inside to the point where once again I realize that I haven't looked down at the speedometer in quite a while. I am so mellowed out that before I do, something catches my attention in the rearview mirror. What I see is the California Highway Patrol pulling me over.

He wanted to know why I was driving so slowly.

MILE MARKER # 4
ARIZONA

ODE TO BOBBIE G

The Sonoran Desert scenery offers it own unique tapestry as we draw closer to Yuma, Arizona. The contrast between the beauty of seaside San Diego and the road through the California desert leading to the south Arizona border is rather startling.

Connie is behind me in the van, trying to conjure up some form of road lunch that we can eat as we drive. My guess is the menu will once again include bananas, granola bars, and bottled water. The meal, coupled with the sameness of the view and the monotonous road, is enough to draw me into a subtle trance. We decide to give our iPods a break and are listening to a formatted '60s station, when Bobbie Gentry's "Ode to Billie Joe" slides languidly out of the car's seven speakers. The listless solo guitar intro and Bobbie's vocal, which barely outdoes the guitar in intensity, drives the rolling quietude inside the van even deeper. The song is a long stretch of tale telling for this equally long stretch of highway. I drift back to another day. I can't believe how much "noise" this simple lament made when Bobbie came on the scene.

※ ※ ※

In 1967 I was called into Capitol general manager Bob York's office and given the assignment to take a new artist on the road to promote a very left-field record. The artist was Mississippi native Bobbie Gentry, and the record was "Ode to Billy Joe."

I didn't like the assignment because this recording was very long. (It was originally seven minutes and the single clocked in at about four and a half minutes.) In order to get airplay, which was very tight in those days, the "no longer than two and a half minutes in length" rule was king at pop radio stations. To be honest, I thought it was a sappy record. In addition to being long and boring, it was just an OK lead vocal with a semi-fair acoustic guitar. Admittedly, it did have a nice Jimmy Haskell string accompaniment, but that was definitely not the key to a hit record in those days. "Ode to Billy Joe" was actually a B-side to "Mississippi Delta," but disc jockeys around the country discovered the tune and turned the record over and made it into a smash.

It was my job to take these assignments, and "no" was not one of the answers available to me. In fact, the only thing I needed to know was when I would be leaving, how long I would be gone, and the approximate budget. I would then plan out a tour working within this framework. The rest was easy—I would place calls to the field staff and have them set up radio interviews, dinners with DJs, and television appearances on the local entertainment shows that were popular in those days.

I met with our new artist at the Tower to go over the schedule and make sure she was all right with everything and free from other commitments in order to go on the road. As it turned out, Bobbie Gentry had all the free time in the world, so off we went. I found it very easy to set up appointments with the guys in the field and the music men in their area when I described what this one-time Las Vegas showgirl looked like. The only thing longer than her legs was the road before me.

Our two-person tour group was on the road barely three weeks when things started exploding to the point where it was like being with the Beatles. I had never experienced anything like this before with a new artist—unless you count Mrs. Miller as an artist. The big difference was that Gentry could have a career. She was gorgeous, had a lot of moxie from her Vegas years, and was indeed a talented songwriter. The record hit a nerve with almost every radio format, and audiences of practically all ages and cultural background. The country market claimed her as their own while the black audience was drawn to the soulfulness of this white girl.

"Ode to Billy Joe" was an instant smash on "Good Music" (also known as "Middle of the Road," "MOR," or "Easy Listening"), Top 40 (Contemporary/Pop), C&W (Country), R&B (Black/Soul) formats, as well as finding its way into the current events and news programming departments at just about every media outlet. The song shot straight to No. 1, where it knocked the Beatles' "All You Need Is Love" off the top of the *Billboard* charts and prevented the Supremes' "Reflections" from moving to the top slot. This was quite a feat for a rookie artist. Our favorite song to sing along with as we rode in the back of limos was "All You Need Is Love." It seemed like that song and hers were taking up about half the radio airplay as we traveled around the nation.

Screaming fans appeared at airports, radio stations were monitoring our every move, and one of the film industry's most famous directors, Elia Kazan, actually tracked us down. He arranged to hook up with us in the Philadelphia airport between flights because he wanted to meet with Bobbie and talk about a film possibility.

With this success the tour dragged on for what seemed an eternity, hitting almost every major U.S. city from Boston to Honolulu. Things were moving so fast in this short period of going from an unknown to a rising star, we were surprised when she was booked to open for the Beach Boys in Hawaii at the Honolulu Bowl. It was put together at the last minute, and we flew straight from St. Louis with just a few days' notice. It was a homey visit to Honolulu in that we were all on Capitol's payroll in one way or another. I escorted the Beach Boys and Bobbie around to the various TV and radio stations for interviews. It was actually a good combination for programming—the California surfer boys and the Southern belle. There was never any problem telling who was answering the questions when it came to the accents.

When the word got out that we were going to be in Hawaii, something special happened. Ray Charles's manager invited us to join them for a late lunch on Waikiki Beach the day of the concert. Ray was appearing in Waikiki at the time, and when he heard she was going to open for the Beach Boys, he wanted to meet her. It was a great feeling to know that Ray Charles was blown away by Bobbie's record. His comment during our lunch was that he could tell by her voice that she was beautiful, which is why he asked his manager to track us down.

Bobbie's record was a huge success and garnered her three Grammy Awards. She became an instant headlining act in Las Vegas and received an incredible offer by the BBC to host her own radio series. The Armed Forces radio invited her to host a weekly show for GIs overseas, and the offers just kept rolling in. It allowed me to understand and experience the phenomenon and mechanics of how a record can swell up out of the heartland and blossom into a hit. It was like following a tornado and being on the front end of a tidal wave at the same time.

I boarded a plane in LA with a total unknown, and when we returned weeks later, I disembarked with a brand-new star. I was amazed how unemotional she was about all the commotion and the skyrocket success ride we were on. As I came to understand her over time, I was able to gain further insight into the various natures and makeup of artists and stars. To everyone in general, and even to myself, this had the appearance of an overnight success. What people don't realize are the hours and years of hard work that the "overnight success" has dedicated to their craft. Bobbie was a very focused and determined young woman, and her achievement was not a surprise to her because she visualized the entire outcome years before it happened. My surprise and her expectations were equal!

When we left on the tour, Bobbie had little in the way of a suitable wardrobe. As the tour progressed, I replaced her one pair of worn dress shoes with new ones and took her shopping for nice outfits along the way. Things became progressively more bizarre as the schedule got crazier. Like the time we lost our luggage in New York City, which forced us to host a formal cocktail party the next night in Boston in our traveling clothes, wrinkled jeans, and sweat shirts. Or getting busted by a nun while smoking a joint on the patio of my ground floor suite at a Marriott hotel in Philadelphia. In almost every city there were managers chasing us in an effort to get Bobbie as a client, which gave our tour *A Hard Day's Night* feel as we became experts at running from them or hiding out when they were near. I finally called legendary entertainment manager Jess Rand (Sam Cooke/The Lettermen) and had him fly into Philadelphia, and on my recommendation Bobbie signed on with Jess for management. Jess joined us for the rest of the tour and handled the onslaught of offers.

A true crisis erupted in Boston when I found Bobbie passed out in her

hotel suite. She suffered food poisoning after the night before at Jimmy's
Harborside Seafood Restaurant. It's a funny story to tell after the fact but a real
scary happening while I was waiting for the ambulance to arrive. I was told
by the hospital to keep her awake by any means necessary until they got there.
So I was frantically doing the James Cagney slap in the face routine, trying to
keep her conscious. I had minimal success until I got her cognizant enough
to look me in the eye, at which point I told her that I could lose my job if she
died on this tour after all the money Capitol Records had spent on her promotion. Her eyes opened wide at the absurdity of my dilemma. I think my
self-centered reaction to her dire straits actually saved her life. She combined
my plight with the show-business mantra of "the show must go on" and mus-
tered up the strength to hang on until the medics showed up and did their
part in saving her life. She survived, and within twenty-four hours we were
back on track and on schedule.

Bobbie brought about a major change in my life during one long plane
trip as we were making some Olympic long jumps between cities and states
on this maddening marathon tour. I asked her what she was reading one
night during a "red-eye." She answered that she was rereading and studying
Ayn Rand's *Atlas Shrugged*. She put the book down and explained in great
depth the whole philosophy of objectivism as developed by Rand and her
student-follower Nathaniel Branden. In street terms, and in Ayn Rand's own
statements, her philosophy exercises its tenets from the basic view that "I
am not my brother's keeper." Interesting how I can reflect back on this
concept as my springboard into spiritual philosophy. In her small book
Anthem, Ms. Rand explains it this way: "I need no warrant for being, and
no word of sanction upon my being. I am the warrant and the sanction."
Bobbie's detailed, almost cold approach and reaction to her success was
now understandable to me.

I bought into this philosophy immediately and completely. This was
right down my one-way, self-centered alley. Objectivism totally worked for
me on every level in the early days. In subsequent years I devoured and
scoured Ayn Rand's books and teachings, accepting them as my personal
gospel and guide. I narrowed her teachings down to a more manageable

credo: "What was good for me—was good!" It worked wonderfully at first. When your goal is simply success and its rewards, it is very helpful to approach things this way—for a while.

I believe this was the fundamental reason I got ahead in the beginning *and* the eventual reason I crash-landed on my behind later on.

WE GOT A GENU WINE
INDIAN GURU WHO'S TEACHING
US A BETTER WAY

Beloved and gentle Guru-ji, please teach us how to pray."

His eyes seemed enormous even when they were almost squinting. His intense gaze into my inquiring eyes had the dual effect of almost burning a hole through mine yet at the same time I experienced healing warmth as the moment lingered. I felt I was experiencing a mental MRI as I awaited an answer to my question.

He finally broke the silence.

"You inspire me," he said.

It was like being shot by a tranquilizer gun with each word hanging softly in the air.

I had become a favored chela (disciple) of the internationally renowned East Indian religious leader called Gururaj Ananda Yogi. Gururaj was the founder and leader of the International Foundation of Spiritual Unfoldment (IFSU). The organization was reflected worldwide as the American Meditation Society, British Meditation Society, Danish Meditation Society, and so on. On this warm day approximately 120 followers of his teachings and practices were seated on the soft ground in a wooded glen that was part of a twenty-acre former nun's retreat in the beautiful Montecito hills above Santa Barbara, California.

He spoke to us from his reclined position atop a pile of colorful cushions placed for his comfort on a makeshift platform beneath a canopy of oaks and pines. We were having a "satsang," the name for those times when you sat at the feet of your guru in meditation and instruction—a spiritual discourse or sacred gathering. It was during these sessions we were given the opportunity as seekers to bask in his learned teachings. Gururaj was a very handsome man in his fifties with a golden bronze complexion beneath beautiful contrasting black and white hair.

I was fascinated with this man. I felt great affection for him and the wisdom that constantly flowed from his soothing voice. I was amazed that out of the thousands of followers worldwide he had chosen me for special guidance.

He told us that the word *guru* comes from the Sanskrit words *gu* (dark) and *ru* (light). A guru leads you out of the darkness into the light. *Raj* stood for king and *Ananda* meant a state of bliss.

When addressing your guru by adding the word "ji" you are saying "my beloved guru." On occasion Gururaj would employ this term of endearment to show his affection and appreciation for one of his chelas. It always made me feel very special when he would address me as Ken-ji.

It is interesting how events and acquaintances tie together moving in and out of our lives in coordinated randomness—that is why I titled this chapter after a line in Dr. Hook and the Medicine Show's song "Cover of the Rolling Stone," an ode to '70s success and excess.

I was in my early forties when life took a "nose" dive for me—they say God invented cocaine for the entertainment industry to let us know we were making too much money. I was miserable and felt very alone in my desperation. I was not only despondent over my life but losing ground on all worldly levels. My despondency was gaining momentum in its downward spiral—I was deeply sad inside and knew I needed something on a spiritual level. I was sharing my sense of disconnect with a well-to-do couple who seemed to have it together. They possessed a certain air of peace and contentment about them at all times. This was a casual conversation, not a counseling session—more of a crying-in-my-beer type of sharing. They informed me they achieved peace through meditation, which they had taken up a year before. They claimed meditation relieved their stress levels and improved their outlook on life. They suggested I give it a try. After all, it didn't cost anything, so what was there to lose?

This caring couple was laying out their plan for inner peace to a born and bred country boy. I was very quick to respond that I wasn't about to sit around in funny positions with my eyes closed, chanting unknown syllables and burning incense, even though I had witnessed George Harrison's involvement with eastern religion and thought he was one of the most gentle and inwardly peaceful people I had ever known. "Oh no," they replied, "you don't have to be a follower of the guru. All you do is learn the mechanics of his meditation techniques. He comes to America about once a year but you never even have to meet with him." My friends informed me they were trained to instruct me in learning his "practices" and once they showed me how to do it, I could come to them if I had any questions. There would be no clock time with the guru.

What did I have to lose? It was worth a shot. I tried it. I loved it. I wanted more. In time I actually sought out more advanced instruction and techniques. But remember, I was still not following one of those weird gurus—I was just "practicing."

A few months into this episode I was informed that Gururaj Ananda Yogi was traveling to LA and would be holding a series of get-togethers at a location in the San Gabriel Mountains. It was free. I should go. It was really fun I was told and this guy was quite fascinating. *(What did I have to lose?)* It was free and . . . you know the story.

It was incredible, the whole event. Everyone was so full of peace and love. The woods and meadows sparkled with a sweet vibrancy. Gururaj was absolutely mesmerizing. I felt I gathered more wisdom in a few days than I had garnered in many years. A specific event at the retreat was so mind boggling that I was totally caught off guard. We were told on the last night of these satsangs we were going to receive a special treat—something the guru did only on special occasion. He was going to hold "communion". That was the only explanation. We were to show up, he would sit before us, and we would watch him meditate. Sounds a lot like watching grass grow or waiting for paint to dry. The last night came and we took our place at the feet of the guru. His only words to us were, "Keep your eyes upon me—I will now meditate." He then closed his eyes and there we were, watching this intriguing man—sit. What I am about to describe to you is so bizarre that I hope the words will stay on the page.

After several minutes of deep silence his left and then his right hand drifted up into an odd position. I learned later this was a traditional pose taken by learned masters when they entered into the ether. Once in this outer world/never space, they are said to be able to see all things from all time. (It is from this space, many lives and thousands of years ago he once told me, that he had seen me. That's when he predetermined I would be drawn to him centuries later. This proclamation shocked me yet drew me nearer to him at the same time.)

He remained in this position for the next hour—left elbow next to his body with the left hand reaching out—palm upward. The right arm was extended slightly above his head with that hand-facing palm out to us while reaching up like we used to do as kids in school when raising our hand to ask a question. After ten minutes more of staring at him in this stance I suddenly began experiencing the most extreme sense of joy I had ever known. This was replaced by an indescribable emotion of the deepest sadness I had ever encountered, tears streaming down my face. These feelings were followed in succession by equally intense emotional stirrings of peace, fear, warmth, and cold. Next, his entire body started glowing and a clearly definable aura surrounded his body—it was like those clear silver waves you see in the hot summer when you look down to the horizon point on an empty highway. It was at this point the event started opening up in grand fashion. The air became saturated with wondrously brilliant celestial music, a symphonic offering beyond anything I had ever heard in any studio or in any state of behavioral enhancement. I was then drawn to the walls in the room. The heretofore beige-matted Spanish stucco walls had turned to gold and they were melting. For purposes of clinical clarification, my basic intake that day had been sprouts and yogurt.

Suddenly Gururaj Ananda's body began jerking mildly and then a moment later his eyes opened. Motionless he slowly looked into our eyes one by one. At that point his arms drifted down almost as if they were weightless until they came to rest in his lap. He waited a minute and then pointed to someone in the middle of the room and asked them what they had just experienced. By the time he had solicited responses from about a half dozen people, they repeated every thing I just described. Without any pre-instruction, we had all shared this same experience. I was hooked. I had a guru.

Gururaj began visiting the U.S. on a more consistent basis. The American Meditation Society (AMS) was growing, and the money and power of the California faction's membership was the driving force behind its expansion. After several retreats at his feet, Gururaj zeroed in on me and our relationship deepened. I began dreaming about how comfortable it would be to dress in flowing white robes. Nirvana was just an astral projection away as I dove headfirst into advanced practices.

I was very devoted to my guru and my "practices." Looking back on that phrase always amazes me as a born-again Christian. As New Agers we faithfully did our meditations, chanting, manifesting, and so forth. We did it in preparation for the thousands of lives ahead, each one guaranteed to improve because of dedication to our "practices" and being better people. Eventually we would become so pure from these good works that once we had paid off all our karmic debt we would one day simply merge away into the mystic mist of a dulcet other world. The mechanics of this process was grounded in the belief in reincarnation. In simplistic form it worked like this: let's say you kicked a dog in this life; when you died you could choose to come back as a dog in the next life to be kicked around and pay that particular tab of your karmic bill. The reason I now find doing "practices" for thousands of lifetimes to get to nirvana so ridiculous is because it only took me a nanosecond to accept Christ as my Savior. Once I did that He truly revealed Himself to my heart and that was it—no practicing, just an acceptance of His unconditional love, mercy, and everlasting grace. I especially like the part where I only have to go through this mess here on earth one time.

I now understand the appeal of the New Age movement. I call it "Chinese restaurant religion," because it actually works like their menu: pick one from Column A, two from Column B, and one from Column C. If you want to remain promiscuous, then some of the New Age belief systems incorporate free love as an expression and facet of God, so that's okay. If you want to keep getting high, then it can be construed that you actually are able to draw closer to God in this manner, so that fits right in too. As it works out you create this personal set of handpicked religious guidelines and suddenly you are holy. The beauty (or should I say deception) of this is that you don't have to change anything about yourself. No wonder I was hooked—I could still have sex, do drugs, and remain close pals with God!

A Prince Among Ruins

Gururaj Ananda and I were going gangbusters. It also looked like my goodness was paying off because my producing career had just been blessed with an important project. I was in the process of producing a major rock project for Geffen Records, a group from Cuba called OXO that the label paid a half a million dollars to sign after a fierce competitive bidding session with A&M Records. (This was 1983 and that amount was big bucks in those days.) A&M was the better choice, but John Lennon had been a Geffen artist and the lead singer of OXO wanted to be on the same label as the former Beatle. In fact, he had just named his newborn son Julian after John and Cynthia Lennon's son.

The sessions for Geffen quickly turned into a nightmare. They had based their enthusiasm to hand over these big bucks on five songs, (the equivalent to one-half a completed album) that I had produced for a grand total of ten thousand dollars at a first-class studio, The Sound Castle in the Silverlake area of LA. My co-pilot on the sessions was my favorite recording engineer, Bill Bottrell, who later produced and engineered projects by Sheryl Crow, Michael Jackson, Madonna, Tom Petty, the Traveling Wilburys, and many more stars.

The chemistry between the band, the studio, Bill, and myself was magic and the resultant master tapes were hot. These recordings were immediately commissioned by a major Hollywood sound reproduction company to demonstrate how good their duplication sound was. Geffen himself, once the deal was signed, made us change studios, the engineer, and the recording concept for the remaining five songs. We also had to re-record the product they paid all that money for. Our master recordings had by executive decision been relegated to being classified as "demos." This seemed a little odd because these demonstration recordings had made the rounds in the offices at Geffen Records and were highly praised by the pros in the industry's most prestigious music company. No one in the group or the record label's general population could understand why we needed to record those five songs over. It appeared to be an ego matter for David Geffen and/or the A&R person assigned to our project, Carol Childs. They knew we had one or two hits in that handful of songs and by recording them anew; they could take credit by putting their stamp on the actual production process. In addition to moving everyone (except for the group members) out of the mix, they also went for me. But the band and their management insisted I stay on board as their producer and we carried on with a minor key cloud hanging over the project.

We were first brought into Sunset Sound Recorders on Sunset Boulevard in Hollywood to begin recording the basic tracks for the ten songs selected to be on the album. We shared the recording complex with another artist, a very strange guy, who called himself "Prince." Our individual studios spilled out onto a small courtyard that had a basketball net at one end—a place where producers, artists, musicians, and staff could hang out between "takes" and during lunch breaks. It was a way to relax, get a little exercise, and get away from the confines and pressures of a recording session. It is typical for artists to hang with each other in these central break areas. When I was producing Waylon at the Sound Labs in Hollywood, we became friends with Olivia Newton-John, Darryl Hall and John Oates, and their respective teams working in the other recording studios in the complex by hanging out in the pinball room. It would be interesting to see a gang of funky cowboys, proper Europeans, and uptown rockers in heated contests in the break room over the Elton John pinball machine. When Dolly Parton joined us as part of our gang, things really got lively. The dialogue and catch-phrases common to each group's culture would combine in some pretty descriptive exchanges. What was unusual about the recordings at Sunset Recorders is that Prince, who was recording his monster album *Purple Rain*, never mingled with the rest of us. I am not sure that he and I exchanged a single word during the weeks we were there.

Donna Summer and David Foster, both "Geffenites," along with other big names, would drop in on our sessions while I was re-producing the original tracks and wonder what the heck was going on. They had heard the original five songs and thought they were incredible. Anyone who has ever spent time recording knows when magic hits a session that no amount of re-recording will ever capture that happening again. Once you nailed it, it's been nailed! For me as the producer and for the band trying to re-create something that we knew we couldn't beat was a discouraging task.

The sessions became music by committee with, shall we say, an engineer with more ego than good ideas and an executive producer overseeing the project under Geffen's guidance who caused the $250,000 recording allotment to go over budget. It was unanimous the finished product never came close to the quality of our $10,000 "demos." In fact, I felt that the final mixes sounded so bad I never kept copies for my personal archives. We did get a top 30 hit in 1983 (No. 28 on *Billboard*'s Hot 100) with a song entitled "Whirly Girl."

Geffen's team punched the final deathblow to the group by finally forcing myself and the management group that created, financed, nurtured, coached, and brought the group to the label, out of the picture. This was simply too much and it tore the heart out of the whole enterprise. This phenomenal group broke up shortly thereafter and never made another record. When I use the phrase "Geffen did . . ." I don't know if these things happened under his direction and with his approval, if it was under management decisions, or if he even cared. His company was a proven major player in the business, and his success to this day is hard to criticize. But what happened to us was sheer lunacy and demonstrates the excesses of the record industry.

We recorded the second half of the album at Lion Share Studios, Kenny Rogers's state-of-the-art facility in the old ABC Paramount studios in Hollywood. It was during this time that Gururaj decided he wanted to record high-quality teaching tapes for worldwide distribution. Kenny honored my request for free studio time for Gururaj because of the large amount of money we were spending on the OXO project. At this time I not only was teaching meditation but also was involved in very advanced techniques and practices, including "tratak" and "mandala" meditations. The recording I was doing with my guru meant that now I was spreading his "teachings" around the world.

As big as the OXO project was and the potential involved for my financial well-being, the politics that broke up the group was the beginning of the inescapable end for me and the life I was trying to hang on to. This event was my exit from the dance of last chances in the circus I had lived in. Shortly thereafter I fell completely off the merry-go-round and sadly watched the merriment gallop away. I lost my home to foreclosure, entered bankruptcy, lost all my property investments and savings. My wife left and I felt like a leper when making the rounds looking for work in the "biz." I eventually lost my Mercedes to the bank. Then as the spiral downward continued, it actually got to the point where I couldn't pay for the parking fees to go to interviews in my remaining asset, a Jeep. I admit I could have hitchhiked or worked out something with local bus transit, but can you imagine a prospective employer seeing me at a bus stop or thumbing a ride while on their way into their office prior to our interview?

It all came to a prideful end one day when I had parked virtually miles away in a residential section where there were no parking meters. As I was traipsing toward tall buildings and working up a sweat, I sensed a certain incongruity in showing up all gritty and grimy for a job interview with the pitch that I was a successful record producer who had decided to shut down his production company in order to return to the corporate world and make their company more successful. I was having trouble convincing myself of my value and had little confidence that anyone else would buy into my story. That day I stopped in my tracks and turned around. It was over and I knew it. This was December 1983. I left LA and moved to the Mendocino coast to work in construction.

WAYWORD SON

The construction business kept my body in shape and food on the table, but I was still me—three chords and an attitude. I just couldn't get the music out of my head. I had to give it another try. Thus began my final musical move—I left the Mendocino coast and moved to Nashville in August 1984.

This is when I met Connie and we fell in love. However, a battle was looming on the horizon. It concerned her Jesus and my guru and it was a hard-fought effort on both sides of the divide.

In mid-battle I decided to call Gururaj in Cape Town, South Africa, where he was residing. I needed guidance, assurance, reassurance, and a lot of answers to the doubts Connie was putting in my head concerning my spiritual choices. It was good to hear his voice as we hadn't communicated for months. I got right to the point, and in his great wisdom he cut right to the chase. He asked me a question he knew would bring me peace and get me right back on track. He was confident my faithfulness to his spiritual "practices" was powerful enough to carry me through this down period. In his sweet, gentle voice and the vision of his dark eyes looking into my hurting heart, he asked, "But Ken-ji my gentle child, how is your inner life?" He was clearly sure after almost a decade under his teaching I would have to confess that I did possess a deep inner peace and would conclude everything was going to be okay if I just kept "practicing."

I thought about it for a minute and was surprised not only by my reaction but my conclusion. The last words I said to my beloved Guru-ji were, "You know what? My life sucks!" It did suck—in and out, all about, here, there, everywhere, up, down, all around, all the day, in every way! At that moment it felt like every vital sign in my body took a rest, and then with the strength of young lions I said to myself, *I am outta here!* I then gently hung up the phone. Ooooom my—gu-bye!

In the months leading up to this momentous occasion in my spiritual migration, Connie had been steadfastly telling me about her Jesus. She would take me to Christian rock concerts and contemporary church services on Music Row where all the insider entertainment people attended. She was appealing to the music side of me, knowing I would dig the worship services where the hot pickers in town played in the bands.

Connie would pray over me, about me, and for me. It was OK if it was in Jesus' name because I believed in Jesus too. I believed in Him as one of the ascended spiritual masters, and I honestly believed He was indeed one of the many paths that led to the mountaintop. I was pressing in harder and harder to God through my prayers while becoming more and more confused about my meditations. I had left my guru but kept on with the procedures. She kept praying and believing I would see the light and know the truth. We were both seeking God's face in our own "way," trying to understand what was going on with my life—sincerely looking for answers. We did have this one very big continuing problem that just wouldn't go away. The problem was in the aforementioned "way."

Connie insisted Jesus was *the* way while I firmly held the position that He was *a* way. We couldn't get past that roadblock. We argued about this constantly, getting up from many unfinished restaurant meals in disgust. She was so bullheaded and inflexible. I, on the other hand, was so willing to meet in the middle. One time before my final conversation with Gururaj Ananda, I even offered to change gurus for her!

This went on for months. We were so in love and knew in our hearts God had brought us together, but there seemed to be no resolve in sight. Finally, one day she came to me with a solution. Because we felt so deeply for each other, she knew where we were headed in our relationship and she could not be unequally yoked. She had to make a decision between Jesus and me. She chose Jesus.

Connie had been witnessing to me, praying for me, introducing me to Christian situations and people, talking to me about her faith. In that moment she reached me because she went beyond talking—she did what is known as walking out her faith. She put into action what she had been saying. There was no question how deeply we cared about each other and we truly had an incredibly exciting and romantic beginning to our relationship. But none of that compared to her commitment to her Savior and her strong faith. I was taken by surprise and my disbelief in what she had been telling me was immediately replaced by this awareness of an incredible act of love that was going down before me. I wanted to love like that. I wanted to believe in someone so immensely I, too, would be willing to give up worldly preferences for that love. I wanted more than a whole bunch of works and struggling through future lives trying to get it right. I wanted the forgiveness, grace, and mercy she had been telling me about. I wanted a fresh start, and in that moment I sensed a new beginning was before me and a lot of wayward ways were now going to be behind me. Her words, which at first seemed so devastating, I now understood were words of pure love. I wanted some of that real bad.

When I dropped to my knees and "surrendered all," the immediate changes that took place in my life were amazing. I don't totally understand why God chose certain items to rework from the first moment, but I do know He knew exactly what He was doing. For example, I automatically became a tither. Now, these were challenging days for me financially so this meant if I had $100 of income and $100 in bills, I had to figure out how I was going to pay those bills with $90. I knew in my heart, not in my head, that the blessings received from tithing was one of His greatest day-to-day working gifts. His instruction and promise were so incredibly clear in this matter, and He does keep His Word!

Other changes took place in my life. For instance, He took foul language out of my mouth. A quarter century of rock and roll and crazy cowboys had added some salt to my vocabulary, but looking back I can see I was "delivered." Another thing He put in my heart was the gift of faithfulness to my relationship with Connie in order to have a dynamic and unsullied marriage. It was a mind, body, and spirit infusion into my makeup. In street terms—God and I had a deal. I be faithful, He be nice.

This also showed me my God had a great sense of humor and irony. If anyone did not deserve a great wife it was "moi" after the way I had handled my prior marriages.

Most of all, God put in my heart I was to begin my days reading His Holy Word. For the first three years as a new believer I replaced magazines, books, and newspapers with the Bible. If I was going to spend time reading, then that was to be my reading material. I read the entire Bible three times in three years. This was not a works thing. I wasn't thinking if I read the Bible a lot that He would see me and like me more. It wasn't playing catch-up; it was something He placed supernaturally in my being. I instinctively knew I needed to know Him better. To this day Connie and I start our day by reading our Bibles and devotionals and spending time in prayer. I have always said God is the greatest economist of all time and He will use our past— good, bad, or indifferent—for His glory once we give our lives to Him.

It is interesting to note that during all those years developing disciplines concerning my New Age (sewage) "practices," I had been trained to set aside a sacred time each morning. I simply replaced my conditioning previously used for meditation, chanting, and sitting funny with Bible reading, Christian studies, and prayer. I also understand how deep the emotions run when being a New Ager because I was there for so long. I had been so deeply involved and deeply committed I know how strong a person's belief system is in this way of life. I have no illusions about how easy it will be to witness to them, because no one could talk me out of it when I was there. But I know the processes and the patterns in this illusion and I know how to relate to them and am able to effectively witness in this matter. I find on my speaking tours God uses me many times in this manner. I think of it as being similar to someone trying to minister to a heroin addict. Who would know better than a recovered heroin addict how to relate and talk to them? God will use for good what the devil meant for evil.

I experienced many sensational moments in my life. I have been where most people will never go when it comes to the heights of the entertainment world and all the rest the world has to offer. However, my worst day as a Christian is far better than the best day I ever experienced when I was lost in that decadent world. I am describing a certain peace that does pass all understanding, a calm that overcomes me in all situations regardless how challenging and devastating they may be. I am relating a sense of security and a sweet *knowing* that I am His child and He is watching over me at all times.

I finally gained what can never be lost.

I don't have to *practice* anymore—I got it!

HOME ON THE RANGE

As the thoughts about my old guru and those extraordinary days evaporate into the arid distance that surrounds Moses on all sides, it's as if they are remnants of an old song fading into silence. I find the sameness around us has ironically caused a meditative state of sorts—an experience reminiscent of what happens when you "go deep." Because of a timeless edge to that form of abstraction, I have no idea how long I have been stumbling down a pensive memory lane. It feels like it has been forever, but it is only a three-and-a-half-hour drive between Yuma and Tucson and we are barely more than halfway. I gaze out the window at the continued nothingness and then a rather obtuse sound in complete contradiction to the current scenery comes pouring out of the speakers. We are listening to Connie's playlist this time and she swears she didn't download the song that was playing. While looking out at scrub, dirt, sand, dried wood, and cactus, the strains of Don Ho's "Tiny Bubbles" breaks the boredom with its tropic incongruity. My mind is having a problem staying in the van. Looking at the parched and desiccated sameness that unfolds from the edge of the road to the horizon is not enough to hold my attention, and so once again I drift back in time . . .

※ ※ ※

The private phone line rang in the antique phone booth at the Hangover House and it was late at night. Very few people had my personal number at home and there was no caller ID in those days. It had to be family or a close friend in order to have called in on that line, especially because of the late hour.

I answered, and the person on the other line responded in a soft voice saying, "Hello, Ken, this is Don Hall." I thought I recognized the voice as being that of Don Hall who had been my A&R guy when I headed up the Verve Records division at MGM. It had been years since we talked and I assumed at one time during our relationship I had given him this number in case of emergency having to do with one of our artists.

He began talking and nothing made sense. I asked once again who it was and once again he said it was Don Hall. He continued on and the conversation still didn't make sense—something about me producing a record with him, something about it being a country record and something about him growing up in a rural area in his home state. By now I was sure this wasn't Don Hall, or at least not the Don Hall I knew. I interrupted my caller once again to ask him his name one more time. This time he said his name very clearly. He even spelled it out for me—DON HO. D-O-N H-O.

Oh, Don Ho! Now I know.

He then explained that Toby Allyn, a mutual friend and artist I produced in the past, had given him my home number. It was several hours earlier in Hawaii, and Don was used to calling anyone he wanted when he wanted. He was, after all, Don Ho, you know, the Elvis Presley of the Hawaiian Islands. This particular night he called just before he was to go on stage for his nightly show in Waikiki Beach.

I was blown away when I finally understood his reason for calling. He continued with his prior attempt at explaining what he wanted. He wanted to record a country album with me at the helm. Don loved country music and told me he had grown up away from the densely populated areas of Oahu, and considered himself a country boy. As I got to know Don better over time, I realized how important that clarification was to him.

Once Hawaii had attained statehood in August 1959, Don became one of our most loyal citizens and was very proud of officially being an American. One thing I learned later when I was working with him on the islands is to never refer to "back in the states" or "stateside." Hawaii was our fiftieth state and the proper phrase was "back on the mainland." So returning to his logic—country people come from the rural areas of our many states and he saw himself as a country boy from the state of Hawaii.

He rang me because he had looked at the *Billboard* magazine country charts and took note of the people I was producing. He was attracted to the fact that I produced two of the top five records on the country charts (Waylon Jennings and Jessi Colter) and he wanted a name producer. Naturally I was thrilled because this dude was already legendary. I also knew that pre-production would most likely take place in his hometown (Hawaii) as opposed to the Hometown Production offices in LA. As excited as I already was, I had no idea how exciting this whole adventure would unfold.

It only took a few phone calls to decide that we could work together. During those conversations we finalized the approach we would take for the sessions. First, he had one severe limitation—his shows were sold out years in advance and he appeared seven nights a week virtually every week of the year. We would have to carefully work out a recording strategy. He also wanted the project to be cut in Nashville. By "cut," I mean that he wanted all the songs to be recorded with Nashville musicians and background singers in "Music City USA."

Don put his complete trust in me by asking that I select all the material— every song on the album, all the arrangements—and by allowing the total overall concept to be in my hands (a producer's dream!). Obviously the logistics had to be worked out, but here's what we came up with: I would select the songs and then fly to Waikiki with the songwriter demos. We'd spend as much time as needed to work on keys to make sure Don was comfortable with singing the songs. Once the performance keys were selected in Hawaii, I would return to Hollywood and work on the arrangements. Next, I would fly to Nashville and record all the tracks using an established country session singer to sing the lead vocals that would become the guide tracks for him to learn the arrangements. I selected a real good ol' boy from Alabama. I mean, the only thing more country than this fellow was week-old ham. The guy's name was Steve Norman. I recorded a small hit with him on a 1972 song Wayne Newton eventually put on the pop chart entitled "Daddy, Don't You Walk So Fast." To add insult to injury, the song was a Top Ten hit and the last time "Mr. Vegas" ever cracked the charts.

I wanted Don to have real hard country vocal phrasings to study as he prepared to record his vocal in place of Steve's. Once the tracks were completed in Nashville, I would fly back to Hollywood where I would book a studio for a solid twenty-four hours. Don would then obtain a release to take a night off, fly in to LA on the last red-eye flight out of Honolulu so he could be there in the morning, record all ten vocals, and then fly back on the last flight that night to Hawaii.

Now, the artist's lead vocal is the heart of the recording. It is the reason for making the record and their performance is what the record is all about. This is the single most crucial item equal to the song selection. In most cases the lead vocal portion of making an album can take days or weeks in crafting each performance and getting it just right. Expecting to accomplish this in one long day was madness.

I flew to Hawaii to begin working on keys for the selected songs just as planned. I was picked up from the airport in a white limousine and taken directly to my oceanfront penthouse suite at the Waikiki Hilton Hotel. That night I was Don's special guest at his show and we met backstage in his dressing room for the first time. We immediately clicked and I realized I was in a special place with a special person getting ready to do a very special project. I was indeed a happy outrigger, floating on tiny bubbles in a sweet Hawaiian sunset.

The next day he made a brief visit to my suite where he informed me: "We no work yet. First you learn how lay on beach." This was a bizarre concept to me, but later I understood it was his way of doing things—that laid-back island way of his. He sensed I had just come off the LA freeways and it was going to take time for me to unwind to the point where we could relax. It was three days before we actually sat down and worked together.

My beach towels were laid out on the beach for me, and for two and a half days I was picked up at predetermined times by the white limo and escorted to lunch with various Hawaiian dignitaries. We were seated in private areas in upscale restaurants, and Don pre-ordered every one of my meals. I had no conversation with the servers; I just sat there and watched as plate after plate was placed before me. Whoever was hosting the meal would explain each item and in many cases its history. I never saw Don during this period.

We finally did get together with a piano player to begin picking keys—I was there nine days picking keys; something that normally takes an afternoon. It wasn't that Don had any problem finding his voice for each song, but we would work for almost a matter of minutes and then it was time, as he would put it, to "go lay on beach." Either that or he would have a driver escort me to historic places on the various islands, places that in some cases only the privileged hierarchy and original descendants were allowed to see and experience. One of the most exciting things was to be taken past all the restricted areas in an active volcano where I was allowed to stand so close that I could feel the scorching heat and magnitude of this incredible act of nature.

Once this bit of paradise living was over and it was time to go to work, I flew back to LA, then on to Nashville, and completed the recordings in preparation for Don's lead vocals. The day set aside for his recording came and I had a lot of trepidation about how this approach to laying down vocals was going to come out. The tracks had turned out magnificent. Psychologically it was empowering knowing that Don had trusted in me to do a job up to his standards and then gave me the freedom and space to do it.

A limo picked Don up at the airport and delivered him to the studio where I was in preparation mode. There could be nothing left to chance that day—everything had to be organized in the most efficient and proper manner in order to pull off this impossible task of recording ten "keeper" lead vocals in one day. Just the amount of physical work was going to be staggering as there are so many time-consuming mechanical moves to make in racking up tapes and preparing electronic settings for each individual song. I also didn't think his voice could hold out that long with doing so many takes.

Don Ho was one of the most professional and talented artists I ever worked with. He came to the studio totally prepared and nailed all ten vocals almost effortlessly. Ten perfect performances, one right after the other. We even had time left over that day to just hang out in the studio before he was going to be picked up and taken back to the airport. We had so much fun that evening listening to playbacks—we had just made a record together and loved the outcome. This is the amazing thing about the music business; experiences like these create friendships that last forever. The myriad of emotions an artist and producer share during the making of a record tends to draw them past the outer attractions that originally brought them together. Typically a deep relationship and personal understanding develops as a result. Although the album, *HOme in the Country*, is no longer in release I believe he sold it at his shows right up until his passing in 2007. The album was named after a song written by one of my publishing company writers and clearly reflected Don's feelings about his homeland. I liked the marketing idea of capitalizing the first two letters to highlight his name. On April 15, 2007, *The Honolulu Advertiser* in writing about his passing listed this album among his most notable recordings.

It was an exhilarating project, but there was also an unexpected event that took place during the preparation of a formal agreement to work with each other. There were, of course, financial and business arrangements to sort out before we could get started. Now, I want to make it very clear that I am writing only about rumor-mill type stuff here but I had heard that there was a thing called the Hawaiian mafia, an inferred counterpart to the Las Vegas mafia. Who knows? Maybe it was something more like the "Memphis Mafia." Don was allegedly "their" man like Sinatra was supposedly "their" man in Vegas. I never saw or empirically witnessed anything of this nature except it was amazing how everything seemed to fall into place when I was being taken around the islands. I don't think I opened a door for myself the whole time I was there and I certainly had no problems wherever I went. There was always someone making my way smooth, shall we say. I must admit there was a bit of romanticism to the idea and it made the project even more exciting to me. This next bit is somewhat curious, though.

Once our initial conversations were over, Don instructed me to meet with his manager to work out the finances for the project and to sort out my percentages and fees. He gave me the address and an appointed time for this meeting. The address was an LA country club, and the meeting was with his manager who also happened to own the country club. We met in a mammoth dining room that overlooked the golf course. The place was absolutely five-star in every way. It was strange that we were the only two people in the restaurant except for two or three heavy-looking dudes sitting in the shadows around the edge of the room. This was not a "get-together at Starbucks with Mr. Peepers" kind of thing. I mean this was straight out of *The Godfather* trilogy.

I would like to have been a cinematographer and been able to set the camera shot that would show two men seated at a single table in a sea of dimly lit tables in the middle of this magnificent restaurant. I was told later that it was rumored ("rumored" must remain the operative word here) *The Godfather* was based on one of three possible people. This guy was reportedly one of them. He was tall, stately, and silver-haired, and he talked just like Marlon Brando in his role as Don Corleone.

We had a light lunch and talked about the project. I felt like I was in another world because this was so out of the movies. With our lunch concluded and an apparent agreement to go ahead with the project, he stood up and invited me to his office to put together some papers.

I walked into his office and, in keeping with *The Godfather* analogy, it was exactly like one would imagine. Everything was massive, the wood-paneled walls, the giant desk, the huge paintings, and all the trimmings were in deep reds, dark browns, and muted gold colors. I became immediately intimidated and found myself on the verge of stuttering. I looked down at the exquisite and obviously expensive carpet that I was standing on. Out of nervousness all I could say was, "Gee, what a beautiful carpet Mr.__."

"You like the carpet, kid?" came the reply in that inimitable Don Corleone voice.

"Yes, sir, it is indeed beautiful," I replied.

"I had it brought over from the old country, kid—this carpet is over a thousand years old, it's priceless."

At that point I was instructed to sit down, and the paperwork he prepared consisted of writing me a big check in complete payment in advance for my services. He handed it to me and said, "You do a good job, kid, OK?" I was then instructed to send the rest of the bills to his attention at the country club. We shook hands and I left.

The next morning I was awakened by a loud knock at the door of the

Hangover House. I came downstairs and opened the door to two big guys standing before me. The really big one motioned to a truck parked down on the street in front of the Hangover House.

"Where do you want us to put the carpet, kid?"

Going Up, Going Down

Interstate 8 stretches out before us in a coquettish manner of detached endlessness. We are west of Tucson, Arizona. I find my thoughts bouncing about, looking for a place to land for refreshment along this lonely stretch of asphalt. My eyes strain for inspiration in the unyielding vista that lies ahead. Nothing outside prompts remembrance, so my mind becomes computerized and by default goes searching within. Eventually the events of the day that possibly birthed this whole excursion creep into the forefront of my mind.

There is an incredible difference between knowing you are dying and actually going about the business of doing it. You don't get a lot of practice over the years—actually putting it off as long as you can. Then it does eventually become your turn to give it a go and you discover a certain unyielding of spirit is juxtaposed with a bewildering acceptance as the whole process sets in.

I was diagnosed in 1996 with a cancer that results in a life expectancy of three to five years. At the time of my diagnosis there was no cure and very little research due to its rarity. As I had been ill and misdiagnosed the two years preceding discovery, the doctors felt I had used up two of those years. That meant when Connie and I got the news I was looking at one to three years of a dwindling existence. My mind automatically latched on to the one-year bit, which made the whole situation even more dramatic. We received the news in late December and drove home in silence. We couldn't bring ourselves to look at each other for a very long time. When we arrived home, neither of us were hungry. We started wrapping Christmas presents, deep in thought as we wrapped our defenses around us in reluctant preparation of what was to come. When we finally ran out of things to keep our heads, hands, and hearts busy, it was finally time to cry. That night I wrote the following in my journal:

Today I found out I have incurable cancer. It is a few days before Christmas and my reaction is one of peace. I am disappointed to hear this news but at the same time I have an uncanny sense of relief. Being a Christian really comes in handy in times like these. It is almost like God is beginning to reveal a new stage in my life. Deep within, where His comforting Holy Spirit dwells, I feel clarity in the mysterious— understanding of the unknown—vision into the unseen. I am in His purpose and that is all I need to know.

I woke up early the next morning and was stunned how I felt—a strange euphoria. I had this sense of peace and was filled with a sweet simple joy. This feeling of serenity and well-being seemed out of place given my devastating diagnosis the day before. It was then I felt God walk up to me, put His arm around my shoulder, and let me know we were going to go through an incredible experience together. He told me this incredible peace I was experiencing was His gift to me and it was a gift available to everyone.

It was the peace that truly did pass all understanding—a peace you can't understand until you have it. To put a finer point on the gift He told me because of the way I felt, it meant that I truly believed in Him—trusted Him. I could rest in the comfort that my faith was real.

Because God knew this was a big deal to me, He let me know He was in it with me—big time. He said I was going to be amazed at how this was all going to play out. He reminded me He was God and He doesn't always let us know what He has in mind.

He described two possible outcomes. If He decided to take me home via my illness, then I would get to be in heaven with Him. That was good news. I already knew heaven is where I wanted to be more than anything, so that was totally cool. He said if He decided to heal me, then I could spend my time in glorifying Him and His miraculous healing ways. I could be used as a witness to His mercy and grace and in the process even more people would end up sharing heaven with me.

God has this great way of presenting things; if you really listen to Him, it all seems so logical. If His audio method isn't available to you He has a real good book that delves deeply into these matters—open it up, read the words, and then listen. He also guarantees 100 percent success rate if you follow ten simple steps. These steps are given fairly early on in the book and it's easy to understand how to go about it all as you carry on through the rest of its fascinating pages.

In retrospect, it seems I have spent most of my adult life on the road, but the unexpected information we received that day took us on an inner journey that was not easy to pack for.

The odd thing about all this is that on an earthly level I felt like I lost my identity. When I didn't know what was before me, when I couldn't make plans, when I didn't have a place to put myself in the worldly plan, I ceased being able to see myself.

My identity was wrapped up in three things—my past, my present, and my future. I knew where I had been, I knew where I was in the present, and up until that point I had a basic idea of where I was going. That was my uniqueness, that was me—a mortal projectile hugging the earth at warp speed, flying low, glancing nervously in my soul's rearview mirror at the wasted years in my past—a trail of sorry smoke left behind. At the same time, I was watching my current movements in the reflections of people's eyes as I made my way along His way, trying to stay on course in my new walk in the Word. Simultaneously with this twisted trek I was looking ahead as I plunged helter skelter for suspended suede into the supposed known. I no longer had a sense of who I was because I couldn't see where I was going. Those were my natural thoughts, but when I pulled my head out of the muck and looked to the heavens, I remembered I was His child and in His eternal plan all I had to do was to trust in Him. But then there I was—I was here hanging on to this giant dirtball called planet earth with my face in the dust of my own guttural reality.

░░ ░░ ░░

I am drawn to King David and what I have seen him do in his many psalms—bouncing between doubting and praise. I grab my Bible and break it open at random. I press it against the center of the steering wheel and delve into its warm interior. I take in the scripture before me and am immediately fed by Jesus' less-than-subtle admonitions—*"we are in the world but not of the world."* In order to take this as one of the core elements of our belief system and understand this spiritual suspension we live in, we have to be true believers. We have to believe Jesus was man and God, God in man and all man while he was all God. Additionally, He was all these things separate, together all in one, one in all and all in all.

I pull myself deeper into the book before me until I find myself inserted into the words. The highway before me, the book in front of me, and the thoughts inside unite in momentum. If I am of the earth then I have all these earthly things in me. In this journey I am a bit of everything. If I were part of a sentence I would be a transitional phrase. I am trying to move from sinful thoughts and bad ideas to the mind of Christ. This concept shouldn't be too hard for me to grasp. If I am able to accept His deity, then I should be able to accept and understand my earthbound position and my child-of-God situation at the same time.

When I leave my natural being, thoughts go beyond the trials and I enter into the God part of me—the joyful and peaceful part. I become less confused now when I catch myself having these basal and heavenly thoughts at the same time. I am a man of the soil; a man of soul who has had a solid core of God and the mind of Christ planted in me when I accepted Jesus as my Savior. I am all these things all at once. I must learn and purpose to deal with them in their proper order and priority. I think when the order of our stuff gets in His proper order; we become more like Him than like us. What an incredible journey—here we go again into the realm of our win-win situation when we become Christians and face everything from that standpoint.

If I get it right I please Him.

If I get it wrong He loves me and gives me another chance.

Because of Him I am filled with joy knowing that I am blessed among men.

Did I ever mention that I have incurable cancer?

I am now over twelve years into the one-to-three-year life expectancy—tell me prayer does not work. Because I have always lived on the edge and shied away from normal things, it would be expected that my cancer is an extremely rare form of bone marrow cancer modestly known as Waldenstrom's macroglobulinemia. I was informed at discovery there are only about seven hundred new cases a year and about four thousand of us alive at any given time. No everyday malady for this cowboy! Fortunately today there is research and new treatments that have lengthened life expectancy although it is still incurable. The name of the cancer is so long I figured I would be gone before I learned to pronounce it. People talk about the big C. For me cancer has a little *c* and Christ has the big C!

I find the strangest things to be prideful about. I guess if there can be righteous anger then there can also be righteous pride.

*   *   *

I come out of this remedial recollection, and a lightness of being invades my senses. I find the road ahead hasn't turned scenic, but the dusk has given it a softness and feeling of being invited along into its extended purpose—I am comforted by its shaded nothingness. I look down at the clock and realize it has been quiet in the van for a long time. Connie knows when I get real quiet, eyes glazed over and locked onto the centerline; she may as well take advantage of the solitude and take a nap.

Ratcheting out of the recesses into roadside reality, I reach up and pan the rearview mirror to find she is in the back, scrunched up next to the side of the van with her head leaning against the window—eyes closed but facing outward as if she was still looking up at the distant hills as they roll by. I connect my iPod and go straight to Pink Floyd's A *Momentary Lapse of*

Reason album, put the volume on 10, and blow away any sense of solitude within Moses' interior. Connie can tell I have come back down to earth when I start playing my space music.

I roll down the window so I can smell the highway. I bet I could make a fortune with a cologne that smells like asphalt. All the retired truck drivers, old rock-and-roll road crews, and motor home mavens who have had to finally pull it over to the side of the road would eat it up as a nostalgic nostril reminder. We could package it with a *Greatest Truck Driver Hits* CD, throw in some No-Doz samples, and call it "Pierre CarVan!"

It has been a few hours since my other self and I left the planet; upon my return I find we are suddenly dealing with Tucson traffic. We hooked up with Interstate 10 a while back and it feels almost liquid the way we seem to be on the move. We stop for gas and a stretch but get right back into the van and wend our way out of town eastward toward El Paso. We don't eat in Tucson because there is a place I have in mind just ahead. But we encounter grand disappointment a few miles east of town when we find that one of my favorite Mexican restaurants from the old road days has burned down. I can't remember its name because it wasn't the kind of establishment where you could call ahead for reservations or inquire as to what the "special of the day" was. This small hole in the wall had, in some obtuse way, been one of the few solid mini-destinations of this portion of our journey. The irony is that the reason we all would seek this funky café out was because the food was so hot. No wonder it burned down.

We have gone too far to turn back into town, and so it is apples, yogurt, and peanut butter from our small grocery stash. With all that in our mouths and a whole lot of Pink Floyd in our ears, we make the Texas border our next goal. The intellectual content of the music evades me at this point in my life and I simply get lost in their creativity and my oblivion.

Finishing off Arizona and the southwest corner of New Mexico will take us approximately five hours. The vistas left, right, behind, and before Moses continue to be less than awe-inspiring, which makes the drive seem even more vacuous. Assured that I have been adequately fed, Connie goes back to her nap.

What Connie refers to as the "Fink Ployd Hour" ends and I am pro-jected out of the music along with my thoughts. I find myself in a strange state of tranquility. Moses' wheels are treated to a new asphalt coating that delivers us from road noise and gives our momentum a sense of silent glid-ing. The magnitude of God's sweet love in granting me these additional years so I can be crossing Arizona in this suspended moment overwhelms me with peace. The vastness that surrounds us, the stillness within, and the immensity of my recent thoughts about His eternal grandeur act as if some giant camera in the sky is pulling away in a supernatural zooming out until I feel like a speck beneath the clouds.

If it feels like I am getting smaller, it is because I am living.

MILE MARKER # 5
MEX-TEX

Run Silent, Run Deep

I was born on the prairies where the wind blew free
And there was nothing to break the light of the sun.
I was born where there were no enclosures.

When a child, my mother taught me to kneel and pray
For strength, health, wisdom and protection.
Sometimes we prayed in silence, sometimes each one prayed aloud;
Sometimes an aged person prayed for all of us...

I cannot think that we are useless or God would not have created us.
There is one God looking down on us all.
We are all the children of one God.
The sun, the darkness, the winds are all listening to what we have to say.

Geronimo
(One Who Yawns)

We don't spend a lot of time in New Mexico on this route, but one thing is for sure: you hear a lot of Waylon Jennings on the radio in this part of the country. This is Apache land and once the stomping grounds of their legendary warrior Geronimo. If it hasn't become obvious by now, it will soon become apparent that when I reflect back on the incredibility of the people and music that filled the deepest crevices in my being, the Beatles and Waylon were the two high points in my musical journey.

Waylon was a soul mate. The two of us had so much in common it was scary. We were the same age. We also possessed a restlessness that pushed us out into a world beyond our understanding and we both carried a special place in our hearts for our Native American brothers and sisters.

No one moved like Waylon, thought like Waylon, or approached things like he did. Not only was he an Outlaw on the outside, but he was a renegade within in his own soul. Waylon wasn't afraid of anything except maybe himself, and he especially didn't care what anyone thought about the way he went about things. The odd thing is, in our closest times together, Waylon admitted that he was running scared just like everyone else. He found safety in his songs and the life he found with the melodies of the road and his band.

Waylon was distant when people got too close to him, while from a distance he could crawl right inside your hide when you heard him sing and play. It is interesting to note some of the people who were his biggest fans. It was the Hell's Angels who rode with us on the road, a sea of motorcycles behind the bus; the Native Americans who as a culture had been moved aside; the "on the fringe" people, and the rebel edge of society. His music transcended so many boundaries. I gained a lot of points with my British buddies as well as the hardcore rockers when I started producing Waylon. He was one of the funniest and scariest people I ever met—sometimes only minutes separating these two aspects of his character. It was so interesting to notice as the Outlaw movement came into vogue how the people in the front rows of our concerts changed—how young they were and expensive their clothes were. You could tell they dressed special for the concerts. We wore the same clothes for days sometimes, and in the confusion, not always our own.

There was a nondescript cowboy hat that tied us Outlaws together in some magical way, and it was with us for about a year. No one knew where it came from, but it symbolized our little bad-boy club. It all started one night when Waylon picked it up from a chair in Tompall's studio and wore it for months. Nobody knew whose it was because none of us had brought it to the session or put it on the back of the chair. He already had a cowboy hat, so we never could figure out why he laid his down and picked this one up. Then one day, quite some time later, he laid it down on the band bus and I picked it up, where it stayed on my head for months.

It left me in the same manner. Eventually this cowboy hat spent time on Tompall's head, Captain Midnight's head, Willie's head, and on and on. We all had our own cowboy hats so it wasn't a matter of trading hats, loaning a hat, or even needing a hat. The hat was this strange happening where we all believed in some odd way it tied us together. The floating irony was that it chose whose head it would sit on and for what duration. Another peculiar thing was that it fit all our heads perfectly. We knew that no one picked it up before his time and no one passed it on at a specific time. Then one day it was gone.

Without discussing it too deeply, I think we all felt it was a symbolic ordination of a band of brothers. There was also a standing joke amongst the Waylors (his road band) and the people associated with Waylon on a daily basis known as being "in the barrel." Known for staying up for six days at a time, Waylon's mood would swing from the loveliest to the lowest during this extended period of craziness. Our phrase for staying up for days was called "going on a roar." During the sweet parts of this time it was incredible being a part of the team. Then suddenly without warning his mood would change and the smallest perceived error of judgment by a team member would land them in the imaginary barrel, and the length of time in the barrel was always excruciating. Everything that went wrong was caused by the person in the barrel, and there was no way to get out of the barrel until Waylon would realize how much he cared for the barrel dweller. Then at that point, the transgressor would be let back out of the barrel into Waylon's world. There was a required ritual that had to be performed in order to officially leave the barrel, which was to figure out some way to explain to Waylon's satisfaction the reason why someone ended up in the barrel in the first place. It should go without saying that it was always their fault and never Waylon's.

In order for a roar to be official, it would have to last a minimum of three days or more; and these were twenty-four-hour days where personal hygiene and wardrobe would be stressed to the max. Waylon would shower and put on fresh clothes during these extended highs and it would seem within less than ten minutes that those clean, freshly pressed duds would look like he had slept in them. I used to tell him that he was the only person I knew who wrinkled his clothes from the inside out. I was only good for staying with him for about two, maybe three days tops and then I would have to beg for mercy, hang it up, and go to bed. He used to tease me for being such a pansy—he called me the "ten-minute roar." While my high of preference was smoking grass, unbeknownst to me his was taking pep pills. It was no wonder I couldn't medicinally hang with the guy. Basically he was doing uppers and I was puffing weed, going in two totally opposite directions of the drug spectrum.

I am reminded that it wasn't far from where Connie and I are on this lonely highway that Waylon and I had one of our most unusual concert experiences. Waylon was legendary to the southwest Indian tribes and one of their biggest heroes. He had been invited to perform at a giant annual gathering of regional tribes that happened at a central meeting place somewhere around here, way out in the middle of nowhere. As we understood it, they built this place for special tribal gatherings. They traveled from all over via truck, horse, wagon, or on foot with some of them taking days to get there. I believe it was built by government funds allocated to a tribal council.

It took us forever to find the location, and it was excitingly eerie when we pulled up in Waylon's bus. The band had heard so much about how much the Indians virtually worshiped Waylon. This was going to be an unusual and exciting experience for these tribes to actually see him in person. We arrived in plenty of time, as everyone in the Waylors was pumped in anticipation of the great greeting and response the concert would create.

Because of our mutual respect for their culture we took an inordinate amount of time setting up for the show. We wanted to give them our best. I have been to a lot of concerts in my time and many with Waylon, so I knew what kind of spell he could weave when he was inspired. This night was definitely going to be magic. There was no opening act and at the prescribed time, Waylon came out and did probably the most exciting opening number I had ever heard performed live by anyone. It was almost like a Bruce Springsteen concert where he just kept going and the song kept building in intensity to the point where you were wiped out when he hit the final chord.

We were all expecting the place to go crazy with applause, but when the first song finished there was nothing but dead silence. I had taken my usual place, off to the side of the stage behind the amps, where I could watch the audience and hear their reaction. As the crowed remained silent, Waylon turned around and looked at me as if to say, "What happened?" We thought he was bombing with the audience and that they didn't like him. Maybe there was something in the lyric of his opener that was offensive to their people and he didn't realize it. Waylon launched immediately into another song, and as we would say when a performance was great, he once again "hooked it" it big time. The song ended and was followed by another round of dead silence. That's the way it went for the entire concert. Waylon came off stage totally confused. It turned out that instead of clapping to show their enthusiasm it was their custom to show the deepest respect by being silent. The Indian community had given their highest compliment to their favorite entertainer that night. It sure would have helped if we had been forewarned with this bit of information.

They called him "Waylown"—stretching out the last syllable so that it sounded very mournful the way it rhymed with *alone*. They would repeat it over and over when in his presence, almost as if in reverence, saying only the name and no more. I can still hear that sound in my ears all these years later. I remember hearing it late that night as we pulled out into the darkness. I hear it now as I drive through the emptiness and alone in my thoughts.

El Paso lies just across the border and we have just enough gas to make it, stopping at rest stops along the way only when necessary. Connie wakes up with the noise of Las Cruces, New Mexico, through the open window, and we ride the edges of the Rio Grande River into El Paso, Texas. The sun has gone beneath the horizon, and there is something romantic about the dusk, the river, and the quiet. We hold hands for the entire drive between the two towns.

THINGS MAY BE CLOSER
THAN THEY APPEAR

As we travel the short distance between Las Cruces and El Paso, the dash lights cast muted reflections on the side windows of Moses' darkened interior. With Connie's small hand as an anchor, I hold on as I begin having vague reflections on what God must think of me, what I have done with my life, and how I used the talents He gave me. I am having one of those "look through a mirror darkly" moments. What makes this episode so interesting is that I am experiencing it in almost a PBS TV special kind of way. You know, that dramatic approach they take when they explore things in a real deep, painful depth-level way of examining someone's life.

From my own distance I see God musing over me. For the most part, it is not real good stuff He is coming up with. I can see Him scratching a wizened chin beneath a furrowed brow. He stays with His "very nature" though, and remains kind and thoughtful as He does a little review of He and me. I can feel a message coming my way, and I can tell it is not going to be too complicated. I have experience with His ways, and I know how efficient He is. He does have a way of getting right to the point.

The way He sees it is that He really went overboard in blessing me with a lot of gifts and talents. Then He stood back as time passed and watched me either waste it, misuse it, or in most cases, dirty it with my selfish ambition and egocentric nature.

I like how He is so open with me. He explains how He has given me a good mind, which enabled me to breeze through academia, graduating as a top student from a major college, but then was disappointed when I muffed all that up by doing a lot of dumb things. As He looks back, I can see this memory was especially agonizing for Him. He recalls opening golden doors of opportunity and then watched as I flew through them, grabbing all the worldly stuff along the way while leaving nothing of value behind except for the torn packaging of His bounteous gifts. He says He was brought to tears when I wasted talents He let few men have, talents that could be used to glorify Him. It hurt Him so much that He had to turn away so He didn't have to watch me gorging myself on selfish frivolities. He was especially ticked off I turned my back for so long on the friend He had for me in His lovely Son.

I am seated in this imaginary front-row center seat as His thoughts unfold before me—panoramic scenes rushing by—transforming Moses' windshield into a Cinerama screen with surround sound. What is interesting about all this is that the bad parts go by in fast forward until He gets to the good part.

You see, when He gets to the good part He zeroes out the counter and in an instant goes back and erases all the bad stuff. He then starts at that point, that special moment when I chose Jesus as the Lord of my life. He hits the slow-motion button when it comes to the place where I was on my knees. Then everything gets real calm. This is when we really start talking. It is an interlude of quiet conversation on a dim-lit highway between the Man Himself and this perpetually naive and aging child-man.

He knew the pain I was going to endure for those mistaken travels. Like that old saying: the punishment I received hurt this Father more than it did me. He knew what was best, and because He is perfect and makes no mistakes He was patient and kind, and at the perfect moment His forgiveness prevailed. That perfect moment is the exact place where He puts the replay on pause; it was when I confessed my sins and accepted Jesus as my Lord and Savior. He then takes the scenario off pause and lets me up off my proverbial knees so we can hug face-to-face. I can see His face, not through the mirror darkly but in the blaze of loving light and pure godly adoration.

Moses has covered many miles on the blackened asphalt that has slipped away beneath us since this whole journey began. It is hard to explain moments like these, because they are wordless encounters and in some ways it's like trying to explain the color of the wind. But like the wind, it is something very real, something you can feel; and each time you experience its mystery it has its own hue and tone. I hate having to retreat out of these moments and wish I could spend more time in their embrace. Suddenly God jumps back into my heart for an ad-lib just to let me know that there is more to this than moments. He tells me that the more I read His Word, fellowship with the saints, and spend in worship of His Holy Name, the more time He and I will spend together like this.

LOST IN AUSTIN

W e cross the New Mexico border into El Paso and stop at the first café with a really big Tex-Mex sign outside. As we eat our chili rellenos and wipe the sweat off our brow from the heat of their version of mild hot sauce, there is a sense of reverse anticipation happening here because tomorrow morning we will begin our long drive across west Texas. As is required with Mexican food, we eat too much. The café is also a gas station, so we fill Moses' tank with petrol and because we started this day twelve hours ago in San Diego, we check into the small motel that is adjacent to the gas-café. The few feet from the pumps to the parking space outside our room is all the driving we can handle at this point. We take absolutely nothing into room 121 except the two Lone Star long necks we picked out of an icy tub at the gas station. Beer and bed—*ése es bastante para nosotros esta noche.*

At 4:45 a.m. we are jolted out of bed by the cheap motel radio blaring loudly with tinny mariachi music. The previous occupants liked their Mexican music loud and had left the radio set for their very early wake-up call from the morning before. Connie dons yesterday's duds and then, first things first, she makes coffee before going out to the van for clean clothing. It is early, but we definitely are up so we make the best of it by showering and going back to the café for breakfast. We both order huevos rancheros and Pepsi. We clean our plates, not out of need for more food but just to prolong the meal. Now that both the van and us are full of gas, we are out of there. As we pile into Moses we agree our craving for Tex-Mex food has been satisfied for the rest of the century.

Even though the city's population is well over half a million, we find the traffic to be surprisingly light. Before the lasting taste of salsa and beans is out of our mouths, we are on the open road heading east; our once-fresh clothes filling the van with the smell of the place we just left. Once we clear El Paso I know from the cowboy band tour bus days what lies ahead. With Austin in our far distant sights we have a long six hundred miles to go, the good news being that it is a fast six hundred miles. The part that dominates this travel evaluation, though, is the "long" part. Even though we are just beginning this leg of the journey, I can describe the landscape to you at most points in this eight- or nine-hour trip. Flat.

I spent a lot of time in the Lone Star state—anyone who has spent time on the road in Texas has spent a lot of time in Texas. You could cover most of Europe in less time or mileage than it takes to go from El Paso to San Antonio. Even then you are only halfway across the state. One thing's for sure, though—you do make good time because it's not often someone asks to stop the car to admire the scenery when you are headed east on highway 10 between Balmorhea and Ozona. Don't get me wrong—I love Texas and *have* spent a lot of time there. I'm not talking about Houston and Dallas. To me, Austin is Texas. It has it all and like Nashville, the minute you enter the "Austin City Limits" you want to do something—usually musical.

Texas does something to you as you venture across its plains and scrublands. Even without the radio on you can hear its music. You can pull over at any truck stop, small town, big city, or country roadhouse and you'll meet its people—the same people it seems—Texans all. They seem to have taken pride, simplicity, arrogance, humility, toughness, kindness, passion, adventure, patriotism, and vision and ground them all up into their own special concoction—drinking deep and becoming one in spirit. It is scary and refreshing all at the same time. You never have to wonder where you are when you are in Texas.

It all looks the same from Moses' vantage point as we seem to be repeating the same stretch of highway no matter how far we have traveled. It feels like the movie *Groundhog Day* with Bob Wills and the Texas Playboys in the background. However, we have a goal—just get through it. Seeing the names of both Austin and Houston taunted on the road signs and hearing the Waylon Jennings and Willie Nelson song that just came on (I have been hogging iPod time) once again throws both of us back into other times. They are playing a Shel Silverstein song "A Couple More Years" that I produced for the RCA album *Waylon and Willie*. Back in other times Shel implied to Connie that he wrote the song for her, and with this irony in tow we both go off into our own little memory-lane side trips. The funny thing is when I go back in my mind to the time in my life that this was all about I have the strange sensation I am back on that same trip with about as much real direction.

▨   ▨   ▨

Hypnotized by the steady yellow line that slides by our motion, I fall into a time trance and end up in my mind probably sometime around 1975. I'm back on the band bus and we are on a long, hard Texas road trip. Waylon is booked to appear at a giant country extravaganza at the Houston Astrodome. Willie is also on the bill as well as about a dozen other major country stars. Even for us this was to be a pretty imposing venue—there were not many spaces bigger than the Astrodome back then without going outdoors.

A strange thing happened this particular time. As big as this event was billed—and you couldn't have gathered a more powerful lineup—for some unknown reason not many people showed up, only around eight thousand. Now that is a pretty good-sized crowd in most places, but here they seemed to be lost in one little section of the giant Astrodome, which has a seating capacity for fifty thousand. Consequently, the concert lacked luster and the sound was terrible. These are hard gigs to do. We were glad when it was time to make tracks out of there. It was the end of a tiresome group of dates. We were going to head straight out to the bus and get back onto Interstate 10 heading east toward Nashville. Then something happened that put this scenario right into qualifying for a movie script or an acid flashback or something in between.

We received a frantic phone call that the legendary Texas Opry House in Austin was going under. The only way to save the place was if Waylon and Willie would go to Austin right away and do a benefit concert the next night to keep the doors from closing. Well, here is that Texas thing again. These two Lone Star cowboys did the expected; they pulled the front tip of their cowboy hats down over their eyes, drew in the dirt with their pointed toes, and did some real deep thinking. They agreed to answer the call to save the shrine. We had a mission and it was a good feeling. It was a cowboy thing and we were on our way to save the day just like in those old western movies.

It was after midnight when we finally headed out for the three- to four-hour drive from Houston to Austin. I figured a pit stop or two would put us into the state capital in the early morn. I also knew that we would not be getting any sleep, so the daytime preceding our life-saving event would be spent conked out in some Holiday Inn. (Waylon always stayed in Holiday Inns because they were all the same and that way he knew how to find everything in the dark.)

The scene that took place as we crossed the terrain in the deep dark was something that wasn't totally foreign to me but in an odd way made me feel like Mary Poppins in a Robert Altman production. The three of us were sitting at a small table in the "living room" area of the bus just behind the driver's seat and I immediately became invisible. It was something akin to when I first went into the navy straight out of the white-bread hills of Idaho and had my first encounter with black guys from the Deep South. When we conversed one on one, there was a normal rhythm to the exchange. Then another black person would join us and the whole dialogue would take on a different slant. Suddenly I found myself no longer a part of the discussion, almost as if I didn't know the language and didn't have the proper credentials to enter into the conversation.

The same thing happened with Waylon and Willie at the little table on the bus. A deck of cards came out and without an exchange of words the poker game began. I was dealt in. So far so good. But then they fell into their Texas cowboy routine—their hats came down over the eyes, and it got real quiet. You could smell the west Texas soil in the air and almost hear strains of Buddy Holly coming from out of the emptiness in the back of the bus. The conversation was deliberately slow-paced. The words were few and everything floated out of their mouths in that easy Texas drawl. Poker pots came and went, some of them even mine, but I was invisible. I had learned a few Texan words and had the boots, hat, and big belt buckle but the admission to the interior of the moment required a shared history. Suffice it to say, I was a few armadillos short at that box office. I finally folded my hand and stretched out on the narrow couch across the narrow aisle and took a narrow nap. I awoke at the air brakes "whoooosh" in the back parking lot of—you guessed it—a Holiday Inn.

"C'mon, hoss," Waylon said grabbing my shoulder, "you're going to need to rest up for tonight's go-round because this isn't going to be a normal *sitchyayshun* when we get to the Opry House."

After a good day's rest we rolled into the parking area at the Texas Opry House in Willie's bus, with Waylon's bus close behind. It was late dusk and I couldn't believe my eyes. It felt like we were the cavalry rolling into town to save every damsel in distress in the whole state of Texas and lower Oklahoma. There were people everywhere crowding around the bus, waving longneck beers and two-fingered longhorn signs at us as we made our way to the back staging area. The shouting, hats in the air, and whooping cattle calls didn't stop until we were past security and safely back stage. These guys were legends, heroes, and hometown favorites all rolled into one. Everyone also knew that there was going to be some mighty music made at the Opry that night.

Waylon opened the show and there was a special edge to his music that night—a Texas edge. These were his people and he was singing their songs. Mamas, babies, and cowboys all danced with their sweet Texas hearts to some of the best and most honest music every played in our great land. Willie closed and got wrapped up in the momentum of the moment and made the two-and-a-half-hour set that he usually did look like a prelude. For all I know he is still there.

We must have broken every fire code in Texas because the place couldn't have held any more people. The building was bursting at the seams while the parking lot had become a small town in itself. Word had gotten out all over the neighboring counties and it looked like everyone and their distant cousins came to help keep the Texas Opry House open and alive. I don't think there has ever been more money taken in for a one-night event at that historic place. We were told before Waylon hit the stage that more than enough tickets had been sold to save this beloved institution. Waylon and I caught a plane back to Nashville and left the band to go home on the bus. The next day Waylon's road manager, Johnna Yurcic, called to give us the sad news that the promoters had run off with the money and the place was closed down. You don't scam road-wise cowboys very easily or often in this business, and two of the shrewdest bit big-time on this one.

   ※ ※ ※

The song that kicked off this whole retro-collection has long faded back into the dashboard. We drive fast. We drive straight. We drive long. I run out of Texas stories and start inserting Texans as the foil in my short list of Italian and blonde jokes. Connie has a few tales to tell about her time exploring a business adventure in Dallas, but eventually we both tire of hearing about Texas.

  Before I give up my turn dictating the musical program in the van I treat Connie to a little more Pink Floyd (*Dark Side of the Moon*), once again turned up to ear-shattering levels. I tell her it will keep Bob Wills away from our door for the rest of our trip.

A Ship Set to Silent Sail

I am startled by the sudden hollow, bellowing sound emanating from a giant semi as it closes in on Moses from behind. Then in gruesome grace it glides by us like we are standing still. This momentum-strained intrusion into our quietude as we bear down on Austin jerks me out of a philosophical fog. As I am already immersed in ethereal deliberation, I go with the mist of this remembrance and without difficulty dive deeper back inside, leaving only my eyes engaged to dictate the driving process.

Moving to the edge of the plank.

There's this part in my inner being that is like a ship set to sail at a moment's notice. It is a hushed interior, occupied by something that is barely anchored down—something that the slightest breeze will set in motion. I feel I almost have to hug the shore and hang on as if it has handles or I will drift away into my dreams. I try to convince myself that I am not hanging on to illusion—that I am actually clinging to a necessary reality. I delude myself into believing that if I don't succumb to this prying-loose episode and just ride it out, I will eventually gain control again. But then just about the time I come to rest in this decision, I find myself in an even more tumultuous vacuum. I face the fact I must never refuse God's gentle urging when it comes time for me to move out of my comfort zone. I cannot ever allow myself to get affixed too securely to a place that is not pleasing to the wonderful plans He has for me.

As we pound our way across the dry lands and highlands of Texas, I miss the shore. I understand the more fearful I become during those sinking times, the more I need Him. There is a left-field pleasure I experience when I have gone off course and run aground as a result of my self-induced collisions, and He rescues me.

It is amazing how stern His reprimands can be, while at the same time, how lovingly gentle His hand is as He once again patiently sets me back on course. No matter how hard I try to listen to His directions, in my life there are always moments I give the devil my best ear. It is so comforting to know God has provided me with an incredible life preserver. It's a promise I know I can count on. He knows my heart and He knows it is His face I seek. Once again I am pulled to the safety of His shoreline. Actually, it is more of a plumb line because I know in His time that He will turn to good what the devil has intended for evil (see Genesis 50:20).

As the highway unfolds before me I am comforted by reflecting on the final words in Donald Miller's introductory chapter to his book *Through Painted Deserts.*

> *We get one story, you and I, and one story alone. God has established the elements, the setting and the climax and the resolution. It would be a crime not to venture out, wouldn't it?*
>
> *It might be time for you to go. It might be time to change, to shine out.*
>
> *I want to repeat one word for you:*
>
> *Leave.*

I like that.

I *have* left, and I know I'm right.

I am a product of my own imagination, which quixotically has never found a place to call home. I feel as if I have been forced to spend an entire existence unerringly adrift and without real roots. Although I am not sure where I am headed at this moment, traffic is light, and I am making good time.

I peer over the hood and can hear the wind bouncing words off the hood ornament. I think Moses is telling me that the last time his name was associated with a long journey, he at least knew where they were going. I reply in like form our excursions actually do share a great similarity in that in the referenced biblical time the destination was the Promised Land and this time we are in search of landing some of God's promises.

Suddenly these roadside reflections upon God's Word take me back to His essence and the sweet knowing that where I am heading is not the point—it is what I am heeding. I have this peaceful and fully unorganized ritual where I mentally morph into recalling the wondrous teachings and promises in the worn Bible that not only holds a special place in my heart but has found a perfect crevice to reside in between the cup holders on the center console. When I get off center in my thinking, it is just a glimpse away. I pick it up, not for reading but just to touch it and feel its warm familiarity.

For many years now I have read it right after I showered and shaved.

I know it is my personal Bible because it smells like my aftershave.

There is a centerline, and it is not always the one on the road ahead.

I said earlier that if it looks like I am getting smaller it is because I am leaving!

Now I am beginning to understand that the reason I am getting smaller is because I'm *learning*.

"T" for Texas

I t is nearing dusk when the Austin city limits sign comes into full view. I see a Holiday Inn ahead and I feel drawn to pull over and check in for the night. I know where everything is in the room . . .

It would be impossible to have spent so much time with Waylon, Willie, and the boys and not have spent some time in Austin. I have many memories there — mostly to do with making music mixed with a proper balance of mayhem and madness.

I had the most fun, though, in the late '80s hanging out at Willie's recording studio in the Perdenales, a small community located in western Travis County near State Highway 71 about twenty-two miles west of Austin. Willie owned a golf course with a recording studio on the property adjacent to the clubhouse. His office was located conveniently near the first tee. When I rode into town with my gang he put us up in a beautiful condo on Lake Travis, and the living was easy. If anyone has ever met Willie on the road, one of the first things they notice is how laid-back he is. Well, you should see him at his studio by the lake or on the golf course in Texas.

I loved recording at his studio because there was such a sense of serenity and a singleness of purpose when I was there. There were so many great pickers in Austin, plus I would bring in a couple of A-list musicians from Nashville. A great chemistry would always develop between the two groups of musicians. They knew each other either from past gigs, tours, and sessions or had heard about the abilities of their fellow pickers.

To run his studio Willie brought in a young engineer from Nashville who I had produced several projects with, including *Homecoming*, my Grammy-winning album by the Gaither Vocal Band. His name was Eric Paul. Eric had worked with esteemed artists such as Pam Tillis, Waylon

Jennings, Willie Nelson, Johnny Cash, Tompall, and the rest of the Outlaws when he was the chief engineer at Tompall's Hillbilly Hotel Studio, just off Music Row in Nashville. Eric was perfect for this set-up. Nothing bothered him. I had worked with a lot of engineers over the years and I liked Eric's sense of acoustic matters.

He majored in overtones, fullness, and clarity, something not teachable at engineering school, which I don't believe he ever attended. He had that innate understanding of sound that few people possess. I could describe what I was looking for in words and he would give it back to me in frequencies. I could change course in the middle of a session, and no matter how involved the new set-up was, Eric was right there with me.

The year was 1990. I had just returned to Nashville after finishing some sessions in Austin the week before with a hot band from the Dallas area called Stallion, who eventually signed with Capitol Records. I was in my Music Row office when Eric called. He sounded as if he was almost out of breath. He said I would never believe what just happened. When Willie Nelson and the IRS were having their little problem, (something about him owing millions in back taxes), the IRS swooped in and closed down Willie's entire operation.

In a matter of minutes they confiscated his possessions and property. Unfortunately when this was going down, Eric was recording a session with a room full of musicians. Eric said a group of government men walked in the studio, pushed the stop button on the tape deck, rewound the tape that they were recording on, and took it off the machine. They placed it in boxes with everything else and began clearing out the complex. The musicians were sitting in the studio hanging on to their instruments wondering what was going on. The IRS officials ushered everyone out, making sure that the musicians left with only their equipment. They emptied the place and put locks on the doors.

Because he was forbidden from using the phone in Willie's office, Eric called from the roadhouse down the street where we used to hang out during session breaks. He was talking a mile a minute with disbelief as he told me about what had just transpired. Besides the bad news of the day, he wanted to let me know about the good news of the day—that he had just shipped out my Stallion tapes to Nashville that very morning, just hours before he went in to do the session the IRS crashed. He didn't want me to be freaked out when I heard the news on TV.

Here's the part I love. One of the perks of working in Willie's Austin studio is he made everything feel so comfortable. He even had a washer and dryer in a room just off the control room for when someone spent extended days and nights there. The day the IRS came in to close things down, Eric had a load in the dryer, and they wouldn't let him fetch his clothes out of the machine. When he went to the IRS sale of Willie's property months later that was being held to help pay off the back taxes, he read the sheets of paper pinned to the walls by the auction site. He noticed a curious item on the "for sale" list: "Maytag washer and dryer *with assorted clothing*." Eric cracked up when he saw that these were his clothes and they were still in the dryer!

Austin wasn't a major part of my past journey, but it was a sweet part. It is easy to make a side trip on the way to Nashville. Connie and I drive downtown and walk up and down Sixth Street right around dusk when the myriad of music clubs are starting to wake up. Out of respect we have a couple of longnecks at one of the places that opened early. Neither one of us are really beer drinkers, but hey, this is Texas, Austin, Sixth Street, country music permeating the air whether you could hear it or not. With a little exploring we find a funky barbecue place and paid gastronomic homage to that bit of Texas lore. When we are finished we drive back up Sixth Street real slowly with the windows down and listen to the music in full swing coming out of the clubs.

That's "T" for Texas—next it's "T" for Tennessee.

SOUTHERN COMFORT

I like driving out of Austin almost as much as I enjoy driving into it. Coming in to the city there is always this wonderful anticipation of all the good things it has to offer in the food, the music, the people, the culture, the hills, the lakes, and the general ambiance of this special place. When I leave Austin, I always go away with that feeling I have when I push myself away from a great meal shared with close friends. I savor the experience Austin always brings to my table.

We are headed straight for Nashville and follow one of the traditional band bus routes taken in the old days when we wanted to make time between the two music capitals. We drive all day and eat truck-stop food in the van. We cross the mighty Mississippi into Memphis on Interstate 40 with the sun setting behind us on the water—I don't slow down because I never really connected with this city. I do make the obligatory reverential bow to Sun Records, but that's it for Memphis and me this time.

I find myself becoming bored because it has grown dark. For anyone in the entertainment business who has spent time on the road, it is not unusual to feel like half your life is spent on Interstate 40, an amazing stretch of pavement that connects the Appalachian Mountains to the California desert. After years of putting in time as a "road dog," a person gets to know every truck stop, Mexican restaurant, Holiday Inn, and speed trap along the way. A few hours go by, and we spot the turnoff for Kingston Springs. That lets us know that we have entered the outskirts of Nashville and are thirty minutes from its heart.

It's not long before we take a familiar ramp off I-40 and head into the middle of Music Row. We cruise by the restaurant where we met, which is no longer there. Then we drive to another restaurant where we had our first date, which is also no longer there. From there, it's to our first house together, which has been torn down and replaced by an ugly McMansion. So . . . it, too, is no longer there. Its darkened exterior gives emphasis to the moment.

We drive around aimlessly, leisurely—almost as if we still lived in this fascinating town—just taking a break from our Music City moves. Things appear quite differently to me now as Moses helps us make our way through its vibrant neighborhoods. I am more subdued and much more introspective as the lights and shadows outside their windows take on a certain familiarity.

This is where I met Connie and became young again—young as in being "born again." Connie brought me to the Lord in the southern softness of this town. That was over twenty years ago, and now one of my favorite things each morning when I wake up is enjoying the fact that the first person I see is the person who saved my life. I have returned to roam the streets once again with her and relive the early days of our courtship.

We turn into the parking lot of our old church where we once wor-shiped—*and it's still there!* I guess that goes to show you what the firm things in life really are.

I turn off the key, and Moses rolls to a stop in the middle of the darkened and empty lot.

We grow silent as we look up at this special place and remember the great times that filled our lives here. As if on cue we lean in to each other and bow our heads. It's midnight, and we fall asleep in prayer.

Because we are the church—we have just come home.

MILE MARKER # 6
NASHVILLE

DIAMONDS AND DIRT: PART 1

Elvis Has (Not) Left the Building

Nashville, Tennessee, was the home of my diamonds and my dirt, my heart and my hurt. It truly was the place of my greatest creative accomplishments as well as the spot on this earth where I reached my lowest points. The most important outcome is that it was the place I found eternal life as well as the girl of my dreams. There was definitely more than one Nashville for me.

I'll never forget the first time I flew into Music City USA. It was my "maiden voyage" business trip there, and I learned quickly the locals move at a different pace in the South. I was used to the high-speed hustle and bustle of New York, London, and LA, and was up to that speed as soon as I hit the curb with my bags. After recovering from the unexpected blast of humidity, I looked to my right where a cab driver was standing outside his driver's side door talking to a fellow cabbie. His vehicle was the first one in line, and we exchanged glances that acknowledged I needed a ride—as tradition had it I proceeded to get into his waiting car. He didn't budge an inch or move to help me with my luggage—he just kept chatting with his buddy. I opened the door, threw my suitcases onto the other side of the back seat, and climbed in. I waited for a few minutes and then began to wonder if his conversation had an ending. I finally stuck my head out of the rear-seat window, excused myself, and politely told him that I needed to get into town. He gave me a look that suggested I had just taken his dog dish away. He turned to his pal, shrugged his shoulders and said, "Well, I guess I better get going—this guy's in some kind of big hurry!" In case I hadn't noticed the "Welcome to Music City" signs at the airport, Bubba let me know for sure that I was in Nashville.

I frequented Nashville most seriously during the early '70s. At the time I was the VP at MGM Records during the early days when the label was building Hank Williams Jr.'s budding music career. This was also a time of planting the seeds that would bear fruit regarding my Outlaw years because Roy Orbison and Tompall and the Glaser Brothers were also part of our Metro-Goldwyn-Mayer country music roster. I planted my feet even more firmly in those fertile rows of music during the time I was president of Barnaby/CBS when I started producing most of the country artists on our label. Barnaby had a branch in Nashville in addition to the main offices located on La Cienega Boulevard in LA.

As Barnaby's president, I had made an announcement to the trade publications that I was going to commit to the country music genre by designating 50 percent of our recording budgets to the country roster. This was a pretty bold step for a small LA-based pop label. In time it was this decision that turned out to be the spark point that put out the fire in my relationship with Andy Williams. Andy owned the company and because we couldn't agree on this business plan I eventually resigned my position to reactivate my own company, Hometown Productions Inc. I wanted to produce artists like Waylon and Tompall. I saw country music getting ready to explode, and I wanted to be part of the fireworks.

It was October 1972, and I was in Nashville for the annual country music convention that almost always fell on my birthday. It had become an unplanned tradition that I never spent that occasion at home or with family. It was there I first met Waylon Jennings. For anyone who used to be a part of or attended these conventions in the '70s there was no doubt as to its main purpose—to party! This particular night featured a big shindig at the Sheraton Hotel located almost exactly midway between Music Row and Tootsies Orchid Lounge where a great part of Nashville's early musical history was written.

I walked into the main ballroom of the Sheraton with Al Coury, the head of Capitol's A&R department. Al and I had become best friends during my five years at Capitol, and we were doing the town that night. We were making our way through the sea of bodies and had a specific destination at the opposite corner of the giant room. As we bumped our way through to about dead center of the ballroom I came face-to-face with Waylon. We both stopped dead in our tracks, and a small circle seemed to clear back, almost like it would in high school when a fight was about to happen.

I was a giant fan of his, and he knew who I was because of my Beatles background. Also, anyone who is president of a record company that was deeply involved in country music was also given a little extra regard in Nashville's music circles. He was already becoming a legend, which was a little odd in that he hadn't actually achieved national stardom yet. We introduced ourselves and before the obvious pregnant silence could develop, I asked him who arranged his records. Waylon gave me a startled look and paused. He stared down at the floor and after a moment's thought looked up and said, "I guess I do." Later I was to understand how weird my inquiry was for him because no one formally arranged his records—he was a complete arrangement within himself. Waylon's music was all Waylon. He had created this unique sound and, although many tried, none could duplicate what Waylon did with a song. There was something magic about the deep-hearted country soul feel he put to his music.

I was in the process of producing Doyle Holly, a new artist I recently signed to my label. Doyle was a member of Buck Owens's famous Buckaroo Band. I had scheduled Ray Stevens, Tompall Glaser, and myself to work on the arrangements, and Andy Williams already agreed to write the album liner notes, so Doyle was going to have some star power backing him. I also decided as the producer that I was going to build the basic overall track sound on a "Waylonesque" approach to the feel of the record. I decided on this approach long before our chance meeting. Waylon was somewhat taken aback when I asked him if he would be willing to work with me on a couple of the tracks on Doyle's debut album. He was actually quite honored, not necessarily because of me but because no one had ever formally asked him before. I think he enjoyed the recognition of his talent and formality of the invitation. Waylon said he would be happy to lend a hand. We exchanged phone numbers right there in the middle of the floor.

Al Coury and I were having a very good time at this convention. We formulated an off-the-wall scheme earlier in the day when we were joking about how many struggling, talented songwriters and singers there were in Nashville, especially at this convention. We agreed that we could probably throw a dart into the air and whomever it came down on would be safe to sign as a potential hit artist. We were putting a fine point to this fuzzy discussion as we entered the ballroom. I suggested that we walk diagonally across the ballroom floor to the exit door on the other corner. I challenged him, if our premise was a true one, to sign the first person we met coming into the ballroom as we exited the building through that door. When Waylon and I finished our business arrangement, Al and I continued on our mission, crossed the ballroom floor, and exited through the predetermined door. As agreed, Al grabbed the first person we met and offered a somewhat stunned person a recording contract. OK, now don't get your fantasy hopes up—nothing ever did come out of it although the person was indeed talented—and coincidentally, very pretty.

A few days later back in LA, my secretary came in to my office to tell me that Waylon was on line one. I didn't think anything of it and picked up the phone. We chatted for a few moments and set up a time for me to come back to Nashville so we could work on Doyle's record together. I learned later that Waylon never called anyone; everyone had to call him, and this whole adventure was uncharted territory for the Outlaw. We had a feeling about each other but I don't really believe that either of us had any idea how much we would end up working together.

I flew to Nashville a couple of weeks later where I produced and Waylon arranged a Shel Silverstein song called "Queen of the Silver Dollar." Waylon and I sensed we had captured something special in the studio during these sessions—a chemistry materialized between us during those first sessions that was fresh and very exciting. In time he taught me how to make a "feel" record while I was able to employ advanced London/LA rock-and-roll recording techniques to his musical offerings. Waylon was truly the greatest artist I ever produced and I was very honored when he told *Los Angeles Times* reporter Bob Hilburn in 1976 I was the only producer he really trusted in the studio. He made a similar comment to reporter Bob Kirsch in a later article published in *Billboard* magazine: "Basically, I'm my own producer but—Ken Mansfield for example understands me and I can work with him. If I make a mistake he tells me and I trust him," Waylon explained to Kirsch.

My longtime association with Waylon had a lot of ironies as well as a lot of incredible experiences. We became family for about five years. I can think of no better example of how close we became than when I took him to a Beverly Hills doctor's office for a minor emergency. Waylon came out into the waiting room and asked if he could list me as his next of kin. Cowboys don't let many people that deep inside, and I was blown away he thought so highly of me. Over time our kids and wives became best friends. (My daughter Lisa from my second wife and Jessi Colter's (Mrs. Waylon Jennings) daughter Jennifer from her marriage to Duane Eddy were the same age and best friends. My oldest son Kevin from my first marriage and Waylon's son Terry from his second marriage were the same age and became best friends. My youngest son Mark had no counterpart and so he ended up with Captain Midnight, Waylon's perennial sidekick and the biggest kid of the bunch.) Maybe the clincher was that we recognized in each other this bizarre mix of believing to the max in our talents and abilities while being incredibly insecure about how we fit in a world that seemed a bit too rigid to us.

A weird series of coincidences began about a year before our first meeting. I was at home in Hollywood late one night getting stoned and watching *Hee Haw* because I had heard Waylon was going to be on the show. Waylon performed a song, and then something happened that brought me right up out of my seat. A beautiful dark-haired young lady named Jessi Colter walked onto the set alone, sat down at the piano, and performed a song she wrote entitled "I'm Not Lisa." Not only did the song mesmerize me but there was magic about the performance. I called my secretary at home well after business hours and woke her up. I gave her Jessi's name and told her when I arrived at the office in the morning I wanted to know who she was, where she lived, and her phone number. I also instructed her to buy me a plane ticket for that afternoon to fly wherever Jessi was so I could meet with her in person. First, though, I needed to know if she had proper representation or was under contract to a record company.

When I arrived the next morning I was informed that Jessi lived in Nashville and was not under contract at the time. She was, however, married to Waylon Jennings. That took care of some of my interests. Waylon had the rep of being a mean motor scooter and someone a sane person wouldn't want to tangle with. I dropped the whole idea, knowing that he probably had things set in place as far as her musical career was concerned. It also explained how Jessi as a relatively unknown performer had acquired a spot on the show—a package deal with Waylon.

Months had passed between their *Hee Haw* appearance and the night Waylon and I hooked up at the Sheraton Hotel ballroom. I had almost forgotten about Jessi Colter until Waylon and I started working together. I was invited over to their house for dinner, and I was surprised to show up at an address that was not in a particularly great part of town and was a nondescript rental. In my mind, Waylon was a superstar, and this was not the kind of digs that I expected for someone of his stature. (I later learned that Waylon was a quarter-million dollars in debt with the IRS in hot pursuit. Waylon had a horrible royalty deal on his records, was forced to tour heavily each year, and never made a dime when it was done. He also had three ex-wives who were receiving alimony. The pressure must have been crushing at times.)

At this point I was spending about half my time in Nashville producing country artists. Much to my surprise, Waylon often hung around my sessions. He was intrigued by my recording techniques and liked the way I worked with the musicians LA style, which was quite different from the way they did things in Nashville in those days.

Recording artist Ray Stevens had recently built a state-of-the-art studio. I came bouncing in from LA while Bob Johnston (who produced Bob Dylan, Simon and Garfunkel, Willie Nelson, and Johnny Cash) came to Nashville from New York, and we simultaneously discovered the magical aura of the new studio. We kept it so booked solid for years that Ray eventually built a smaller version of this studio across the street just for himself. Bob and I joked that we paid for Stevens's second studio, and in a way that statement wasn't far from the truth. I would haul in outboard electronics from LA on a regular basis to add to Ray's top-drawer equipment. The sound we created was very sweet and solid. Waylon liked that and the freedom-of-expression approach to making the music was right up his alley.

In Nashville you could walk into any one of the traditional studios and when you looked down at the recording console, you could see all the channels were pre-assigned to specific instruments. For example, the bass could always be on Track 5 with the same EQ (sound equalization) settings, etc. Even the faders were marked with tape or grease pencil so that the levels were always the same on each instrument for each record. It was called the "Nashville Sound," and that is why all the records from that time period sounded somewhat the same.

Things were done much differently in Los Angeles. We booked the studios by the month, handpicked different musicians for each session, and selected the appropriate arranger to fit the artist's unique style. Sometimes we'd spend months finding and going over the material with the artist and choosing the studio, musicians, arranger, engineer, as well as a time schedule that worked with their touring schedules. Once the sessions began, it could take many hours getting the perfect sound for each instrument and acclimating ourselves to the environment of the project and the crew selected. For example, we'd try new microphone techniques to match a drummer's particular style of playing as well as working to the specific qualities of his brand of drum kit. Each musician had their unique instrument and their own approach to how they played it. To "get the best" out of them we had to "give our best" in order to determine on an individual basis how each one should be approached when recording.

Putting down the instrumental tracks took days—sometimes weeks. These tracks were called "basics"—typically drums, bass, piano, and rhythm guitar. It was a starting point from which we would build the record. In these tracking sessions my ears mainly focused on the drummer's performance because if their part was not perfect, it would be like constructing a building with the foundation out of square. I always booked the drummer first and then asked him which bass player he liked recording with best. Go to any producer who booked a drummer and bass player who didn't like playing with each other and ask how their tracking session came out. If one of the tracking musicians was out of tune or missed a beat, I knew I could replace their part of the track later. Forget doing it the other way around. I am not the only producer who has gone back into the studio to try and replace a drum track to match the rest of the musician's performance. That little song and dance is not a pretty sight to behold or hear.

Once a tight basic was locked in, then I started doing the overdubs, working with one instrument at a time and stacking takes until we got the exact sound and texture we were looking for. This was a long and deliciously tedious process, but it was important to build the proper platform for the whole reason we were there—to prepare the musical setting for the artist's vocals. As a side note, this is not the only way to produce a record. There is nothing more exciting than nailing a session where everything is recorded live. That's magic time for all of us in the music business, but there are only certain artists who could pull this off. Waylon Jennings and Jessi Colter were the masters of recording this way—the *Let It Be* sessions were the personification of "live" sessions until Phil Spector came in and neutered them.

As a producer I hardly ever sat down in my producer's chair because I was so busy working the session. I was out in the studio, under the piano, or behind the drum kit adjusting microphones and working with the musicians. In the control room I constantly leaned over the engineer getting in his way, pushing faders, and suggesting new echo pans, EQ (frequency equalization) tweaks, and the like.

Producers are a wacky brotherhood. We are very supportive of our comrades in arms and are the first to bow to each other's success and prowess. We share ideas and encourage one another. We do cover up the settings on our recording consoles, though, when one of these dear associates enters the control booth. As much as we share we never want to give up our secrets. We don't want anyone copping our moves.

※ ※ ※

In the early days Nashville artists were basically slaves of the record company. They were told which songs to record at which studio with which producer and which musicians would be playing on the session. They would go in and cut a whole album via the Nashville formula for the "Nashville Sound" in three days top to bottom. That included the recording, overdubbing, and mixing. Of course, this was always a problem for Waylon with RCA, his record label. I think he did most of his recording in those days angry and planning his escape.

Waylon would stand against the back wall of the studio during my sessions. He watched me spend hours on one steel-guitar passage with seasoned pros like Weldon Myrick who did incredible things every time, first time through. But there was always that certain performance I was looking for on every record, and I could tell the Nashville pickers loved working in this creative setting. They were musicians, not machines.

Waylon asked me more than once if I would like to produce him. Each time I politely declined, much to his amazement. No one ever turned the "Hoss" down. I think it was frustrating for Waylon because (his band told me) he thought I didn't think he was good enough for me to produce. This was hilarious because I was in such awe of his talent that I felt I wasn't ready to take on someone of his caliber. I was also afraid if I did agree to produce him and blew it that it would be the end of my producing career in Nashville. I wanted to work my way up through the system and establish a reputation as an innovator. I was being cautious and wanted to get a few hits under my belt before I made such a bold step.

Producing Doyle Holly's "Queen of the Silver Dollar" with Waylon as arranger was perfect because it was a different sound for Nashville. It was a hit, and I was on my way. I had established a new artist career on my own—as an outsider. These sessions gave Waylon and me a chance to feel each other out in the studio. In this one project I had now worked with some of Nashville's very best in Waylon, Ray Stevens, and Tompall. Over time "Queen of the Silver Dollar" was covered by two other established artists (Emmy Lou Harris and Dave and Sugar) who had subsequent hits with the same song.

One night I was finishing up an album at Ray's studio when Waylon popped in unexpectedly. He announced that he and I were going to make a record that night. I told him I would be working until about 2 a.m. and so it just wouldn't be possible. Also he knew as president of a CBS label, I was prohibited from producing artists for other labels, especially RCA. He stayed for a few minutes and then quietly left without saying good-bye. Around 1 a.m. a few of the guys from his crew came by the studio and sat down on the couch in front of the console. I was used to them dropping in and thought they were just hanging out for a while. When I announced to my engineer Ben Tallant that we were finished and he could wrap things up, Waylon's guys stood up and took me by the arms. One of them gathered up my stuff, and they hauled me out the door. I was put in Waylon's orange Cadillac and driven a few blocks to the RCA building where Waylon and the Waylors were waiting in Studio A all set up and ready to go.

Waylon introduced me to Al Pachucki (Elvis Presley's engineer) and told me to take a seat in the producer's chair. The session started around 2:30 a.m. and we worked for about eight hours straight. We cut four songs, live and hot, and walked out with one of his finest hits, a Donnie Fritz song entitled "We Had It All." His *Honky Tonk Heroes* album was already in the can and ready for release, but Waylon was so excited about the session that he went over to the RCA offices the next day. He had them pull a song from *Honky Tonk Heroes* and add ours so that he could have a hit single. He called me at my hotel, woke me up to tell me the good news. He set up a string session for the next afternoon and also booked time with Al Pachucki at the RCA studios so that I could mix the single that same night at 6 p.m.

Let's back up a little—when Waylon's band, the Waylors, brought me over to the studio the night before to produce the session and introduced me to Al Pachucki, he made it very clear that he was Elvis's engineer. The impression he gave was that I should be honored to work with such an "artiste" and high-ranking official in the recording studio pecking order. I am being kind when I say he did have somewhat of an attitude.

Just to make things clear—there is a hierarchy in a recording session, and the engineer, although crucially important, is not at the top. The minute you enter the room with the red light above the double door, the artist (Waylon in this case) is definitely the unchallengeable top dog of the whole affair. Second in command at the session but first in command in the recording booth (the other side of the heavy glass partition that separates the artists and musicians in the studio from the equipment and sound crew) is the producer, which was me in this case. Next comes the engineer (Al for this session) followed by the second engineer. Then, if you are lucky, there will be gofers and runners filling up the bottom rungs of the ladder. There is an understanding that this order is not to be altered and is always respectfully honored. A producer guards his position with great care because without this respect, a recording session can go awry very quickly. There are about a million elements going on at all times, and if the producer lets go of the handle for just a second, the whole train can permanently go off the track.

OK, now we can talk more about the situation with the third man from the top of this totem pole—Al Pachucki. Pachucki did not like the idea of the California kid being brought into his territory, and he was not about to do things any differently than he had always done. As I set the sounds, pans, and EQs for the instruments, he would either not move the appropriate knob the way I instructed or move it right back after I looked away to work with one of the pickers. When I told him about a recording technique I wanted to employ, he informed me that we were going to do it another way—the way Elvis liked him to do it. The inference being that if Elvis liked things done a certain way, then there could be no better way.

Our little chat took place at 3 a.m. and I saw Waylon staring into the booth from the studio. He wanted to make some music, but he also was waiting to see what the hot-shot LA guy was going to pull off in the control room to make his music better. I needed to get things rolling, so I told Pachucki to cut everything dry when he printed it to tape and whatever he did to make sure that we didn't print any echo on the tracks. When you record an instrument or vocal to tape, you can't change what you have recorded (printed) because it is indelibly on the tape—but you can alter its sound. By instructing Pachucki to record in this manner (dry) meant that when it came time to mix the final recordings I could use any engineer and any studio's electronic gadgets to make the record sound the way I wanted it to. There is one thing you absolutely can't reverse, and that is when echo has been added to a particular instrument and then recorded to the master tape. That becomes a permanent part of the sound of that instrument.

The session was magic, and we recorded four great tracks that morning followed by a wonderful string session the next afternoon. As I mentioned previously, Waylon had set it up for Pachucki and me to mix the single the next night at RCA.

The string session was a breeze, and I got a break to rest my weary ears before the mixing session. I walked into the mixing room at 6 p.m. and Pachucki was already there and tape was rolling. Before I sat down at the soundboard, he said, "Here, what do you think of this?" and hit the play button on the two-track machine. (The reason for a mixing session is that you record all the instruments, vocals, etc. on multi-tracks. In this case we had sixteen tracks of information, and the next step would be to combine them, called mixing, down to the two-track stereo version, which is used to make the final copy for commercial distribution. Ask any producer, artist, arranger, or engineer in the business and they will all agree that the final mix process is where a successful record can be made or lost.)

I listened to what I assumed was a rough mix. Al had done some preliminary work on the tracks to show me some of his ideas in preparation for the final mix. I was used to my engineers doing this because it gave them a chance to submit their ideas early. I liked this process because I was often presented with creative approaches to a mix that I may have never thought of doing. I anticipated a challenging working relationship with Al because of his attitude at the tracking session, so I was determined to be diplomatic and make our producer-engineer relationship a successful one. There was no doubt this man had earned his stripes to become Elvis's engineer and he had a mile-long credit sheet of accomplishments at RCA. I did have good reason to hear him out.

When the playback ended, I thanked him for coming in early and told him that I really liked some of his ideas. His response to my compliment wasn't what I expected. "Well, I think that's it. I don't see any reason to make any more passes at creating a final mix," Pachucki said. I was stunned.

I repeated my original comment in more concrete form and that I would consider some of his ideas as we commenced work on the final mix. With that I said, "Let's get started" and told him that he didn't need to save the one he'd just done. His response was even more pointed than his first announcement. My next comment was less cordial, and things got worse from there. I held my ground and he finally sat down at the board, pouting like a child, and started "putting up" the mix.

Typically when constructing a mix, the engineer will bring up the drum tracks first. Along with the producer, the engineer works toward getting the desired sound, pannings, echo, and so forth before moving on to the bass guitar. We actually developed a good sound on the drum kit. That had a lot to do with Waylon's drummer, Richie Albright, who basically delivered the sound I wanted (which in great part was a signature to Waylon's music). We then moved on to the bass. Al played the bass track over the monitors, and before the first four bars of the song had passed I told him to take the echo off the bass. It was a sound that I definitely didn't want on the record. It was at that point Al informed me he couldn't take the echo off because that was how he'd recorded it, regardless of my prior instructions. He added that was the way he heard it being done and that is how Elvis liked the bass to sound. Flabbergasted and stunned even further, I pushed back my chair and stood up. Like synchronized dancing, he matched my movement bit for bit. We were standing face-to-face, clenched fists at both our sides, and his face went deep red. I was younger than him, a little taller, and ready to go the distance in this musical melodrama. The thing I didn't know was that Al was an ex-boxing champion and it would have taken him seconds to completely dismantle me and throw me out the door.

At about this point Waylon walked into the room and instinctively knew we were ready to go toe-to-toe. Without a moment's hesitation, Waylon picked me up from behind by the waist, carried me out the door, set me in the hallway, and told me to "stay!" He went back in the mixing room and closed the door. Although I couldn't hear what was being said, I could see through the soundproof window that Waylon was doing all the talking. When he came out he motioned for me to come in and told both of us to sit down and "mix the damn record" Waylon pulled up a chair in the middle of the room directly behind the two of us and folded his arms.

We did get a final mix that night, but in all honesty, I don't think either Pachucki or I were happy with what we came up with. Waylon and RCA liked it, though, and the *Honky Tonk Heroes* album had a new hit single— "We Had It All." (According to Alan Stoker, audio and video curator at the Country Music Foundation/Country Music Hall of Fame: "I've heard Waylon in an interview say that this was one of the best records he ever did.") Nashville had a new team in town, and this was the beginning of my five-year relationship with Waylon, his band, and our families. We were two desperadoes no longer waiting for the train—our ship had just come in!

We left Elvis's echo in that building. Waylon and I never recorded there again.

DIAMONDS AND DIRT: PART 2

The Lady and the Outlaws

O utlaws don't go by the same rules as ordinary folks, so we made our own and were prompted and encouraged by other peoples' expectations. In a way the fans became our guide to this insanity and told us what to do, and we happily complied. People, it seemed, wanted us to be crazy because they didn't have the guts to do it themselves. We were foolish enough to bow to the exultation of their hero worship. In the long run, even though we were having a heck of a time, we were the ones who had to pay the consequences.

Although there were a lot of wannabe Outlaws, the core group mainly consisted of Waylon Jennings, Willie Nelson, Tompall Glaser, Kinky Friedman, Shel Silverstein, Billy Ray Reynolds, Roger Schutt (a.k.a., "Captain Midnight"), and the relative band members and producers. Richie Albright, Waylon's drummer, was the heart of the Waylors, and a partner to the madness. The resident lady of the Outlaws was Jessi Colter, a.k.a. Mrs. Jennings. The man who held it all together was Johnna Yurcic, the consummate manager, friend, bodyguard, and trusted confidant who went before us to make the way clear while magically watching our backsides at the same time. He was a highly qualified jack-of-all-trades and a mirror image of what Mal Evans and Neil Aspinall were to the Beatles. For five years, Johnna took care of all the details, disasters, and derailments that came the Outlaw way—then one day he went back home to New Mexico and slept.

As Captain Midnight so aptly put it, "Often we stayed up for six nights, and it felt like a week."

Recording sessions with Waylon and Tompall happened whenever the inspiration hit. In order to be their producer, you had to be in the immediate vicinity when the creative rush came on. Whether you got credit or royalties for your work depended on someone's mood at that time. Over time I produced a lot of recordings with the Outlaws, and have been credited in various ways via gold and platinum records, royalty statements, trade reviews, session tape legends, liner notes, etc. Credit was so sporadic that any given source may or may not have me listed. Jessi Colter was a different story in terms of legal ceremony. Jessi was signed to my production company, Hometown Productions Inc., and because of the formality of my contract with Capitol, all her sessions were very organized, clearly annotated, and scheduled. We always had very tight release dates to adhere to because of the success we were having with her hits.

Waylon's career was getting ready to bust wide open, and during this period he recorded what I consider his best work, beginning with *This Time*, the album he co-produced with Willie Nelson. Next came *The Ramblin' Man*, which was basically a co-produced album with Tompall Glaser except for the two tracks I co-produced with him ("Amanda" and "It'll Be Her"). There was something electric going on with his music, and I knew the next album was going to be a classic regardless of what the songs were. I sensed Waylon was getting ready to peak artistically and commercially.

I enjoyed the whole Outlaw scene and never thought of our relationship in a formal way. The drawback for me in this haphazard way of doing business was, as I just mentioned, that I didn't always make the liner note credits. However, RCA knew my involvement and still sent me the gold and platinum albums. What I am getting to here is a mind shift on my part—I wanted to produce his next album, which turned out to be *Dreaming My Dreams*, in its entirety. For the first time I made it very clear to Waylon I was the perfect choice to be the official producer on that project. I wanted it all—the credit, the experience, the formal contract, the financial gain, the bragging rights, and the memory.

Technically, relationally, and conceptually this was not a problem— except for one minor fact—Waylon had already asked Jack "Cowboy" Clements to be the producer for this classic work. My heartfelt request put us in an awkward position. Coincidentally, during this time, I had been virtually begging him to let me take Jessi into the studio to cut "I'm Not Lisa" and a couple other songs she had written. One night he grabbed me after I had just finished a session at Tompall's studio and suggested we go for a ride and afterward he would drop me off at my hotel. We drove around the edges of Music Row talking about nothing in particular. When we pulled up to the King of the Road (Roger Miller's hotel) that's when Waylon told me that Cowboy was going to produce *Dreaming My Dreams*. He knew how much I wanted to do the project, so without giving me a chance to respond, he threw me a bone. He said he was going on the road the next day for about a week and suggested I take Jessi into the studio while he was gone.

The next morning I was on the phone booking the sessions for Jessi. Talk about magic. When Waylon returned from those road dates, I played four recorded and final mixed tracks—he practically fell on the floor because he was so excited about how good they turned out. He knew I had nailed it, but the more he thought about it, the less he liked the idea of the potential of having two stars in the same family. After a few days of stewing, Waylon called me. He told me he didn't like Jessi's new tracks after all and wanted to "can" the recordings. Waylon's decision was a double-edge stab. My gut told me I had produced at least two major hits out of the four songs ("I'm Not Lisa" and "What's Happened to Blue Eyes") and I had personally bankrolled the sessions. I spared no expense hiring the best musicians in Nashville, even flying in a keyboardist and string arranger from LA.

Jessi knew the songs I produced with her were special and didn't want this opportunity to go away. She suggested that Waylon start co-producing with me, which got him back on track with her project. I agreed that I would come back to Nashville and remix the masters together as co-producers. Now I was back in LA when all this was going down on the phone and had already put a plan into action that would further distance the Outlaws from the Nashville establishment. I had scheduled an appointment with Al Coury, Capitol's A&R vice president, to play Jessi's songs that very day. I decided to keep it even though the songs were to be remixed in Nashville with Waylon.

Al and I had history as I originally brought him in from Boston to Hollywood to head up the Artist Relations department at Capitol Records when that position was under my jurisdiction. After my departure, Al worked his way up to the head of A&R for the company. I kept the appointment and played my tapes for Al and he was knocked out with the recordings. That day I signed Jessi to Capitol's contemporary music division as a pop artist. Our plan was to release "I'm Not Lisa" to the public simultaneously via the country and pop division. Signing Jessi to Capitol's pop division was a blatant act of throwing down the gauntlet to the Nashville good ol' boy way of doing business.

Al kept my demo of the mix I had done on "I'm Not Lisa" while I went back to Nashville to present the deal to Waylon and Jessi. Unbeknownst to Al, while I was there I remixed the song with Waylon. When I returned, and contracts were signed and in order, I gave Al the master tape of our remix. After listening to it he was very disappointed. Al told me the second version was not what he paid for. He insisted on my original mix. We went with that first version and the rest is history. Waylon never said a word.

Country music stations fell in love with the single. In the process of soaring to No. 1 on their charts, we were getting such strong sales reports at the retail level that it got heavy rotation on the contemporary stations. We ended up with a Top 5 pop record. We had a good chance of making it to No. 1 on the pop charts, too, except Captain & Tennille's "Love Will Keep Us Together" hogged that position for a month.

What disappointed me was that because of Waylon's star power, he was listed as the primary producer on forty of the forty-four major record reviews we received on "I'm Not Lisa"—and he wasn't even there. This was unintentional on his and Jessi's part, and none of that really mattered anyway because we had a hit. We were family and that's just how it worked.

So here we have Jessi in 1975 with her No. 1 single ("I'm Not Lisa") and No. 1 album (*I'm Jessi Colter*) and Waylon scoring with the first of his No. 1 records, *Dreaming My Dreams*, with two No. 1 singles. These two country albums by husband and wife accounted for three No. 1 singles and six Top 5 singles. I followed *Dreaming My Dreams* with his classic *Are You Ready for the Country*, which shot to No. 1 on three separate occasions during 1976.

It also yielded two Top 5 singles and two more Top 10 hits. *Record World Magazine* 1977 Country Music Awards voted *Are You Ready for the County* as the No. 1 album of the year. (Various music critics have also stated that this particular work was one of his greatest. This was Waylon's "on fire" era — five other albums in this particular six-album, three-year (1973–76) run — *Lonesome, On'ry and Mean/Honky Tonk Heroes/This Time/The Ramblin' Man/Dreaming My Dreams/Are You Ready for the Country* — all received this accolade at one time or another. To this day I feel blessed to have been involved as a producer on three of these.

It was a magical time period for me as a producer and Waylon and I as friends. We were young, rich, crazy, successful, and having the time of our lives. Hooking up with the Outlaws was like jumping on a rocket. We were soaring in more ways than one, and there was no turning back or turning us off.

DIAMONDS AND DIRT: PART 3

Fools Reshen In

Waylon reminded me of the Beatles during this rich harvest in that each new album was refreshingly different and creative. He had the same core to his music but would always craft something new into the mix of things, be it the producer, the location, musicians, etc.

Waylon was hot now, and Jessi was on fire too. Following her 1975 No. 3 album *I'm Jessi Colter* she charted two more Top 5 albums in 1976 (*Jessi* and *Diamond in the Rough* which went to No. 1) with the two of us at the helm. We were in the studio, on the road, and completely out of touch with reality. It was madness—a cowboy version of the extravagance and craziness of my Beatle days. It seemed as if everything we touched turned to gold. Tours went from small country venues to large mainstream auditoriums. Waylon went from opening for supposedly bigger name stars to headlining his own shows. Jessi would walk out unannounced during his shows, and the crowd would go bonkers.

I'll never forget the night he was the opener for Commander Cody and His Lost Planet Airmen at Santa Monica Civic Auditorium. I believe that being a warm-up act to Commander Cody wasn't setting right in Waylon's craw, and he had every right to be upset. Waylon was in the process of rewriting music history while Commander Cody was basically a one-hit wonder—1972's "Hot Rod Lincoln."

Waylon went out on stage that night and blew the roof off the auditorium. When Waylon would decide to be "on" it was infectious and his band would automatically crank up the intensity. I was in my usual spot, stage right leaning on an amp with a Lone Star beer, when he finished the last number. He walked past me with a look on his face like "just try and follow that, Commander!" I was told later that Commander Cody said he would never follow that Texas cowboy on stage again. It was also, to my memory, the end of Waylon's stint as an opening act.

The fourth album I produced with Jessi Colter, a concept by her insistence that Capitol was very unhappy about but finally conceded to, was a gospel album entitled *Miriam*. Miriam was Jessi's given name and she dedicated the album to her mother's memory.

My friendship with Roy Orbison had deepened over the years since the MGM days, and he invited me to record this project in his studio on Music Row. It was a wonderful place to record because Roy did things right. The furnishings, the sound equipment, and the layout were first-class. It was a producer's dream to work in such a relaxed and yet creative atmosphere. I had spent time at Roy and Barbara's house out on Old Hickory Lake in Hendersonville, Tennessee, and this studio felt like an extension of their home.

Picture this if you will—a bunch of Outlaws stoned out of their minds recording a gospel album. I think the only person in the room who wasn't wasted was Roy, who hung out during some of the sessions. One night we were putting the final touches on the album when Waylon decided to sing a duet to Jessi's lead on the choruses of "I Belong to Him," a beautiful and haunting hymn.

Roy had stopped by earlier and was leaning against the control room wall just behind me—off to my right where I could see his reflection in the glass between the control room and the studio. I noticed how intently he watched Waylon, and could see he was mouthing the words to the chorus. I pushed back from the recording console and swung my chair around to face Roy. I casually said to him the chorus would sound good as a trio—you know, Jessi, Waylon, and him. Roy shook his head in that gentle easy way he had and said softly, "Yeah that might sound *real* good" (drawing out the word *real* as only a true Texan can do). I turned back to the board, pressed down the talkback button, and asked Waylon if he would mind if Roy came out and joined him. He agreed and Roy took his place at the microphone with Waylon. One take and it was beautiful. Jessi's vocal was already recorded on another track, so the mixing would be easy when it came time to blend the voices. As it turned out, Waylon and Roy's voices melded together like sweet Texas butter.

Barbara Orbison walked in the studio about this time and couldn't believe her eyes. She said that Roy never sang on other people's records so he sure must like me. I felt honored that we were friends but this comment made me feel special. (Years later Roy would visit LA and was very reclusive while in town. I don't think he was comfortable there—with the city, the scene, and the people. He and Barbara would call the house and come by to just hang out. Sometimes we'd meet for dinner at his favorite place—Trader Vic's located inside the Beverly Hilton Hotel. He liked the restaurant because he was able to enjoy his dinner there rather incognito. Nobody expected to see this legendary Texas rocker eating in a glitzy Polynesian place.

While my friendship with the Orbisons blossomed, the same couldn't be said for my relationship with the Jenningses. Jessi's gospel sessions turned out to be the beginning of the end for Waylon and me. Enter Neil Reshen.

Right around the time of those sessions, a New York manager named Neil Reshen began appearing on the scene. Much like Allen Klein in the '60s, Reshen came with a heavy-duty reputation. *Country Music* scribe Bob Campbell wrote in 1979 that Reshen was "a man with a sinister reputation." Neil's management style included being controlling and manipulative. He didn't like how intertwined mine and Waylon's musical and personal relationship had become. This was obviously due to the fact that the musical success portion caused me to enter into the money pot.

One night during Jessi's *Miriam* sessions, Neil showed up at the studio and pulled me into the tape locker for a chat. A tape locker in a recording studio is typically a long, narrow closet-like place with extra structure and ventilation in order to preserve previously recorded master tapes. Neil was an imposing character, a bit scary in appearance and even scarier in reputation. I was like a cautious dog walking in a pasture of mean bulls whenever Neil was around. I figured the least amount of interaction we had, the less chance there would be of getting on his wrong side. It was unusual for him to cut me out of the herd during playbacks and it was a calculated move. I was very uncomfortable in that very confined space, standing face-to-face with the bearer of bad tidings. Reshen spoke first and last.

"Ken, I know I have a reputation and some people have said that I am a crook," he started off. "I want you to know that I don't care what people think of me because I do what is best for my artists and if it pleases people to classify me that way—then fine. If they are right, I do want you to know that I am an honest crook and I am going to lay it out straight for you. The fact is that I'm taking over and you have become too important in this organization—I will have you out of here within months. I want you to know that it isn't personal, it's just my way of doing business." He concluded with, "And because I actually do like you, I wanted to let you know this upfront so you can make other plans." I was astonished and thought him to be a fool because he didn't realize how close we all were. I felt as if he was making a big mistake and that Waylon would see through his act in time.

It's astounding to reflect back on how close we all were. Waylon was the best man at my wedding. This is interesting because I hadn't asked him to stand up with me but just as the ceremony was starting he walked up and positioned himself behind me and to my left side. I asked him what he was doing and he informed he was my best man. I told him I decided not to have a best man and he answered; "Don' matter hoss, I'm it—now le's get married"!

We spent holidays together as families. I remember one Christmas was spent at Waylon and Jessi's new home in Nashville. We enjoyed the spoils of our new success and went crazy sharing our financial rewards. They bought my wife and me a vintage jukebox that was too big to wrap, so it was hidden in the garage and presented as the final gift. But the scene you had to see was their very big and long living room on Christmas morning. With all the various marriages involved, we had an army of kids there that day and the presents flowed out from under the Christmas tree and filled the entire room. It was madness when it came time to open the presents. Wrapping paper was flying everywhere and happy screams filled the air. When it was all over we couldn't even walk through the waist deep, wall-to-wall gift-wrappings without the fear of stepping on an expensive toy or small child.

Another Christmas we loaded this same gang, plus Captain Midnight and Jessi's dad, into Waylon's bus. We decided to take a tour of Littlefield, Texas—Waylon's hometown. There we were, tooling down the highway with the busload of people with Captain Midnight and the older kids following in Waylon's orange Cadillac. (We were used to seeing someone following Waylon's bus while on tour, but the vision from the rearview mirrors was usually the sight of about a dozen or so Hell's Angels riding herd behind us. They loved Waylon and the whole Outlaw image and appointed themselves as our personal and concert bodyguards.) This Christmas we left Nashville for Texas and attended several family reunions and homecomings for Waylon in Littlefield and Lubbock. We played in the snow in New Mexico and ended up in Arizona where Jessi was raised and where she and Waylon began their relationship. This bizarre scenario was decadent and yet so innocent at the same time.

I think the craziest get-together was when Jack "Cowboy" Clements and Jessi's sister, Sharon, got hitched. It was winter and they decided to tie the knot at Jessi's parents' cabin, which was located out in the middle of the Arizona desert somewhere along the Gila River.

Tompall and June, my wife and I, Waylon and Jessi, Cowboy and his bride to be, Jessi's folks and some kids were all crammed in this little three-room cabin with limited facilities. Of course, the one bathroom quit working the first day—and we were there for four days. Three couples, the Jennings, Mansfields, and Glasers flew into Phoenix Sky Harbor International Airport and rented a brand new baby blue Lincoln Continental with soft plush cloth fabric seats. I mention the absorbent seat covers because just about everyone on this excursion was a heavy-duty smoker. If I remember correctly, the ride to the cabin was around three hours. The last leg of our journey was similar to a wilderness trip and was basically non-road type travel. We drove down creek gullies and cattle trails through heavy brush that reached out and scratched the paint job every step of the way. This was dry desert land so it wasn't long before there was about a foot of dust and mud caked on the outside of the car. The inside didn't fare much better. Because no one was allowed to smoke in the cabin, and it was freezing in the desert, the Lincoln became the smoker's lounge for the next few days.

The night of the wedding came and Cowboy drove into the nearest town that afternoon to find a preacher to marry them. Only Jessi and her folks were professed Christians at that time. Because of the limited options, availability, and willingness of the local religious leaders to venture out to this desolate place filled with weird looking strangers, it was no surprise that Cowboy came back with some off-the-wall cult leader or left-field prophet that he most likely dragged out of a bar. To add to the insanity of that day, the wedding was held outside on the edge of the property in the freezing cold. It was beginning to look like a Fellini movie the way it was unfolding. So here we are—this gaggle of very funky, unshaven, wrinkled, smelly group of curious looking people, shivering in almost total darkness. Tompall, played the guitar with his cowboy hat pulled down over his eyes, and sang Don Williams' "Lay Down Beside Me." It was a sight that shall forever remain tattooed on my brain: Tompall had a cigarette hanging out of his mouth and a bottle of Jack Daniels between his boots while Jack and Sharon exchanged vows. It was so cold Tompall said he needed the cigarette to keep his mouth warm so he could sing and the Jack Daniels to keep his body furnace stoked. In a way, that scene perfectly summed up this decade of decadence.

Jack and Sharon had somehow driven a Winnebago into the canyon where the cabin was situated. It was their plan to head out that night on their honeymoon. It was to be their "Honeymoon Suite." As there were only two bedrooms, everybody pretty much slept in the same room, on the floors, couch, and dining room table. Jessi's mom was a preacher and wouldn't let my wife and I sleep together in the bedroom because she thought we weren't married. ironically, Tompall and June were not married and got the bedroom because she assumed they were husband and wife. Waylon and Jessi slept in the kitchen.

After the ceremony and a very small celebration, the newlyweds climbed into the Winnebago and headed off into the night down the small ravine that would eventually take them out to the highway. We couldn't believe they were able to negotiate that house on wheels into the area in the first place. The Winnebago could barely scrape through the gully when it rolled up to the cabin. But what comes in doesn't always necessarily go out, and they got that baby stuck no further than about 300 yards away. It was firmly entrenched and leaning heavily to one side. They ended up spending the night in the cabin with the rest of us.

Cowboy and Sharon made it out the next morning and Tompall, Waylon, and I spent the next day wandering the hills above the river shooting guns. The desolate landscape didn't provide much in the way of target practice—we shot at the river, any bush that moved in the wind, and an occasional tin can on a pile of rocks. The next morning the migration headed out for reality and back to our day jobs. Because of the extreme temperature, I contracted a cold and spent three hours suffocating in the Lincoln, which was baby brown inside and out after its four days in the Arizona wilds. I coughed all the way to the Phoenix airport because of the cigarette smoke and several layers of dust I congested while at the cabin. No way was anyone going to turn the car into the Hertz lot looking like it did. Keeping true to our Outlaw ways, we pulled up to the curb, got out with our luggage, checked it at curbside and dropped off the keys at the Hertz counter inside and told them where it was parked. Waylon called road manager, Johnna Yurcic, who had made the reservations and instructed him to deal with the car company. It definitely wasn't the first time he had to handle something like this. I'll bet it cost a small fortune.

Boy, did I ever underestimate Reshen. With the years of struggle, success, family experiences, and deep emotional ties I had with the Outlaws, I never imagined that this individual could come in and break it up. He was nothing like us, but he was the best at what he did and what he did wasn't always good. He basically took the approach that Allen Klein did at Apple by coming into an organization and messing everything up. Then as the creator of the chaos, he was the only one who knew how to straighten it out. He had decided it was time for me to go, and over time erased as much as he could of my historical involvement. To this day you won't find my name as producer on any of Waylon's albums except *Are You Ready for the Country*, *Honky Tonk Heroes*, and *I've Always Been Crazy*. The biggest single record I produced with Waylon was his No. 1 hit "Amanda" on *The Ramblin' Man*. Although I have received acknowledgment from RCA and select discographies, my official producer's credit is missing from the song. To this day, that still stings.

I want to make it clear that I don't see Waylon and Jessi as the heavies. Waylon had a tendency to look the other way when it came to business matters and was fond of delegating delicate situations. None of us in those days were financial wizards, and Reshen has explained to the world that he came in when the Jenningses were supposedly $600,000 in the hole. We all knew that figure was highly exaggerated. This was another example of Reshen rewriting history. He offered to clear their mess up via the record company contracts and cutting corners in other areas. I should know: I was in the corner with the other areas.

Knowing that Waylon and I had a deep friendship and a unique way of making records together, be it his or Jessi's, Reshen took the low road by going to Waylon with one of the few things that he knew would damage our relationship. As Jessi was signed to Capitol via my company Hometown Productions Inc., Waylon was told that I was stealing royalties from his wife. Now, I could have driven his new Cadillac off a cliff, killed his dog, and even said bad things about Texas, but the one thing that was indefensible would be stealing from his wife. Like any bad seed planted and watered, Reshen had accomplished a damage that couldn't be undone. It was a suspicion that couldn't be erased.

The irony in this accusation was the fact that Jessi's royalties never came to me for distribution. As with all of my Hometown Production Company acts, I hired an entertainment industry financial institution called Talent Payments Inc. (TPI) and instructed Capitol to submit all royalty payments and statements directly to them. I did this for the very reason that I could never be accused of or tempted to mishandle my client's monies. Once received by TPI, they would in turn make payments to artist and producer according to the terms of the production contract between Capitol, the artist, and me. The only royalty checks I received for Jessi's records came in the mail to me as a producer the same day hers came to her.

Reshen knew what he told the Jenningses didn't have to be true—all he needed to do was paint that picture in Waylon's mind just the one time.

Waylon and I had a final encounter over this matter in the Sheraton Universal Hotel in Studio City one night after both of us had been up for days. Richie Albright said when he got off the elevator he could hear us all the way down at the other end of the hall on that floor. As bad as our fallout was that night, I never dreamed that it was the end of our long run. But Waylon developed this strange loyalty to Reshen, whom he believed saved him from financial ruin. His loyalty to Reshen's promises was stronger than his loyalty to our history, and so I had to go.

Captain Midnight went to his grave with the greatest of distaste for Reshen for rewriting himself into Outlaw history and our lives. Willie ended up suing Reshen. And no great surprise, as the story goes, Reshen ended up abandoning Waylon a few years later when he faced financial problems again.

The roller-coaster ride that started in 1973 finally collapsed in a heap by 1978. Sadly, finding myself on the outs with the Outlaws, I moseyed back to LA to resume my forgotten rock-and-roll career.

In some ways it's hard recalling some of these happenings, because I will always love everyone who was there and know I was blessed to even ride on that bus. I did feel with the passage of time that Waylon and I would renew our friendship and bury the hatchet. As it turned out, we didn't talk for more than two decades and never had the opportunity to mend fences. I found out about his death on Fox News and was crestfallen. When all is said and done, Waylon is still my favorite singer. I used to tease him that even though he only knew four licks, he was also one of my favorite guitar players.

I did leave with a special feeling about my contribution to the Outlaws, because when it came to the Beatles and the other famous acts I had worked with, I was never in the birthing room of these superstar careers. The Outlaw movement was a groundbreaking era in the country music movement, and it felt good to know I was one of the producers at the heart of it all.

DIAMONDS AND DIRT: PART 4

The Heart and the Hurt

In 1978, basically "outlawed" in Nashville, I put my focus back on California where I thought I'd pick up where I left off in LA's rock-and-roll scene, but I couldn't seem to get reestablished. Ironically, the pop labels saw me now as a country producer and were reluctant to assign me projects working with their marquee artists. Neil Reshen, in the meantime, had put the kibosh on my long-time association with Capitol and RCA by tagging me as persona non-grata for all his artists, which certainly didn't help things.

I did produce a few name artists (David Cassidy, Sam Neely, Don Ho, Nick Gilder, Byron Berline, and Sundance) but except for Don Ho, their careers were struggling like mine. I couldn't seem to get on track in Hollywood and there was no real cohesiveness or direction to my work. I didn't deliver the hits, which was exactly what I needed to do to get back on top. My heart was still in the progressive country-rock genre and I had been exiled and blackballed. I didn't realize how much I had been thrown for a loop by what happened in Tennessee, and I dealt with it by getting my highs from drugs and partying instead of creativity and accomplishment. I can explain why things fell apart in Nashville, but my disappointing role in the aftermath falls totally on my shoulders.

For the first time in my life since I left Idaho, almost three decades earlier, I was no longer, as we say in the business, "happening." I had made success my god and when failure came my way I found myself alone and confused in a godless world.

In time it all fell apart. I certainly wasn't alone as there were a lot of us who couldn't handle the combination of success, drugs, and rock 'n' roll.

You could find us late at night on the Sunset Strip figuratively carrying our awards, gold records, and top-of-the-chart clippings around in garbage bags.

In 1984 I figured the Tennessee wounds had healed and I headed back to Nashville to give it another go. My life was a mess, my career was in the commode, and I was pretty screwed up. The bucks I had made during the good years had all evaporated via the upkeep and monthly expenses of owning a Hollywood estate and properties, the oceanfront summer home on the northern California coast, the Mercedes, and other expensive toys. My wife ran off with a friend of mine who also took some of my favorite clothes. (I really miss that blue jacket.) I landed in Tompall's studio on 19th Avenue (just off Music Row) with three cardboard boxes and three suitcases. I had no car, no money, no jobs, and nothing going for me except a whole lot of desperate determination—a Hollywood casualty looking for another shot at the big-time.

I spent the next nine years in Nashville. As I look back on my life during that time, I am somewhat amazed at the person I see. I was a pathetic mess at first, graduated to being pitiful, and then spent a long time being borderline hopeless until I got in step with my walk with the Lord. I spent the first four years without a car and kept that fact hidden by the way I made my moves. I rented an apartment in Hillsboro Village, which was situated strategically a short distance from Music Row. I could walk the streets of that part of town making my rounds with the record companies, publishing houses, and recording studios without anyone knowing that I was without wheels. Connie and I were dating then, and in those situations where a car was essential I would borrow her wheels.

There were times I'd be hanging out at a club late at night trying to network or find work, and when it came closing time I'd be standing outside with no way to get home. I had some very insightful late-night chats with myself as I walked long distances across town at one or two in the morning. Let me tell you, it was cold and dark and I wasn't very good company. Even after I generated some income, I vowed that I wouldn't buy a car of any kind unless I could pay cash for it, and even then, not before I had paid off 100 percent of every dime I owed from the days past. It was amazing how I never got busted for not having transportation. If I had a business luncheon I would suggest a cafe in Hillsboro Village. If I couldn't pull that off, I'd simply leave for my meeting an hour or so ahead of time and hike to my destination. There was a bank, a grocery store, a post office, and just about everything else I needed to live a normal life within three blocks of my apartment. My small dwelling was furnished with cast-off furniture from Tompall's studio and some extra pieces from a few friends' places. My total budget was $500 a month—$350 for rent, $150 went to food and necessities anything above that was used to pay off old debts. I lived this way for over two years.

Nashville simply became a country-fried version of my return to LA. I couldn't break into the system this time and hit total bottom. My anti-establishment stance with the Outlaws had left me with few friends at the record companies. The excesses, the drugs, my guru, and quirky cohorts had finally let me down. I was thrown unprepared into the "real world"—lost between "rock and roll" and "heartbreak hotel."

What makes the story about my second stint in Nashville interesting is that I hit my worldly bottom and experienced the heavenly high of my eternal salvation simultaneously in Nashville. I met Connie, my wife to be, shortly after arriving back in town, and in time she brought me to the Lord. (To find out more about this, read *The Beatles, the Bible, and Bodega Bay*. My future was taken care of (eternally), but the here and now of the Nashville skyline was still dark.

The doors of the music business were closed to me. I could hear opportunity running out the back door to get away from me. I couldn't get a job in the mailrooms of the companies I had once managed as a top executive. Desperate to make a living, I applied to sell used cars down on Broadway and was turned down there as well. At least they could have said I was overqualified! On the verge of becoming homeless, I finally scored a job in my profession. It wasn't quite as glamorous as some of my previous positions, but it did pay a bit above minimum wage and required maximum endurance. I got a job at the new Starwood Amphitheater doing what we call in the business "humping amps."

This gigantic outdoor venue brought in the biggest acts in the country, and I was a part of the stage crew. We started at five in the morning on the day of the show unloading the giant semitrucks that backed up to the staging area with the sets, sound, and lights for the evening concert. We unloaded heavy equipment and set up non-stop for about twelve hours except for short lunch breaks. Picture this—Nashville in mid-August, 95 degrees with 90 percent humidity, and here I am working in the bowels of these trucks unloading heavy equipment. I got the job through a friend of a friend and I was definitely different than the rest of the crew. They typically didn't hire fifty-year-old men to do work usually reserved for the twenty-somethings. In *The White Book* I tell of humbling experiences I had with James Taylor and Julian Lennon while working at the Starwood Amphitheater, but these were more related to worldly matters and thinking. One of my most moving spiritual experiences took place on that stage the night of a Whitney Houston concert.

During Whitney's first song, she was uncomfortable with the sound emanating from her stage monitors. It was vital to the performance because she needed to hear herself in order to stay on pitch and in time with the band. At the end of her opening number, she turned to the wings and motioned for a stagehand to come out and rearrange the physical location of the monitors directly in front of her. I was the nearest person to her position—therefore I was the one she motioned to join her on stage and move the equipment. I was already embarrassed about my current employment situation and wasn't excited about music industry people knowing what I was doing for a living. I also wasn't about to go out in front of thousands of people looking like I had just escaped from a chain gang.

I turned to push one of the young guys standing behind me out onto the stage when God stopped me in my tracks and gave me very clear instructions. I was still a baby Christian and not used to having one-on-one dialogue with my Maker. In this suspended time in Starwood space He told me to get my prideful buns out on that stage and do the job I was being paid to do. He told me I was working for Him now, and He didn't like slackers. You see, among my many problems and one of the things He felt it was time to start sorting out big-time was my pride and vanity.

I realized at that moment what He was after. I wasn't about to defy Him when He had made Himself perfectly clear about what was going on here. So I sucked it up and walked out onto the stage and got down on my knees in front of thousands of concertgoers and repositioned the monitors to Whitney's liking. While on my knees I looked out at the first row, which was about twelve feet in front of me. I looked directly into the faces of the record company presidents and executives, most of whom were former associates. They were sitting in the seats that in better times I used to sit in alongside of them. They sat there stunned, staring up at me. From my knees and with my dirty, sweating face I looked up at the sky beyond the crowd and into the sparkling stars that were my heavenly Father's eyes. I silently prayed, *Lord, this is the single most humiliating moment of my entire life, but Lord Father God, I love You more than anything I have ever known. I want what You want more than anything I ever wanted and so Abba Father—game on!* I arranged those monitors like monitors have never been arranged in the history of rock-and-roll concerts. To this day they tell of how the stage monitors at the Whitney Houston concert were arranged to unbeatable supreme placement. I looked back out at the well-dressed executives and could see the look of disbelief in their eyes—many of them had wondered whatever happened to Ken Mansfield. Now they knew.

Before getting up from my knees I looked straight at them and smiled, tipping my head to them in a "there now, isn't this a lovely row of monitors?" manner. I got up, proudly turned to Whitney for her approval, and when I walked off the stage and cleared the wing curtains I felt as if God gave me this big high-five. A giant weight had been lifted from me, and I had attained a new understanding of this incredible relationship. God knew my pride was really in the way of my relationship with Him and it was time to take a big chunk out of it. In our two decades of marriage, Connie and I have experienced some incredible moments together as husband and wife. She was there that night when God took a big piece out of my stubborn, human pride. She has told me that to this day it is the proudest she has ever been of me.

(I understand that the Starwood was demolished in February 2007 to make way for a sixty-five-acre home subdivision. I'll bet, though, that they kept those monitors just the way I left them.)

The Starwood experience lasted for two seasons, and then God moved me into a new phase. I was deeper into my walk with Him and being richly fed by the pastor at the church that had become our spiritual home. Some good friends from the church were led by the Lord to fund our new company, Main Mansfield Associates. They set us up in a United Artist Tower corner suite of offices from whence we looked out on the 17th Avenue half of Music Row. That is when I reestablished my business relationship with Ringo and produced and managed the Flying Burrito Bros., as well as a small stable of cutting-edge contemporary and country music acts. It was also from this vantage that I was commissioned to produce the Gaither Vocal Band's classic Grammy-winning *Homecoming* album as well as the legendary Imperials and their *Big God* album.

My second stint in Nashville was filled with surprises, disappointments, victories, failures, joy, and tears. I was there nine years, and during this time both my mother and father passed away in Idaho. Both times I was too late to say good-bye.

▨ ▨ ▨

But that's there, and now we are here.

The miles separate these two places but the memories draw them together.

The tears and the triumphs have become the fabric that covers and combines us like a coat of many colors.

Connie became the thread that mended my broken heart.

I am no longer all tied up in loose ends.

We have a lot of great friends in Nashville and are able to leave the confines of the van for a few days to stay in some very nice homes. One of the advantages of having been successful is that not all the old friends had blown it like I did, so we get to enjoy their continued blessings when we visit. We make the rounds and hang out for a week or so, but Connie is anxious to head north to Kentucky to visit her folks in the Paducah area. She spent most of her life there and in Nashville, save for some short stints in Dallas and LA. She feels at home by being back in Nashville but at the same time is getting homesick for "home" in Mayfield, Kentucky.

I was ready to leave Nashville too, but for different reasons. There is a certain sense of overload that overtakes me while there. There was just too much deeply intense stuff that went down in my life. The rush of memories and surging of old feelings leaves me wiped out after a while. It *was* the lowest point of my life and it *was* the most exciting period of my life. I lost both my parents while there; but I found my closest friends there. I was rejected by my peers; I was accepted by my Lord. I lost my love for making music; I found my love and married her—all within earshot of the sound of the music I once made there. There were times I couldn't afford to eat; yet it was there that I was fed the Bread of Life and became full and refreshed.

Nashville is both the heart and the unofficial center point of this journey, and continuing on from here gives us the sense of starting out all over again. It is late afternoon when we depart.

If it looks like we are getting bigger as we are leaving, it's because of all those meat and threes and home-cooked meals we have been eating for the last week or so. Our cups *and* plates continually ranneth over and we did empty them.

MILE MARKER # 7
KENTUCKY

HER OLD KENTUCKY HOME

Connie knows "by heart" (cliché intended) the road from Nashville to the one-hundred-acre place her folks have called home for many years. I envy that feeling she has of having a real home; that one place she has been able to come back to for so long.

Connie could drive there from Nashville blindfolded, but I take command of Moses so she can look out the window and have her private time with her memories. This is a role reversal of sorts because this whole trip has been about me. For the first time we are in her territory, both physically and mentally. It is the back of Connie's curly head I see for most of the trip as she leans into the passenger door peering out the window.

I love to gaze at the South as we drive along. For some inexplicable reason when I get out to walk in it and live in it, I am not as comfortable as I am on the western slopes, valleys, and shores of this great country. I like the western dirt, weeds, rivers, and ocean edges much more than I do the southern versions of these landscapes. Western river beaches have sand and no snakes in the water; the bugs are fewer and more polite and the ground seems friendlier. (A slight disagreement doth abound between Connie and me concerning my version of the two geographies.) The South does have us beat when it comes to the massive lawns on the southern plantations and rich residential areas of its gracious cities. I also have to give it to the South when it comes to its hospitality and its food—aah, yes, there's that "meat and three" thing again.

We leave Nashville heading north for a few miles on Interstate 65 before veering northwest on Interstate 24 for the longest part of our trip to her home. Once we cross the Tennessee line into Kentucky, there is a faster route we could take, but that would keep us on the freeways longer. We choose to turn off at a quaint little town called Cadiz and travel the back roads through the beautiful "Land Between the Lakes" area.

I've always found this drive refreshing for a couple of reasons, one being that we get to drive through Golden Pond. Do you think you could drive through a place called Golden Pond without having beautiful flashbacks on that luscious film regardless of what the place looked like? The other reason is that Connie comes alive here. She regales me with stories about her times on the lakes with her family and their boat outings. I have my Idaho rivers— the Clearwater with its pristine waters and the Snake with its deep canyons and rushing rapids. She has her greenery and the verdant land between the two giant lakes—Kentucky Lake and Lake Barkley. The Tennessee and Cumberland rivers have formed the two bodies of water as they pass through the southwestern corner of Kentucky on their separate ways to music centers like Nashville, Tennessee, and Muscle Shoals, Alabama.

We arrive home right around dusk, a time in the South that is different than anyplace else on earth. There's a light edge of darkness that has a certain softness about it I have never experienced anywhere else. It is like God personally takes responsibility for dimming the light of day in the South, and everything takes on a quiet hush. We get out of the car, and before we even see anybody, I can tell that Connie has called ahead. I smell the fresh cornbread cooking in the kitchen—a dead giveaway. I wasn't sure her folks liked me at first, but I never doubted how much her mom loved the way I scarfed up her homemade cornbread. I will never forget the first Thanksgiving I spent at their home when Connie and I were dating. I wasn't used to what Thanksgiving dinner meant in the South. It meant about forty different mouth-watering food dishes on the table. It meant that your eyes were bigger than your stomach, and after about an hour at the table it meant your only thought would be to find the closest place possible to lie down.

Connie's dad, Doug, is a proud Kentuckian, and loves his land. He can find more pleasure out of crawling around on some old tractors than my California friends could ever have from spending a week at an oceanfront resort. Years later when I got a job in California it was necessary for me to go ahead while Connie stayed behind to wrap things up with our Nashville house and honor commitments to some television shows where she was the Directors Guild Association associate director. Two months later she and Doug drove out together in a large furniture van and had a wonderful cross-country father-daughter experience. Doug stayed only one day. Our home in Bodega Bay was big and beautiful and overlooked the whole sweep of the long beach that fronted the bay, but Doug wanted to get right back to Kentucky and the level green lands surrounded by heavy brush and lots of trees. To quote him, "This just feels too darn lonely here!"

As usual, the next day Connie drives me around her old haunts in Paducah. Later we find a place to sit on the banks of the Ohio River, which runs through this picturesque little town. I am especially chilled out and laid-back. I look at her river and tell her about mine.

We arrive back to the house at that perfect moment of muted darkness and the aroma of fresh cornbread. We share grace and dinner and white cake dessert, Connie's favorite food item. After our meal I turn in early to read and write while Connie spends long hours into the night catching up with her folks.

We stay less than a week. She hardly gets out of her pajamas some days and spends a lot of time simply resting and talking to her mom while her dad tinkers in his shed. The time comes and she knows that we will leave in the morning. She really doesn't want to go, but I promise her when our trip is over she can use the air miles we have earned with our gas credit cards and fly back home to stay as long as she wants. It is hard for Connie to live so far from her roots, but there is another part of her that has grown to know distances. This is a gut knowledge that grows out of spending many years in the entertainment business. Connie and I have a common understanding of the dichotomy that invades our senses—the desire to settle down that lives side-by-side with a certain restlessness that never seems to go away.

I can feel a change in us as we drive away. Without discussing it, I think there is a shared comfort in knowing that the staying-in-one-place part of our lives is gaining in importance. We are both tired of saying good-bye to the people and places we love. She knows she is blessed because she has something to miss and something that misses her.

That something is a special place called home.

In some unexplainable way I believe that Moses is taking us—*home*.

NEW YORK NO YORK

I can still see the tops of the trees that line the front yard of Connie's folk's house in Moses' side mirror. Connie is facing out the passenger side window, but this time she is not looking at the scenery.

I keep an appropriate silence that pervades moments like these. Connie doesn't know how long it will be before she returns, so she knows this very moment is the longest point in time from when she will see her mom and dad again. We leave the country road and turn west toward Highway 80 instead of getting on the Parkway heading toward Lexington and New York. Noticing the change in direction, she turns to ask what's going on. Women have this sense about things and Connie knew something was brewing the minute we got up that morning. But whatever it was that her radar picked up was relegated to a lower priority until we got to this exit. Enough miles have passed and the revised route, coupled with her intuition, indicates a change in not only our physical direction but also the emotional bent of our trip. She turns from the window and joins me for the first time since we left the house.

"So what's up?"

Being at Connie's home for a few days got me to thinking. We had been doing the home dynamic and the variations thereof for quite a while and I was no longer in a New York state of mind. We had visited five "homes" during the last couple of months and there was only one home missing—the one that was pulling at the hand on Moses' steering wheel. We left home in Bodega Bay, drove to the Hangover House in LA, then to my first California hometown of San Diego, and on to Nashville, a place we both had called home. Now we had just left her "old Kentucky home."

I tell her that for the first time since we left Bodega Bay, I want to go back to my hometown in Idaho and then back to our home in California. She immediately says OK and that she understands. I am relieved but do harbor the feeling her gentle response may have more to do with the fact this new plan means there will be fewer nights sleeping in a van.

This was intended to be a yearlong trip, but I am cutting it short. It was a good idea romantically and on paper, but like a rodeo rider with too many years ridin' the circuit, it was time to climb down and tie the leathers up to one secure post. Because we are skipping the visual and geographical of our scheduled visit to the East Coast, I recount some of my New York memories. There is going to be a lot of time to fill as we head north and west toward some of the highways and states a lot of people never see or hear about. A part of me feels relieved, because in all those years I had never driven a car in Manhattan, and this cowboy was actually fearful of the experience.

▨ ▨ ▨

When I think of New York, it is like a sifting of recollections to where you finally are left with the finest grains in the sands of time past. Robin Leach, host of *Lifestyles of the Rich and Famous* was my favorite part of the "Big Apple." We shared a fairytale existence, and I bless the day we were thrown together in the concrete canyons of the most exciting place on earth.

Manhattan sizzles, especially if you are young, naïve, and able to have the bucks to make it work. Robin and I grew up less than privileged and had fought our way against all odds to the center of a tough business—one with a lot of perks for those who were doing well. We easily adapted to the new lifestyle with a certain air of sophistication that was surprisingly easy to don for two scruffs from different continental versions of backwater beginnings.

Robin was the president of *Go* magazine, which was based in Manhattan. In the late '60s, the publication had positioned itself into a "rag" of great importance to the record companies. It was the cutting-edge East Coast tabloid for the contemporary rock scene in those days. The publication was particularly important to Capitol Records, because even though we had big offices in New York, we were still primarily known as a West Coast label. We needed to boost our East Coast image and prowess. I was the head of promotion for Capitol when Robin and I met. It was important to get as much editorial space in his magazine as possible on our new artists, especially the contemporary part of the roster. I had an unlimited expense account to hustle Robin Leach in order to entice him to give our artists good editorial space in his magazine. Robin, on the other hand, had to keep the magazine profitable. He did this by obtaining as much advertising dollars as he could from the big record companies, Capitol being his primary target. He had an unlimited entertainment budget to spend on hustling me for ad space. Do I need to paint this picture any clearer?

We were two young men in our twenties who had just been given free rein to do whatever we wanted in New York, LA, or any place else by just tying it into our dual and mutual assignments. Well, we hustled and wined and dined each other all over this land, knowing we were just a few scant years away from making less money in a month than we would spend in an evening. You have seen him on TV and heard him laugh and know how ebullient he can be. If you pull that back into a youthful mind and body and let her rip, you can imagine what it was like. We are still close friends today, and he and the memory of those days are some of my favorite recollections. We still have mini reunions in Las Vegas and San Francisco and make the rounds like the old days, except the pace and intake is slower and lower.

In my years at the record labels, working with so many different campaigns with major artists, New York became a second home to me. I was there so much that I had my own room at the Warwick Hotel. In those days the Warwick was the hip hotel, and it boasted a great bar right on the corner of 54th street and the Avenue of the Americas. It was also perfectly and strategically placed to do business with the heart of the entertainment world.

Working with the network TV shows was a natural part of my job description, and in those days *The Tonight Show Starring Johnny Carson* was the top of the ladder in establishing or maintaining an artist's career. A specific incident involving that show is another one of my favorite remembrances when it comes to the big city.

Michael Parks was an MGM artist who was busting wide open because of his hit TV show *Then Came Bronson*. His James Dean–style character in the television series hit the zeitgeist of just about every nine-to-five working man in the late '60s and early '70s. The basic premise of the show was a guy who walked off the job one day, hopped on his Harley, and headed out across the country free as a bird leaving all the stress of worldly pressure behind. Check out the opening scene of the first episode that begins with Bronson (Parks) driving up to a red light in San Francisco. He briefly chats with a commuter and introduces his signature phrase, "Hang in there," which he used often in the episodes.

DRIVER: "Taking a trip?"

BRONSON: "Yeah."

DRIVER: "Where to?"

BRONSON: "Oh, I don't know. Wherever I end up, I guess."

DRIVER: "Pal, I wish I was you."

BRONSON: "Really?"

DRIVER: "Yeah."

BRONSON: "Well, hang in there."

He then roars away from the stoplight leaving the commuting worker wistfully sitting in his commuter car.

Michael was also a recording artist and had a hit record on MGM from the show. It was a smooth pop-country song called "Long Lonesome Highway." It turned out that the song was becoming a crossover hit and making inroads on the pop charts and the country charts. MGM was able to get him booked on the *The Tonight Show* and this appearance would obviously put the whole thing over the top.

I flew with him into New York for the show, and we brought hot musician/arranger Mike Rubini with us to prepare the music charts for Carson's conductor, the talented Doc Severinsen. Both Rubini and I were in for a shocker when we got to New York. Mr. Parks explained to us that we would stay at a different hotel than him. After all, he was the star and didn't feel that it was appropriate we stay in the same place. Even though I was a bit taken aback, I didn't have a problem with his request because I had heard pretty much everything up to that point in my career.

Here's the best part of the story: I went to Michael's hotel room to escort him to the NBC Studios, which was just around the corner. I was surprised to see how fidgety "Mr. Cool" was. He was open about the fact that he was nervous about going on *Carson*. I told him that I had a little grass on me and maybe if he took a couple of tokes it might calm him down. He said he wasn't much into smoking grass but maybe one or two small hits might make him feel better. He took a couple of tokes and we headed out to the studio. We arrived with just enough time for him to get his makeup done. Michael literally got up from that chair and walked onto the set because we had cut it so close.

He bowed to the thunderous applause from his introduction and sat down in the guest chair where he and Johnny exchange greetings. Carson shuffled his cue cards for a second and then asked him a question. I guess the weed kicked in about that time, because Michael went off on a strange tangent that had nothing to do with him, Carson, the question, or even any recognizable event of this century. Carson stared blankly at Michael while I was bent over with laughter in the green room. Finally Carson was able to tactfully end the interview. When Michael's segment was over he informed me as he picked up his coat in the green room that he would return to his hotel on his own.

We also flew back to LA on separate flights.

If memory serves me correctly, he did sing well that night.

MILE MARKER # 8
THE MIDWEST

Maybe Missouri

The Mississippi River is only forty-five miles away, and Connie and I cross the mighty muddy into Illinois just south of Cairo, Illinois. From Cairo we head straight west on Highway 60 to Springfield, Missouri, which should take about four to five hours with minimal stops. Because we crossed the big river almost without comment, I sense this is going to be a quiet ride—and minimal everything.

There has always been a part of me that goes running off in search of some lost thing when I couldn't find solace where I was standing. Once again I have left my moorings so I can find *it*, that precious treasure, lying alongside some crumbling highway like a shiny vintage hubcap. If I can find *it* I will pull over, pick *it* up, and hold *it* before me and maybe I will be able to see the truth in *its* skewed reflection.

Author/pastor Lee Strobel once told me when we face things about ourselves that are hard to sort out, the best place to start looking for answers is to discover the root cause. Logically everything else grows out of that like a tree or a bacterial infection. (The germ reference is my example, not his.) What finally hit me in Kentucky is that what I have been looking for has to be simple. Perhaps it grew out of the dirt of my upbringing or has to do with something somewhere off in space where I landed later on because I didn't have a Captain of my soul, no spiritual Spock for my spacecraft. So far I have been looking at the time slot in between instead of the inaugural moment or the final destination.

I guess it's time to go back to the drawing board, or as in this case, back to the potato fields, to the "Gem State"—to the Idaho riverbanks and rolling hills of my youth.

I am starting to get a little squirrelly; somewhat of a placid counterpart to the Jekyll and Hyde syndrome where in the movies the hair starts growing out real fast. But in my case, it feels like it is growing inward and tickling the inside of my head. Fortunately my madness stays internal instead of thumping out on other people. Connie is passing the time trying to avoid catching my absurdity by jumping back and forth between actively probing me with questions about what we are doing and dropping out for long periods of time. She says she feels like a deer thrown over the front fender of an old truck—she is definitely along for the ride but maybe not quite the one she had in mind.

This scenario melts away as I focus in on the beautiful Missouri scenery. I escape by letting the rolling hills and greenness all around us fill my field of vision and the open spaces left in my mind. I purpose to remember the last bit that just went through my brain, recognizing it as a precious little piece in the puzzle I am trying to put together. The scenery does overtake the senses—we seem to be gliding in a simple space in time as we close in on Springfield, Missouri.

It is late afternoon, and knowing Kansas City is only three hours away, we decide the big city might be a nice place to culture up for a day before we sail westward across midwestern barren lands. We gas up in Springfield and purchase sandwiches at the deli next door. We sit down at a picnic table outside along the highway, which we rarely do, and eat while watching the traffic go by. We agree a nice California Fumé Blanc would go better with our chicken salad than Missouri truck fumes, but it is getting late and we have some more driving to do.

We agree during this interlude that sleeping in the van is not as scary as it was in the beginning—as long as we can find a spot that feels safe to Connie. That usually means a designated area set aside just for that purpose. (We put "Bible Wagon" placards in our window before turning in so no one will try and break in to rob us in the night.) I can usually get up to three nights in a row in the van before Connie jumps out and sits immovably on the curb until I promise that we will spend that night in a motel of her choosing.

All she asks for is my heart and a king-sized bed. My heart is forever— the bed is for the night. Maybe Missouri isn't such a bad place after all.

LINCOLN LOG

We are hopscotching on back roads now with Lincoln, Nebraska, as our next destination point. We enjoyed a brief layover in Kansas City, finding it to be a refreshing interlude because of the straightforwardness of the people, but we are on our way once again. We will barely skirt the northeast corner of Kansas, just enough to say we have been there. We are avoiding the main highways for a while because when we hit Lincoln, it will begin our commitment to a long, straight shot into southern Wyoming via Interstate 80.

The towns along the way are very small, few, and somewhat far between. I find it odd that, here we are, officially in Kansas, with neither iPod hooked up to the sound system, and I am hearing Glen Campbell's "Wichita Lineman" loud and clear in my mind. Connie is driving, and I have my seat leaning back looking up through the telephone lines at a blue-gray sky. I find myself being pulled back to Hollywood for another cerebral reunion.

☒ ☒ ☒

People involved with artist careers at Capitol Records considered Glen Campbell one of the label's most potentially successful artists. Even after many years of failed attempts to make him a star, we kept releasing his records because the label wholeheartedly believed in his talent. Capitol eventually scored with his first major hit, "By the Time I Get to Phoenix," in 1968.

This wasn't Glen's first big score, actually not even his first climb up the charts, because he had preceded "Phoenix" with the classic "Gentle on My Mind" the year before. "Gentle" was unquestionably an important record for Glen, but at that point in his career it didn't completely establish him as a hit artist. (It charted two times for Glen, and the first time peaked at No. 62 on the *Billboard*). There was the fear at Capitol his recording career could still potentially return to its old pattern of mediocre sales and success. As it turned out, "Gentle's" success helped propel "By the Time I Get to Phoenix," which then set up "Gentle" to become an all-around hit on its re-release. "Phoenix" was the catalyst, in our minds, that set the whole artist power ball rolling. I also believe this record was the eventual reason for Glen being invited to host the summer replacement (CBS's *The Glen Campbell Goodtime Hour*) for the highly successful *Smothers Brothers Comedy Hour*.

By the end of the '60s, Glen was an internationally famous singer, a TV star, and picked for a plum role in *True Grit* starring John Wayne. They didn't get much bigger than Glen Campbell back then.

It was a slow and unsteady climb for the superstar. Glen was an unusual artist in that he wasn't quite as motivated to get to the top as most were. He found that working as a session guitarist was quite lucrative and this allowed him to spend a lot of time on the golf course where he would much rather be. Not only was Glen known as an incredible guitar player, but he was also well respected in entertainment circles as a fine golfer. It appeared as if he really didn't care that much if he became a star because life was good in the hood—in the "HollyHood" that is.

A musician friend told me when Glen first started getting calls as a session musician that he didn't know how to read music. As the story goes, he'd sit down with his guitar in front of the sheet music on the music stand at a recording session and pretend like he was having a problem with tuning or some other mechanical problem in order to stall for a while. He was such a quick learner that during the time he was supposedly fumbling around, he'd learn the complete arrangement while the other musicians were running through the song. Then he'd sit back and be note perfect for the rest of the takes. I never asked him if this was true, but I like the cowboy git-'er-done angle of this tale.

Not only was "By the Time I Get to Phoenix" a classic record, but it also had a classic story of how it became a hit. It was amazing how incredible a talent Glen was and how well received he was by the entire music industry, especially at the radio station level where they loved him. Station music directors and DJs' acceptance is the key to chart success, and we could always count on them to play his new records practically every time out. I was national promotion manager for Capitol at the time and I believed in his enormous potential. Glen absolutely had the whole package—he was unique and possessed an incredible voice with a phenomenal range (especially when he incorporated his falsetto). He was also a guitar player who could hold his own with the best. It didn't hurt that he was good looking, had a great personality, and a smile and demeanor that welcomed everyone into his world. There was nothing missing when it came to his resume. Because of his enormous talent and star potential, I put a lot of effort into promoting his career with my field guys. But even with the Capitol Records star-making machinery behind Glen, we were frustrated because we could not bring it all the way home.

Capitol had originally signed Glen to a contract in 1962 after hearing a regional single the year before called, "Turn Around, Look at Me." He produced two instrumental albums as well as several vocal albums, and every single one of them tanked. Even the legendary Brian Wilson could not sprinkle any of his stardust on Glen, though try he did. Brian had a hand in one of Glen's records either as a writer, producer, or arranger. I can't remember the exact involvement, but the name of the record was "Guess I'm Dumb." It was released as a single in 1965. It was an excellent record and the DJs loved it. Capitol decided to back up its release with a special promotion by sending out traditional yellow pencils with Glen's name and the name of the record stamped down the length of the pencil—"Guess I'm Dumb." The kicker was that the pencil had an eraser on both ends.

Regardless of the airplay and the promotion team's enthusiasm, that record also went the way of all the others and died in the stretch. We just couldn't get the public to go into the record stores and buy a Glen Campbell record. When "By the Time I Get to Phoenix" came out after a few weeks of hard promotion, I was getting that "here we go again" feeling. We had a knockout record, a super response, a great airplay, and now a semi-established artist because of "Gentle on My Mind"; but once again it looked like it was going to follow suit and disappear from lack of sales. As it was heaving its dying gasps on the priority list of records to feature, our efforts in the promotion department waned. But a curious thing happened: I noticed whenever I got off the elevator to my office floor at Capitol, I kept hearing the song playing somewhere on the floor.

The layout of the Capitol Tower offices was unique because of the building's round design. Each of the executives had sound systems in their offices, and when we were not in the building, the secretaries would often play current releases while they worked, leaving the door to their boss's office open. I noticed several of them kept playing this one record over and over. This song had obviously hit a nerve with the young ladies who worked there and they were logically representative of the general public's listening tastes.

After about two weeks of mulling this over, I stepped out of the elevator with the strains of "By the Time I Get to Phoenix" coming out of my office. I asked my secretary why she was playing the song and her reply was quite insightful. She said it was a "gal" thing. I went straight to my desk and sent a memo to the field staff that we were back "on" the Glen Campbell single. I wanted them to pull in favors and stay with it until we brought it home. They did and it became a big hit. The song even became a part of music history—Glen won a Grammy in both country and pop categories for "Gentle on My Mind" (country) and "By the Time I Get to Phoenix" (pop).

An interesting footnote to this story: Capitol had tried for almost seven years to establish Glen Campbell and Lou Rawls as successful artists. We continually received great feedback and encouragement from the radio stations on their releases but without follow-up success from the record-buying public. In both cases we had giant hits ("By the Time I Get to Phoenix" and Rawls's "Love Is a Hurtin' Thing") just before renegotiation time on their contracts. You can imagine the headache and empty wallets that created for the company in sorting out new deals for both artists. I happen to know there was serious consideration at Capitol concerning dropping Glen from the label in 1966 just prior to his success with "Phoenix." However, the good news is that Capitol stayed the course with Glen, and in the end, Glen ended up paying off in silver dollars. He even outsold the Beatles for a few years because he was a crossover artist.

✐ ✐ ✐

The telephone lines have crossed to the other side of the road. I hold my vantage position by the window—clear skies spread to the edges of my vision. Soft white clouds drift across the heavenly blue meadow above and I hear music . . .

> *I hear you singing in the wires*
> *I can hear you through the whine*
> *And the Wichita lineman is still on the line*

BETWEEN WYOMINGS

When we pull on to Interstate 80 in Lincoln, it will be all about making time and distance until we reach Cheyenne, Wyoming. As a young boy growing up in Idaho, everything before puberty had to do with the Wild West, Indians, cowboys, and shooting at things. Wyoming seemed to epitomize all those adventures with the desperado sounding towns like Cheyenne, Laramie, Casper, and Cody. When I was twelve years old we drove from our home in northern Idaho to Pennsylvania to visit where my mom and dad grew up—the little town of Noxen where I was born. Noxen is located in Pennsylvania's Wyoming County. Moving west I find myself between those two Wyomings.

Back then my family drove through Cheyenne, Laramie, and Cody; and now Connie and I are retracing those exact steps in returning to the Nez Perce Indian lands that surround the small Idaho panhandle town I grew up in. To include Cody in our route means we'll drive through the heart of Yellowstone National Park, which is in direct line to Montana and Idaho.

The drive between Kansas City and Lincoln was, according to MapQuest, 189 miles and the estimated driving time was supposed to be about three hours. Because of my misguided back-road plan, it has taken us six hours so far, and we are just now seeing the signs for Lincoln and Interstate 80. I don't know what happened, but the bottom drops out of the whole adventure for both of us precisely at this point—ten miles outside of Lincoln. The search that in the beginning was somewhat diffused in rationale is in jeopardy of losing whatever focus it had. We both draw deeper into our individual forms of emptiness. I am becoming more desperate for answers and she is losing enthusiasm as a willing passenger in the mounting vagueness of the voyage. She is staring at me, I am staring at the road, and we are both carrying on inner conversations with God.

We find ourselves in the midpoint of America and at a low point in my big idea. It didn't take a genius to suggest to her that we stay in a nice hotel that night instead of the van.

I pray for a romantic bistro with fresh seafood—in Lincoln, Nebraska.

PARTON PARCEL

Our momentum has definitely slowed considerably, and by mutual lack of communication Connie and I have purposely avoided setting a timetable for leaving in the morning. We sleep in and then order room service. It is almost as if we need some time away from Moses and the whole idea.

The day begins with an undefined flow where the sequence of events fold seamlessly one into the next without words. I know it sounds strange, because by most standards we are already doing nothing, but it feels good to do even less for a while.

It is noon when we are ready to leave, and once again we pile into Moses. That doesn't feel quite right, so we "unpile," delay our departure a bit longer, and eat a small lunch at a café near the hotel. When we finally do leave, we are rested, well fed, and "good to go." (Those are my words and possibly a solo opinion.)

In a matter of minutes we are out of Lincoln and straight-lining it west on Interstate 80. I am doing everything I can to improve relations, so Connie's iPod is dictating the music. Just about the time the expected boredom normally starts building, Dolly Parton comes on with her beautiful "Coat of Many Colors." It has the effect of calming us both into our mission, as undefined as it seems. Strangely, it also brings our thoughts back to the center of our lives, the God part, the One that our story, this story, and every story is really all about. We both knew and had worked with Dolly, and we love what she is singing about in this song. We are back on track, heading the same direction and traveling together again. Knowing Dolly is a happy thing, and hearing her sing makes you feel even happier.

◨ ◨ ◨

In *The White Book*, I tell the story about the night I invited Dolly Parton and Ringo Starr to the Hangover House for dinner and how Dolly pulled one of her little stunts on Simply Red's producer Stewart Levine. Dolly is a master put-on artist, but she does it in a fun and kind way. The night with Ringo wasn't the only time she pulled off one of these stunts in my life.

This is a "beg your Parton" bonus story. In 1994 Dolly was recording the *Trio II* album project with Emmylou Harris and Linda Ronstadt in Marin County. She had taken a break from the sessions in Sausalito, a beautiful little seaside town that lies just across the Golden Gate Bridge from San Francisco. Dolly was having lunch with one of the musicians from the recording sessions at a restaurant called Mikayla, which sat atop the romantic old Casa Madrone hotel on the main street of the town. I had an important meeting that day with Gary Chappell, an executive with a bay area-based record distribution company called Real Music. We had also chosen Mikayla as our place to dine that day.

I arrived first and spotted Dolly sitting a few tables away. We exchanged greetings, chatted for a minute, and then I let her go back to her lunch and conversation. I was a few minutes early and reviewed my notes and sales pitch as I waited for my meeting. Gary arrived a few minutes later, and after the usual small talk I launched into my spiel. I was trying to close a deal between Real Music and a record company I was representing at the time called Clubhouse Records. Gary hadn't noticed Dolly was in the room and I was so intent on my purpose that I forgot to point out she was there. I didn't stop to think that it might be rather impressive to show off the fact Dolly and I were friends. Without my realizing it, Dolly had been observing what was going down with me. Our tables were not that far apart, so Dolly could hear parts of our conversation and picked up on my situation.

At one point in our meeting Gary got up to go to the restroom. Dolly had a fairly good idea what was going on, and I think her interpretation was that I wasn't doing too well in making my case. She excused herself from her table and followed Gary to the men's room where she waited outside until he was finished. Dolly stopped him as he exited and said she noticed that he was having lunch with Ken Mansfield. She wanted to know if he (Gary) was a friend of mine. Of course, he was taken aback by the encounter with the world's most famous blonde. After catching his breath, Gary replied that, yes, he was indeed a friend of mine. Dolly then gave Gary a big hug and a kiss on the cheek and said that if he was a friend of Ken Mansfield, then she was a friend of his. At this point she turned and disappeared into the ladies' room.

Now, I had no idea what had just gone down—all I knew was that when Gary came back to the table he was in a daze and could hardly talk. He finally gathered himself together and told me what happened. I looked over at Dolly's table and she smiled and gave me a little wink. She knew what it was like to scramble and just wanted to help out an old friend.

PS: I didn't make the deal.

MILE MARKER # 9
THE NORTHWEST

Mystery Moments

Entering Wyoming brings about a sensation that is a little off the wall. When you cross the state line it doesn't look that different from Nebraska outside the window, and yet it somehow feels different. Here is where my childhood romanticism hooks up with a part of me that remembers the beauty ahead.

Wyoming—its lyric name is like a new world cowboy concerto.

There are so many movements to the landscape, such a wide vibrato in its history, so much harmonic mystery in its distances, and an unexpected sweet crescendo when you find yourself entering the gates of Yellowstone National Park. Our passage through Cheyenne, Laramie, and Cody were sonatas—romantic interludes along the way.

This is one of the states where I roll down the window as we drive into its interior. I do this even though it is slightly cool outside and I am always cold, but my senses warm my body and I feel safe here. I am in the northwest and there's an undercurrent running through my insides that seems to level out and go smooth when I am in this enchanting land.

Our itinerary becomes exciting and at the same time any sense of a time line goes out the window. Moses feels like a trusty stallion that has carried its master and mistress safely through mountains and deserts and now seems to have slowed down to a soft canter upon crossing the state line. We see from the signpost that Cheyenne lies about half an hour away. We were in such a hurry before, but now I expect Connie and me to start talking in a slow drawl as the speedometer needle points to the left of center for the first time since we left Lincoln. We both come alive and are sitting up straight in our seats. Although we have been sitting in the van forever, it has been a long time since we both actually occupied its interior 100 percent mind, body, and spirit. The clear mountain air offers an awareness that we not only are over the hump in traveled distance but have traversed an ethereal line in our journey. Our endurance has been replenished, and as we roll into Cheyenne we perk up and take notice of this almost other world that quietly resides in our vast nation.

We find a picturesque western downtown street where we pull over and walk about. We order burgers and fries to go, discover a nice park, and sit in the shade of a western tree. We are settlers because we are settling down. We are adventurers because we feel discovery. We are explorers because so much to be uncovered lies ahead. We are youngsters because everything suddenly feels new again. We are lovers because we are His and He is love and it is His heart that beats inside our chests. We finish our repast, lie back, and become silent as we stare through the leaves into a clear blue sky. We say nothing, but in the quiet we are together—no longer apart.

There is something going on inside of us right now and I don't know if it is an awareness that can't be explained or a feeling that can't be described. It is so hard at times to put these impressions into words. I look at Connie and she concurs with my thoughts through those soft, green, knowing eyes. I guess one could call this the mystery moment—that space in time we yearn to dwell in for much longer periods.

Then there are those counter moments when I am feeling so far away from Him and then suddenly everything suddenly flips and I get this sweet feeling that fills my bones and flows deep into my most secret parts. It is a sweetness that lets me know the only thing I could be feeling is . . . Him. He is with me, around me, and about me. At my lowest points He essentially seeps into my innermost being and fills me with this aroma, this pristine presence that is more than comfort; it is blessed assurance. *Don't quit*, He tells me. *Press in and I will smooth it out. Hold on and I will see that it is all held together*, my heart is told. *I am for you and when you are with Me it matters not who is against you*, He tells me. *I will give you bread when the fallen world feeds you stones.*

Connie and I know we are lying in His green pasture at this moment in this park. He has provided us with living water; comforted us with His daily bread—we know we are never alone for He is with us. We shall drive through the valleys before us and He will provide cover during the days ahead. He will shine His light upon us in the nights to come, and we have no need to be afraid.

The reverie ends and we sit up as if two tightly coiled springs had just been turned into dandelion fluff. We rise up on a soft breeze from the cool earth knowing that in the stillness we had just covered a lot of ground. We realize we have been slowly drifting apart as we traveled together these past few weeks, but as we laid beneath that tree, it was almost as if we had come to the foot of the cross. All things were made right at this moment—just like it had been done two thousand years before this sweet moment in time.

God put Connie and me together over twenty years ago and we did become one. Any distance between us was never His way with us. We know in our one heart that we do not need worldly definition to go about our ways—we simply need divine guidance and each other to keep on track.

Mysterious? No, it is actually very simple when you don't think about it.

PLAYBACK

I always knew I would be a record producer.

I could hear it in my head and my heart—"Produced by Ken Mansfield."

I could see it on records and in magazines—"Produced by Ken Mansfield."

When I first heard those words—"produced by so and so"—that was it for me. I wanted to be a record producer. As far back as I can remember I envisioned reading my name on a Capitol Records label. Capitol epitomized the music business to me. When I was a teenager and collected 45-rpm singles, I categorized them by record companies instead of artists or genre. I had a shelf where I kept all my records organized in this manner. The stack to the left was the tallest followed by the others in descending order. There were five stacks. The biggest was Capitol, then RCA, Columbia, and Decca, with the "short stack" being "miscellaneous."

The first time I drove by the Capitol Tower on the Hollywood freeway I got chills. It was like seeing a childhood fantasy materialize before my eyes. It is so bizarre to think back upon this backwoods kid in Idaho with his little piles of records—this same kid who one day would occupy an executive office in that building. I honestly believe if we simply let go and follow our dreams they will lead us to where they know we should be.

A year or two before I landed my dream job at Capitol Records I had an interview with Karl Engemann, the VP of A&R. This came about through prior contacts made during my Town Crier days and the group's association with the Beverly Hills management group Artist Consultants. The meeting was a favor set up by our manager, Lou Robin, who also managed the Gateway Trio, a Capitol act. Mr. Engemann made short work of the interview by opening up our discussion with a couple of pertinent questions. First, he asked why I was applying for a producer position at Capitol. I answered, "I have always wanted to produce records for Capitol Records." He then asked if I had ever produced any records and I told him, "No, but I sure want to." His third and final question was if I knew what a producer did. I innocently replied, "No, but it's what I want to do." It was a short meeting. Years later when I was producing records for the label he reminded me of my answers. He said even though my last comment was an interview ender, it had actually impressed him and he knew he would see me again some day.

The first record I officially produced was a success of sorts. It was a Top 5 regional record, a big hit on the West Coast, but because of its folk-rock California sound it did not fare very well on the eastern seaboard. We made it to No. 65 on Ted Randall's Tip Sheet (one of the national charts used by the industry at the time), but it just touched the bottom of *Billboard*'s Hot 100. The record was called "Rising Sun" by the Deep Six (five guys and a girl).

The Deep Six was a group I had handpicked and put together in San Diego from musicians who had graced the stage of my club, the Land of Oden. I was working with the band trying to get them a record deal when Capitol hired me. Because of my new employment I was immediately able to get them a listen at the label but the band was turned down. This was frustrating because I was involved with them financially and emotionally. Attorney Denny Bond and I were partners in managing the group, and when I came on board at Capitol I had to go underground with my involvement. Thus, Denny became the group's spokesman. A few months after being turned down by Capitol he got married and went on a six-month world cruise for his honeymoon. He had basically given up on our quest because of so many rejections.

I was bemoaning the band's lack of success to a fellow record promoter, Tom Sawyer, one night at Martonis. I truly believed in them and couldn't let it go. I was also in a compromising position. I either had to give them up or get them signed to my company's roster. He suggested I produce a demo and then take it to Capitol. Maybe that would be the way to get them signed. He said he knew how we could go about making a two-song demo very inexpensively. We ended up making the record for a total of $250. Sawyer arranged for us to book a studio for a $150 flat fee to make the record. To get this price, though, we could only use the studio between 2 and 6 a.m., the good news being we would have as many of those "off" hours as we needed until we were done. He knew of a young guitar player who had some experience at producing who could show me the ropes. Additionally, he knew an engineer friend who would work for us for next to nothing. These two people agreed to do the entire record for $50 each. The engineer's name was Mike Dorrough and the guitar player was a new kid about town making his bones named Jimmy Messina, later of Buffalo Springfield, Poco, and Loggins and Messina. A team was now in place, and we began working on the songs.

Keep in mind I was pulling full daytime duty at Capitol, doing my promotion thing in the evenings with the disc jockeys at local Hollywood hotspots, *and* producing my first record in the wee hours of the morning. We finished everything on the record except for a guitar overdub that Messina wanted to do. During the overdub of "Rising Sun" we blew a small capacitor or some other inexpensive part of the studio equipment and it put this wild electronic sound on the tape. It was so cool we left that mistake in and blew out a few more pieces of electronics to get the same sound for the other sections of the record. This accident was one of the things that helped make the record a hit.

I presented "Rising Sun" to Capitol, and once again they turned the band down. This scenario was not turning out at all the way I wanted it to— but I couldn't give up. Sawyer then suggested we print up five hundred copies and he as an independent would start promoting the record to the West Coast radio stations. The purpose of plan B was to garner some airplay and then take the record back to Capitol who would have to take the act on at that point. We created a phony record company—SawMan Records (SAWyerMANsfield). The picture on the label showed a log that looked like a 45-rpm record on the end. A man was sawing a record from the end of the log. The little blurb under the logo said, "We're cuttin' hits at SawMan."

"Rising Sun" began getting airplay and it started to take off. We were getting "on" the playlists of big rock stations in LA and other major West Coast markets, and listener demand started building for sales. I immediately went back to Capitol confident the group would be signed and I would be a hero. They were still unreceptive. I could not believe they were passing on a sure thing. I would have given them the record. Meanwhile Bill Gavin, who had the nation's hottest record industry tip sheet out of San Francisco, called Bob Skaff, president of Liberty Records, and told him "there's a record out there that's becoming a hit and no one has it." Skaff tracked Sawyer down, and because of Capitol's rejection, he made an overnight deal with Liberty so the record could stay on the radio to meet the sales demand. It doesn't take too many calls from listeners to a radio station complaining they heard a record on the air that they can't buy before it gets pulled off "rotation."

Suddenly I was in a precarious situation where I had a hit I couldn't put my name on or take credit for and my business partner with the Deep Six was somewhere on the other side of the world. I was also the producer of a record that was on a competing label. This was not good for another reason. Capitol was not doing well at pop stations at the time and my record on Liberty Records was taking up one of the valuable slots on the short playlists. In the middle of my personal pandemonium, Liberty A&R director Dave Pell was knocked out with "Rising Sun's" innovative sound and found out who produced it. He called me into his office and offered me a job as a producer of contemporary product at Liberty. I reluctantly turned his offer down, one of the hardest things I had ever done. During this time I was moving swiftly through the ranks at Capitol and had just been promoted into a national position in the Tower. Capitol was still a bigger dream for me than record producing. I just knew in time I would be able to meld these two desires into one place—Capitol Records!

Denny Bond was tanning on a beach in Australia with a portable radio and almost jumped out of his bathing suit when they played this hot hit song from California by the Deep Six. He ran to a phone and called me in the middle of a California night to find out what was happening. It took me about an hour to fill him in on everything that had transpired while he was honeymooning. He could hardly believe what I was telling him. He cut his honeymoon short and flew back to California so I could quit double-dancing between my real job and trying to hold the group together. This all broke in 1965—which is also when I first began developing my relationship with the Beatles.

Fortunately Karl Engemann knew how hard I had tried to put the band on Capitol and kept the situation from spiraling out of control for me at the label. I also think he felt we should have this little secret because he had turned down the band twice and now it was becoming a smash hit west of the Rockies.

These were the formative years of the Buffalo Springfield, the We Five, Poco, the Flying Burrito Bros, the Byrds, and the Association. The Deep Six was poised to be equally famous. We were booked into the hungry i in San Francisco by owner Enrico Banducci for an unlimited run. I had put the band together two years earlier, and they were the house band at my club in San Diego in addition to having played other major Southern California gigs such as the Ice House. By the time the record hit and this offer came they were seasoned performers. The San Francisco venue was the pinnacle of success for new artists on the West Coast. The club, located in the North Beach section of the city, was instrumental in launching the careers of singer Barbra Streisand and comedians Lenny Bruce, Mort Sahl, Jonathan Winters, Woody Allen, Dick Cavett, Phyllis Diller, the Smothers Brothers, and Joan Rivers. It was also the home of famous "live" recordings by Bill Cosby, the Kingston Trio, and the Limelighters.

Opening night was a great success and the Deep Six were on their way. They were the perennial opening act for the big-name headliners for many months in the future. The exposure was more than a management team could ask for in establishing an artist. Denny and I flew up to San Francisco for the New Year's performance as a matter of celebration. They had been performing at the "i" for a few weeks and had already shared the stage with Pat Paulson, Mort Sahl, and Professor Irwin Corey.

Something else was taking place at this time. One of the Deep Six members (Tony McCashen) had been approached by a more established hit group (The Nitty Gritty Dirt Band) to discuss leaving the Deep Six to join them to replace a departing member. Without telling his Deep Six band mates, Tony decided to meet with the other group to see what they had to offer. Somehow this information came to light between the second and third sets at the hungry i on New Year's Eve. Lead singer Dean Cannon was infuriated with Tony's actions. During the middle of the third set she had finally processed the information and came to the conclusion this was not right. The band had been together as a single unit for years and she felt betrayed. In Tony's defense he didn't feel he was doing anything out of order and fully intended to disclose his activities. He had no plans to abandon the group. I think it just felt good to be wanted and recognized, and Tony thought it would be nice to see what they had to say.

Between the third and fourth songs Dean decided Tony's actions sucked, the music business sucked, nightlife in clubs sucked, sleeping in a van with five guys really sucked, and she was through. Dean decided at that very moment to leave the group. She was dating bass player Dann Lottermoser at the time and turned to him on stage, gave him a good-bye kiss, and walked off. She headed to the dressing room, packed her stuff, and was gone before the set was over. Their long-term booking at the hungry i was also over that night, and it was the beginning of the end for the group. Attempts to hold the group together with new members failed and the Deep Six eventually did just that—"deep sixed" themselves.

Cool Clear Water

"I am tired of fighting....
My heart is sick and sad.
From where the sun now stands,
I will fight no more forever."

Chief Joseph of the Nez Perce
In-mut-too-yah-lat-lat
(Thunder Coming Up Over the Land from the Water)

From Cheyenne to Cody is about a six-hour drive. Because I wanted to go through Laramie, and also because we were both drinking in the beauty of the journey, it took much longer.

Cody, Wyoming, is situated about fifty miles from the eastern edge of Yellowstone National Park and the perfect spot to spend the night before venturing out into a place that special. The combination of wonderful Wyoming and sweet Connie has mellowed me. Once again we leave Moses alone in the still of the night while we stay at a quiet motel. The shortened trip has left us with a larger travel budget. We sleep in and take long showers in the morning.

Wyoming is probably not as pretty as we think it is, but close. The towns are maybe not as romantic as we imagine, but close. Yellowstone can't actually be that incredible, but it turns out that it is. We stock up our mini-kitchen in the van with enough food for the rest of the trip before we leave Cody. By the time we head out for the park it is shortly before noon.

Two hours later we are in the very center of Yellowstone enjoying our picnic lunch by the lake. I have the feeling that everyone knew we were coming and politely cleared out of the area so we could have the place to ourselves to enjoy our fried chicken and potato salad. This is starting to get way too fine for me, and I am having trouble maintaining my introspection. I remember from my New Age days that hippie guru Ram Das used to teach his misguided followers to "be here now," which is actually a good thing and with very little tweaking it can fit right into the Christian belief system. (I have modified it a little—"Kneel here—bow.") Well, with a full tummy and a sense of inner calm, we were "being here" as "now-ish" as anyone could be. Once again we find ourselves on our backs under another western tree looking skyward.

A lot of mountain driving lies ahead, and after this pleasant interlude we rise to our task and buckle into Moses, ready for the ride. We drive straight north out of Yellowstone with the southwest corner of Montana in mind. Butte, Montana, is our next destination. It is about a four-hour drive and will take us through a lot of ups and downs—valley after valley after mountain after mountain. Butte doesn't win a lot of beauty contests even though it does have its moments. The rolling hills that surround it in their bareness and quiet are beginning to suggest home. We find an official camping facility and stake out our spot. Once again, we eat our own food at a picnic table and turn in. We are closing in.

When we get up in the morning we have a mutual desire for a cup of good old-fashioned Starbucks coffee. We head downtown only to be told that downtown is called uptown in Butte. We learned that looking for a Starbucks is not a visitor friendly occupation in Montana. We're told the municipality managed to stave off the roasted bean giant until late 2004. We did find a good cup of java at Wetona's Coffee House & Deli in Butte just a few blocks off Interstate 90. I-90 is the beckoning string of asphalt and cement that will take us to Missoula and the final leg home to Lewiston. We are on our way and picking up speed once again—Missoula is about an hour and a half away. We are less than vaguely interested in its offerings beyond more strong coffee. We discover Butterfly Herbs, a downtown coffee bar where we find a sticker on the cash register that reads, "Friends Don't Let Friends Drink Starbucks."

We leave Missoula with fresh java in hand and turn west at Lolo where

Highway 12 cuts away from Highway 93. Once we cross into the northern Idaho panhandle and are headed into the Lolo Pass, we will follow the Lochsa and Selway rivers for more than a hundred miles with no towns—only breath-taking wilderness, rugged ravines, and thick forestland. Once we arrive at the Clearwater River and I am officially driving between Kooskia and Kamiah, I know I am nearing home. This is Indian territory. We see it in the names of the towns and the images of better days that our mind creates as Moses almost glides reverently through this pristine landscape.

Anyone who has driven along the Clearwater becomes rejuvenated by the crisp, sparkling waters that began their journey in the Selway-Bitterroot Mountain Range. The road clings to the banks of the narrow river as it and the road carry on in tandem toward their eventual meeting with the Snake River. The "Snake" is the defining border between Idaho and Washington and the place we are headed—Lewiston, Idaho, where I grew up.

As I drive down these canyons and along the rivers, it is not the beauty that overwhelms me as much as a presence I feel. This is the land of the proud Nez Perce Indian tribe and its great Chief Joseph.* Although their original tribal areas covered a much broader expanse, this is where the

---

*. Joseph was chief of the Nez Perce, a Native American tribe in the northwest. In 1877 the Nez Perce along with other tribes were ordered to a reservation, or special land reserved for Native Americans. The Nez Perce refused to go. Instead, Chief Joseph tried to lead eight hundred of his people to Canada. Fighting the U.S. Army all along their eleven-hundred-mile journey, they crossed Idaho and Montana. He became known as "The Father of Military Strategy" because of his genius in standing against large cavalry troops with his small ragged group of warriors. They were trapped just forty miles from Canada. After a five-day fight, the remaining 431 Nez Perce were beaten. It was then, on October 5, 1877, at Bears Paw Montana, that Chief Joseph made his historic and touching speech of surrender:

> I am tired of fighting. Our chiefs are killed. Looking Glass is dead. Toohulhulsote is dead. The old men are all dead. It is the young men who say yes or no. He [Joseph, his oldest son] who led the young men is dead. It is cold and we have no blankets. The little children are freezing to death. My people, some of them, have run away to the hills and have no blankets, no food. No one knows where they are—perhaps freezing to death. I want to have time to look for my children and see how many I can find. Maybe I shall find them among the dead. Hear me, my chiefs. I am tired. My heart is sick and sad. From where the sun now stands, I will fight no more forever.

government placed them to live out their days and quietly continue their history. I can feel them in the flow of the streams, sense them in the shadows of the trees, and feel their heart beat in the soft wind that blows by Moses' open window.

I have no Indian blood that I am aware of but I never realized until I went away and then returned how much the essence of their spirit had filtered into my being during the years I grew up on the borders of their lands. We have been on the reservation since we arrived at the river just west of Syringa and will be a part of it all the way to Lewiston. Approximately fifty miles west of our destination we enter Orofino, the town I lived in when my family first moved to Idaho. We came to this picturesque town when we left Pennsylvania because when I was five years old my brother was born with a bad case of asthma. My parents were told in order for him to survive his childhood that they would need to move to a dryer climate. The doctor recommended Idaho or Arizona. It was a sudden move, and the only immediate work my dad could find was lumberjacking in the forests that bordered the river we are traveling along now.

I was about to enter first grade when we moved to Orofino. Finances were very short for our young family because of being uprooted and having to relocate so quickly without any real planning or preparation. We moved in just before the new school year, and on the first day of school my mother dressed me in the clothes that she had already purchased in Noxen, Pennsylvania, and then sent me off. Now here's the problem—it was the custom to basically dress in uniforms in the somewhat Pennsylvania Dutch area we had just left and the mode-o-day for first graders there was what would be known as "Lord Fauntleroy" outfits. You know, the little dark blue, short pants with the white fluff lapel shirt, little dark blue jacket, and patent leather shoes—there may have been a little bow to go with it as well. That may not be an exact description of the outfit, but that is how I remember it and definitely how I felt wearing it that day. Well, this was lumberjack country and these were very rugged people. Rugged people tend to raise rugged kids. I have to tell you, none of the other kids were dressed quite as nice as I was. As can be imagined, the little sissy (me) came home that day with a red, white, blue outfit because of the nosebleeds from the beatings I took that day. I would not leave the house after that shakeup until my mom went into town and bought me some jeans and checkered shirts.

Because my first days of school were so rough I became a real mean kid. Before the year was out I was sent home for good because I kept getting in fights—as the instigator and for beating up on someone on a regular basis after school. Being isolated and different from the others at the school from day one made me mad and I stayed mad. I learned at a very young age how to survive as a loner. Fortunately we moved into Lewiston before the next school year when my dad found a job at the sawmill on the Clearwater River.

These were hard years, but because I was young it wasn't a problem for me until I hit my teens. We ended up living in what was called the Orchards, the area on the outskirts of town. The Orchards was bordered on one side by Lewiston and on the other by the Nez Perce Indian Reservation. Actually, to be specific, we lived in the country outside a country town.

I have often wondered what it was that drew me out of that rugged backcountry into the glamorous world of the music industry. It is almost like a slightly altered version of the clichéd "you can't get there from there"—but somehow I did.

I was common and didn't like being so. Deep down, even as a young child, I knew that one day I would gather my daydreams of shinier things and put the little pieces into a ragged bag I would unload in Hollywood.

※　※　※

We cruise Orofino for a few minutes and then pull Moses over to the side of the road, parking the van as close to the river as we can. We grab the last of the leftovers Connie had gathered together in Cody, walk down to the river, sit on some rocks, and enjoy our potpourri lunch to the sound of the lightly rushing waters of the Clearwater River. I am coming home and it feels good.

FINAL MIX

As mentioned earlier my first record as a producer was a minor success. Sadly, it was a long time before I hit the charts again.

I had backed away from my main desire by becoming successful in the business end of the music world—something to do with the Beatles taking up a lot of my time and my upward executive progression years through Capitol, Apple, MGM, and Barnaby/CBS. Finally the overload in taking on production tasks in addition to my executive responsibilities eventually led me to the decision to leave the corporate world and set up Hometown Productions Inc. My heart started dictating to my head. I took the big step and finally committed to producing full-time. "Produced by Ken Mansfield" began showing up a lot more on those little black discs with holes in the middle. I have often wondered what would have happened if I had followed my heart earlier and taken the job producing records for Liberty. My head won over that time because I had put so much into working my way through college to earn a Bachelor of Science degree in Marketing. I felt all that effort would have been wasted. Historically my decision was a correct one and in the long run I landed where I belonged, producing, but now I had an advantage because I also had acquired the executive background needed to manage my own company.

Producers are a unique cast of people. It takes a multitude of abilities with head smarts and gut feel being necessary requirements. A producer has to have tons of intuitive sense. In addition to musical and technical talents, one of the most important skills is becoming a psychiatrist to whimsy and abstraction. It is like playing patty-cake with a nervous octopus. So many things are coming at you at the same time. You need to know how to pick songs to fit your artist's talents and abilities. You have to gain and maintain their trust and confidence at all times while being as crazy as they are. You have to become a marketing genius so you can read the minds of the consumers in order to know what kind of music they are looking for. You need to find that special place right on top of current trends or carve out a spot at the cutting edge of the ever-moving, ever-fickle tastes of the fans. You need to learn how to dance faster than everyone in the room at all times.

There are budgets, schedules, finances, politics, and egos to deal with at the record companies. Odds are that your artist is going to bring a Hummer load of quirks and emotional baggage to work around—stuff most people have never dreamed of dealing with. You are fighting for songs and the enthusiasm of the musicians, engineers, and back-up people to the project. All this and we aren't even in the studio yet *and* we haven't introduced drugs and paranoia into the mix of things to come. That said, there is this pulsating undercurrent running inside all of us drawn to this glorious enterprise, that pulls a certain calm into the madness. It is addictive—the thrill of coming up with something tangible that has virtually been created out of the air. We live for that lovely point in time when we can sit back in our chairs in the control room and hear the final playback—a final mix of all the emotions and music we have put into something that has never been heard before. The hits, money, and success that follow this are just the gravy. Being from Idaho we ate a lot of potatoes and I always liked a lot of gravy on my plate!

Any time a record producer and an artist commit to do an album together, they set out on a journey that will become a moving part of their lives. I have always maintained that each project I did took a piece right out of my being. The hours are long and very intense, and there is always a lot riding on each record. The artist and producer have to be in sync on so many levels with the most important one being the creative melding of their musical imaginations. It takes a real connection and singleness of purpose when two extreme personalities decide to take this ride together. A small example of this was understanding Don Ho's deep pride in being an American. In time you become sensitive to each other's priorities, which areas are of the deepest importance, and also the buttons that are never to be pushed. Don was the perfect artist because he was a pro and very gifted. In looking back at my recording career I believe that he, along with David Cassidy, were the two artists I enjoyed producing the most. I don't list Waylon here in that he was more of a force of nature, a life experience than a recording project. One fact never changes—artist egos always remain intact and active even if on the subtlest levels. I once mentioned to Don Ho that I saw similarities between him and Waylon. Don thoughtfully paused for a second and replied, "Yeah, he does come off a lot like me."

⚅ ⚅ ⚅

I've discovered over the years that each recording session has its own dynamics. I was once hired by MCA Records to produce a new band they had just signed called Byron Berline and Sundance. Byron was a three-time national fiddle champion and the group was composed of top-notch blue-grass pickers. The record company concept was to add Neil Young's old drummer from *Harvest* album fame (Dallas Taylor) and a contemporary country producer (me) to this group of authentic, purist bluegrassers in order to make a cutting-edge, progressive country album.

It was a great idea except the pickers in the band were a little suspicious about recording with drums and a rock-oriented producer. One member who stood out in his paranoia was Jack Skinner, the group's lead singer and bass player. Jack was a leathered veteran in the music circuit and had his own recording studio. In other words—he knew it all. He came off a bit surly and rightfully earned the nickname "Coyote." After a rather brief preproduction phase, we began recording at the state-of-the-art Sound Labs in Hollywood. Skinner from the get-go scowled and stared at me from the studio with a look of disgust on his face. During playbacks in the control room he stood alongside me at the recording console (traditionally a rather private space) and looked at settings like they had vomit on them. I could see that this "big dog–little dog" positioning stance was not a healthy thing for the general tenor of the sessions. In time this animosity could spread to everyone and poison the whole endeavor.

A producer has to maintain control at all times or the session will eventually fall apart. The situation with Skinner had to be resolved immediately or this album was never going to make it to the final mix. I had to dig deep into my psychiatric abilities and scope this surly coyote out and do it quick. I had an idea. When the next take finished I pressed down the talk-back button and told the band to come into the control room for a playback. I quickly got out of my chair and stood by the air lock that separates the studio from the control room. In order to sound-proof the control room from the recording studio, the construction separating the two spaces is typically made up of two walls with extra sound insulation. This prevents the music from the control room speakers "leaking" into the studio and "bleeding" onto the tape. Therefore the door between the studio and the control room is actually two doors with a narrow, approximately three-feet-deep air space between the two. I waited until Skinner entered the space and before he opened the second door into the control room I jumped in and closed the door behind me. Here we were, face-to-face in the air lock. I looked him straight in the eye and told him he was driving me crazy. He was making it near impossible for me to concentrate on doing my job. I curtly told him how we would proceed from this particular point forward.

"You are going back out to the studio, and on the next take you will play bass for me like you have never played before. You will startle me with how good you can play. I am going back into the control room where I am going to turn those knobs and whip the engineer into a creative frenzy. When you come for the next playback, I will be thrilled with your performance and you will be blown away by how I have knocked your socks off with how great I am producing the band."

The old "coyote" tilted his head back slightly and got this look in his eyes (which were inches from mine) that said, *OK, I got it*. He went back to his chair and on the next take absolutely played bass like he was on fire. He loved my playback and our friendship was cemented. In time, Jack and I became best friends. We produced, wrote, and recorded two movie soundtracks together and created a new modern cowboy band called Wide Open Spaces with him as the lead singer. I would have trusted him with my life.

I was once asked in a radio interview how to describe the perfect recording session from the standpoint of the producer. My answer came quickly. I described it as being one where all I did was turn on the lights at the beginning and then at the end said goodnight to the musicians and artists as they left. The only other thing for me to do would be to turn out the lights and also leave. The interviewer was puzzled by my response. I went on to explain the perfect session was an impossibility. We all strive for perfection, but just imagine how awful it would be if we ever achieved it. Where do you go from there? My simplistic description of the perfect recording session meant that I, as the producer, had planned the entire project perfectly, done all my homework, and communicated every aspect of the session clearly with my artist beforehand. This also meant I had selected the right material, arranger, musicians, engineer, studio, pizza, and everything else that went into making a great record. My answer suggested I had anticipated and prepared for every curve ball that would come our way during the day. If I had done all this perfectly the session would have run itself.

▨ ▨ ▨

I awaken from these thoughts realizing I have this giant smile on my face. I look in the rearview mirror hoping that Connie hadn't noticed my gawking state of euphoria as I drove down this lonely stretch of highway. As I have done since 1965, I begin pushing the buttons on the dash radio. I am listening for one of my songs to be played. Even though I haven't produced a record for almost fifteen years this motion is automatic and has become a part of my DNA.

I would probably drive off this country road if I heard one of those masterpieces I had recorded at one of my near-perfect sessions.

THE DRUM IS LIFE

The drum is life.
*   It is the sound of life within you.*
When the world ends,
*   The drumbeat will sound just once for you*
Like it sounded for me.
*   It will sound bad or good.*
It will ask you if you have been bad or good;
*   And you can answer only one way.*

Smohala
Wanapum prophet
1898

About halfway between Orofino and Lewiston the road crosses over the Clearwater River to the other side at a place called Spalding. It is just down the road from Lapwai, the main town for the Nez Perce Indian Reservation. Spalding is not actually a town but a very historic spot on the river where the tribe has a small museum.

We pull into the parking lot to check it out. We sit for a while under the coolness of the trees in the park that borders the river. When I was a kid we swam across the river at this spot as a rite of passage. In the macho madness of our youth it was important to say you had done it. The second step in this ritual was to eventually swim the much wider Snake River between Lewiston, Idaho, and Clarkston, Washington.

The museum is small and quiet and not very dramatic, but I come across a saying posted on one of its walls that stops me in my tracks. (The

Wanapum Tribe was from an area not far away from these lands along the Columbia River and mouth of the Snake River. Their spiritual leader Smohala believed that they could pray the white man away and in this process never participated in armed conflict. This was good in terms of peace but resulted in no treaties ever being signed and the tribe ended up with no federally recognized land rights. This may be the reason that their history was being shared with the Nez Perce.) The wisdom in this ancient poem immediately becomes a part of me. Not only do I identify with its inherent truth, but I feel that it came out of the same soil that I grew up on. (I would later send a copy of it to Ringo thinking he would also find great meaning in its gentle discourse but he never commented. I guess you had to be there—on the river—in the moment.)

We leave the park and cross back over to the other side and are within a few miles of Lewiston. The wind must be blowing the other way because we have yet to get a whiff of the pulp mill that joins the sawmill along the river. This river road was a major part of my youth. When we were small our parents drove us to Spalding to swim in the river. Sometimes they'd take us even further up the river toward Orofino for more pristine beaches where the Indians came down from the reservation lands to swim and cool off.

If we didn't stop at the Spalding Beach we'd stay on the north side of the river, instead of crossing over, and continue on a gravel road that took us to a place we called Arrow Beach. This is where we would hang out as teenagers during the hot Idaho summer school vacations. We claimed it as our own, and any families or older couples who came there to swim and relax were soon vibed out by our noise and domination of the entire beach. We could lie back on the sand looking up into the clear blue sky while digging our hands into the soft sand at our side, knowing we would probably come up with an arrowhead or two. That beach, in some odd way, is my best memory of growing up in the canyons along the edge of the great Camas Prairies. It represents a time in my life when everything was just right—that period of time after high school graduation—before things got too serious.

Moses doesn't get to go to Arrow Beach this day. This is the second time he has gotten close to a cool place without actually going there. I think the reason I don't turn the van up that road is that I don't want to be disappointed by the possibility it might not look as I remember. We bear west instead, staying on Highway 12, and are now almost to Lewiston. As we drive into the outskirts and cross the river into town, I can already tell that it is not the same. For some reason it doesn't matter because I become acutely aware I am not here on a sightseeing trip. I am here . . . well, I am here because . . . because . . . I am here.

It seems like I should select a relevant genre of music from one of our iPod collections that represents the area. Maybe a little Lefty Frizzell (the music my dad played when we were growing up), Bill Haley and the Comets (the rock-and-roll music of my high school years), Elvis (the music that drew me away from here), or something that makes no relevant sense like Pink Floyd (at least I admit it). (Actually it *would* have to be Pink Floyd because I don't have the others downloaded.) But I find silence seems to be the most appropriate and conducive sound at the moment. Once we cross the bridge into the east end of town we encounter a new one-way street system, so we pull Moses to the curb and walk down the street that goes straight through the middle of town.

The town looks old but still nice. It isn't one of those downtowns that has completely withered away. Fortunately, it has been blessed by restoration and we are drawn in by the coffee shops, boutiques, and cafes that dot the old brick building's exteriors. I like it. I am neither saddened with melancholy nor excited to be here. I know it was important to return to this place with Connie at this time, however, I am not sure of the significance of my visit. It was a major destination and now that I am at its heart I appear to have nothing specific to recapture. I have come this far without thinking things through too clearly, so why should I start now?

We tour the shuttered movie theaters and soda fountains where I hung out as a kid. We return to Moses and drive up the hill to the residential areas above the town and along Prospect Avenue that looks out across the Snake River to the other side where the smaller town of Clarkston, Washington, is situated. Although Lewiston and Clarkston are twin cities, they would have been one town if it wasn't for the river that acts as the state line and separates them. Lewiston became considerably bigger because Idaho never charged sales tax as they do in Washington. Naturally, businesses located on the Idaho side and homes were built in their proximity.

Prospect Avenue was where the rich kids lived. As we drive by the homes I can't remember ever being invited into any of them.

We drive by my old high school, grade school, and junior high school. We then turn on one of the roads that lead up the hill and out of town to the Orchards. It used to be several miles between the two places, Lewiston and the Lewiston Orchards, but the decades have almost joined them together with homes and businesses.

We drive down the dead-end road to the house I grew up in but we don't stop—we just slow down because a stranger lives there now. My home used to be at the end of a dirt road and sat alone in the middle of vast wheat fields. In those days when we looked west and north, the fields dropped away into big canyons that went all the way down to the rivers. From our tiny back porch we watched the sunsets beyond the rivers where they came together, the Snake and the Clearwater. My dad joked that you could see as far as Colorado from our house even though it was in the other direction.

Instead of the road ending at the old place, we are now able to go about a quarter mile past the house on an asphalt road that boasts several upscale homes on both sides where the wheat fields once were. The old house looks tiny huddled between the other homes that are three to four times larger. The only way to see the rivers from that place now is by trespassing over a neighbor's property to get a glimpse of what used to be ours and ours alone. We have only been in Lewiston for about an hour and a half and we have just one place to go—to surprise my eighty-four-year-old aunt Evelyn, the sweet matriarch of the Mansfield family.

As always, it is quiet and loving at Aunt Evelyn's. We talk and she fills in some mysteries of my youth—the little things that seemed unimportant when growing up but now have bearing on understanding my heritage. I want to know more about my mom and dad and what they were like when they were young. I specifically want to know why there was this chasm between my father and me that we were never able to cross before he died. She is able to impart an image of their youth back in Pennsylvania but doesn't know what to say about my dad and me. That question will remain unanswered. Then we go.

I have some cousins in the area but they are not around and we call it a day. I am beginning to find a little obtuse humor unfolding here. The emotional intensity that this whole excursion started out with seems to be dissipating in the quiet of the Idaho panhandle's vast openness.

As we drive out the backside of the Orchards and down to the Idaho side of the Snake River, I get the sense that we are emptying out. If I were a baseball game I would have just touched home base without scoring. We reach a place I know where we can give Moses a rest. We will spend the night parked next to the fast-moving water, listening to its soft roar as it comes out of the canyon.

As I sit on the edge of the river the rush of the rough waters over the rocks feels like it has developed a rhythm pattern, a kind of steady drum beat. The brown barren hills that rise up from the water's edge counter with wind words from the natives who caressed its surfaces and I could hear their beat. The sounds come to me from earlier in the day and rest in my core.

> *The drum is life.*
> *It is the sound of life within you. . . .*
> *It will ask you if you have been bad or good;*
> *And you can answer only one way.*

The river has darkened and softened in its flow. I look across to the other side to a grove of trees that appear almost liquid as they flow in the breeze in the settling dusk. I know an answer is required. It might be possible to ignore the question for a while, but there is a deeper knowledge that requires I must someday respond to the prophet's inner pleadings. Moses can take me to a lot of places, but I will never get away without someday giving a clear and perfect answer to this ancient offering.

I awaken from the depths of this deliberation into a realization a little less ethereal. For the first time I embrace the irony that I am on a spiritual quest, and yet tonight we will be sleeping at the official "Gateway to Hell's Canyon." Hell's Canyon—another of my hometown's many claims to fame.

I am standing on a silent stage this night, but the drum of life and the rhythm of the river are telling me that the song isn't over yet. We still haven't reached the final chorus—the beat goes on.

JESUS AND 14 CENTS

We arise early in the morning, grab a cup of coffee, crawl on top of Moses' roof rack wrapped in blankets, and watch the river as it flows out of Hell's Canyon.

In certain places the canyon floor is over a mile deep and is listed as the deepest gorge in North America. Along its edges tower a group of peaks known as the Seven Devils Mountain Range. It is said to be named for a vision of seven dancing devils that appeared to an Indian lost in the area many years ago. This magnificent work of nature is about fifty miles up the river from Lewiston and Clarkston.

I tell Connie about how incredible it was when I would return home from college to work summers on the state highway crews. It got so hot in the afternoons that we started work at 4:30 in the morning. The upside was that we were off the job by noon and soon we were on the river soaking in the sun's marvelous rays. On weekends we loaded up three boats—one with food and beer; one with gas tanks, tents, and supplies; and the third with six or eight good friends. We then headed up into the canyon early in the morning to where the ravine would get so deep in places it appeared we were looking up through a slit to see the sky. We parked our boats on pristine beaches that had no footprints other than the animals that would come down for a drink during the night.

The river was wide in places, rough in places, smooth as glass in others, and made exciting by some incredible rapids in other sections. We could water-ski for miles in a straight line if we wanted. Sometimes we would find a wide glassy spot and do circles and amateur acrobatics until the gas ran out. Our favorite feat was attempting to ski the rapids, something that was near impossible, but like a dog chasing its tail, we never gave up on it or got tired of trying. The outcome was always the same—the boat losing speed when its motor came up out of the water (called capitation for some reason). When that would happen the resultant slack in the ski rope would send us falling backward into the rushing rapids. The biggest thrill was swooshing down the river at breakneck speed back through the rapids knowing that we were not in peril because we never got very far in our attempt at conquering them. After a short, exciting ride we would soon be delivered out the lower end of the turbulence into calm waters. The driver of the boat would cut the engine and drift back to our original starting point so that we could hook up and go at it again. The sweet reward at the end of the day was the campfire, the beer and burgers, and feeling the warmth of the canyon give way to the coolness of the Idaho night. The sand was warmed for the evening's sleep, and the next day we would rise with the morning light and begin chasing our tails again with no one watching.

▨ ▨ ▨

The sun is almost in full bloom now, and its early warmth strikes me like an old snake lying on a rock, so I feel like moving once again. The memory of the warm sand and being on the river brings us off the roof of the van and out onto the road. We cross over to the Washington side of the river and drive to another beach I used to hang out at as a teenager. It was the best beach on the river and they've added a nature walk that goes for miles along the river. It is a perfect day to walk by its side and the exercise will do us good.

Just being by the river makes me talkative and evokes lots of memories. Connie listens quietly because it is a chance for her to match the stories up to the locale. Before we begin our walk she asks if we could kneel at the river's edge to pray for guidance.

Her prayer has a simple childlike honesty about it and drives me further into the peace of the moment. With her "Amen," I am drawn to remembering how my parents brought my brother and me up in a country church and how nothing there ever penetrated me. This was in spite of the fact I attended Sunday school and church services every week as well as Thursday night choir practice, summer Vacation Bible School, and any other time the doors were open. I earned my monogrammed Bible by learning Scripture verses and maintaining good attendance, but Jesus was never real to me. It was just what I did, the whole church bit. I understood it as part of being a kid who did what he was told.

The town didn't have enough people for denominations, so it just had a "community church." We all went to the same general church—you know, like a country general store. It was all hellfire and brimstone at that old church. When I left home, I was eighteen years old and I purposed the church, God, and Jesus were not going to take up any more of my time. To this day, looking back at years spent in front of that pastor's face, I cannot for the life of me conjure up any lingering impression of a smile on those lips. I came home from that stark white building scared to death of what was going to happen to me some day because of fibbing or cheating on a test at school. The pastor put a nail in the coffin of my already feeble faith one Sunday when he told the congregation that when Jesus came back He was going to walk down the middle of the main street in Lewiston, Idaho, and take everyone to heaven with Him except for those in the bars and the movie theaters.

This was truly devastating news to me because I didn't have a lot going for me entertainment-wise out "in the sticks" where we lived. This geographical location and the fairly bleak financial situation at our house did not offer forth a lot of social situations. When I was twelve, I did receive a weekly allowance of fifty cents based on obedience to my chores, and I carefully worked out how I would spend this. When Saturday came I headed for town where I blew the whole wad down to the last penny!

The downtown movie theater was called the Roxy and each Saturday they held a matinee for kids. It featured two westerns, a cartoon, and a serial feature. We didn't have running TV sitcoms in those days, but a serial was an adventure story where each week it would leave you with some sort of cliffhanger ending. It was done on purpose so that you had to come back the next week to see how the hero escaped from an obviously fatal train wreck. Of course, the villain had strapped him to the cowcatcher on the front and we were left with the vision of our hero and the train going over a thousand-foot cliff in the closing scene.

The movie was fourteen cents, the bus ride was a dime, and the remainder of my allowance was divided up differently each week. In addition to the movie I could get a comic book and a hamburger, or a hamburger and a soda, or a milkshake and a comic book, or two comic books and a soda—you get the picture. Sometimes I would walk or hitchhike home from town in order to stretch my budget. There was such a thing as penny candy then, which would turn my fourteen-cent movie into a fifteen-cent financial package. The candy was my sustenance for the trek home if I decided to walk. I lived for this break away from what I considered a very boring existence out in the Orchards. I loved going into town where I would meet up with the town kids and live in this fantasy world as it unfolded from the screen before me in a front-row seat.

As the pastor preached this message about Jesus not taking us moviegoers to heaven if we made the mistake of being in the movie theater on the day He came back, I became so scared that I was afraid to go to the movies the following weekend. I was so sure after hearing that sermon that Jesus was indeed coming to Lewiston that next Saturday if I went to the movies. I just knew that He was going to pick that day to come back. As a result of the apocalyptic message, I didn't go.

What compounded this particular situation was that I was going to miss the movie event of the year. It was a Roy Rogers and Gene Autry doubleheader with a special treat, a "Cartoon Carnival." A carnival consisted of three cartoons instead of one, and it was the final episode of the serial where we would find out the answers to all the mysteries that had mesmerized us for three months of faithful attendance. As a result of the pastor's foreboding, I didn't go to town that Saturday. It was a true test of my faith. I sat home up there in the Orchards—and Jesus didn't come. I was so mad at the pastor and the whole church thing that I vowed that I was getting out of that town as soon as I could and that I was never going to fall for that bull again.

I remember how I would come home to visit my folks in later years. By then they were very involved in this great little baptist church that had moved into the Orchards. It was the typical small-town church and was pastored by a super guy—Reverend Carpenter. One time when I was visiting home, Reverend Carpenter and his daughter sang "How Great Thou Art" during the offering. It really touched me and actually brought tears to my eyes. In looking back on the feeling I experienced that day, I recognize it now as the same one I get when the Holy Spirit climbs inside me and gives me a hug in the middle of my trials and confusion. My mom noticed my reaction and without fail, every time I would come home for a visit and go to church with them the pastor and his daughter would sing that song. I attended church with them because I knew it meant a lot to my mom—it was also part of my upbringing to be dutiful in matters such as these.

The part I didn't like was that I wasn't saved and it was a small church with the same people in attendance every Sunday. The denomination was duty bound by tradition to give an altar call after every service. They'd sing "I Surrender All" for what seemed like hours. I sat there with my head bowed knowing everyone was looking at me. I know my mom would have given her right arm for me to go forward but I just couldn't do it. I always wished that someone would please step out of their pew and put an end to the endless song even if it meant them being saved again. But there I was, the only person who was new to the place and everyone knew I hadn't been saved and they all were. I can remember almost "going forward" just so it would make my mom happy. But I never could go forward because it would be a lie and I would think instead of being saved I would be hell bound for fibbing, according to the pastor of my youth.

I speak of my growing up in terms of my mom and not my dad so much. Although he was truly a good man in every sense of the word, he just didn't have much to do with me. It was with him and me as it had been with him and his father and the generations before him. It was the Mansfield way and a pattern I made sure I broke when my kids came along. Of course, they always knew I loved them because I let them know it all the time. I found my own ways to let my kids down, but not knowing if they were loved wasn't one of them.

My mom prayed for my brother's and my salvation for three decades. She never judged me for my complete rejection of the gospel nor condemned me for my New Age years. She just kept praying for us. My mother spent the last decade of her life very ill and a great share of that in bed living in sheer pain. She should have passed on from her illnesses long before she did, but she lived on for her boys. As soon as my brother and I were both saved she passed on shortly afterward. I know deep down in my heart that she wasn't going anyplace until she knew her boys were safe—until all her children were in. There is an old song written by Craig Starret, entitled "Are All the Children In," which says it all when it comes to my mom:

> When I'm alone I often think of an old house on the hill
> Of a big yard hedged in roses where we ran and played at will
> And when the nighttime brought us home hushing our merry din
> Mother would look around and ask—are all the children in
>
> Well it's been many a year now and the old house on the hill
> No longer has my mother's care and the yard is still so still
> But if I listen I can hear it all no matter how long it's been
> I seem to hear my mother ask—are all the children in
>
> And I wonder when the curtain falls on that last earthly day
> When we say goodbye to all of this to our pain and work and play
> When we step across the river where mother so long has been
> Will we hear her ask a final time—are all the children in

Unichappell Music Inc. (BMI)

I was living in Nashville when my folks died, and I didn't make it home in time in either case to say good-bye. That is a sadness I will carry with me to my dying day.

I remember being in New York many years later on business. My meetings carried over to the following week and I was forced to stay in the city, alone for the weekend. There is an incredible church in Manhattan called the Times Square Church situated in a historic movie theater. Located directly off Times Square (51st Street and Broadway) its membership is made up of the rich, the poor, the famous, the homeless, the city's high-steppers and low-ballers from the surrounding area. When you walk into the sanctuary, there is an overwhelming sense of the power of God in that place. The first thing that hits you is the anointing in the sanctuary caused by a heavy murmur coming from the front of the auditorium. Before the service begins the walls on both sides of the stage area are lined with people praying just as they do at the Wailing Wall in Jerusalem. The world-renowned choir must have over a hundred people in it, and they sing with that "Sunday go-to-meetin'" kind of feeling. There's a lot of hand clappin', bodies swayin', and arms lifted high to the Lord. As you can tell, I love this church and have visited it many times.

It turned out that particular Sunday was Mother's Day. I was alone and Mom was on my mind. I was saddened over how much I missed her and how little time I had spent with this marvelous woman because I left home at such an early age. I decided to go to Times Square Church, and when I walked in I went straight to the wall and in prayer told her I loved her. I told her that I wished she were there with me on this special day. I sat down and bowed my head saying another prayer to her sweet memory. Just as I finished praying the service started and the choir began singing "How Great Thou Art." The tears started streaming down my face because I knew she had figured out a way to let me know she was with me that day, that she would always be with me and that I was never alone.

I also knew she was happy because—all her children were in.

Idaho Now I Know

Connie and I tire of our walk and our talk, and return to Moses. We drive back through Clarkston and continue a few miles west down the river where it heads away from town on its way to the Columbia. There is a marina and a café on the western edge of town, and we hope for some fresh fish. The fish is from the river and the servings are large enough for a Boy Scout troop, so we fill our tummy tanks for the day.

Over lunch I decide to visit my parents' graves in a cemetery on the backside of the Orchards. It is a symbolic spot because not only is the earth that the blood of my blood lies beneath on the edge of the place I grew up, but standing before their headstones I am able to look out over the canyons and fields that border the Nez Perce reservation lands. I am not a person who has a lot of ritual when visiting a cemetery. In fact, I always feel a little uncomfortable because there appears to be some sort of required response when visiting the graveside of a loved one. They are not really here, as far as I'm concerned, so I find it hard to talk to them. I don't picture them being in these two dirt holes before me. Instead, I find them to be in my memory, my prayers, and my expectations of the day I will join them.

As I stand there I get the sense that I am in a long shot in a Sergio Leone Spaghetti Western. I picture myself looking like Clint Eastwood squinting against the sun in a wistful moment. Connie stands back and to my left. I can tell moments like these hold more meaning for her than for me. After a few minutes we walk away and I am pressed to have lighter thoughts as we climb into Moses. These little ramblings I have been offering forth in remembrance of other times are going to be a light preamble to what I have decided I need to tell Connie later.

As we drive away from the graveyard and head toward town to check into

Lewiston's finest, the Red Lion Inn, I continue with stories about simple times when my showbiz career touched upon the two people whose names were carved in the stones at the place we just left.

I tell her stories about when I was growing up—how we grew our own food, raised our own chickens for eggs, goats for milk, and pigs for eventual bacon. I tell her how the only thing between us, the wheat fields, the canyons, and the rivers in the valleys below was a certain loneliness down at the end of that dirt road.

I tell her how my dad would sit patiently on our little stoop at the back of the house with a Winchester rifle across his lap. He took advantage of his good aim and the timing misfortunes of some unlucky pheasants that wandered too close to the house. It wasn't fried chicken but it was close and it was free. He was a good shot and never failed to get his deer when he went hunting. Because he didn't like steak or other fancy food, he would take it down to the meatpacking place and have it ground up into hamburger, the only kind of meat my dad liked. We didn't have a freezer so he paid a minimal fee to have it stored there and then picked up packages on his way home from the mill.

The first time my parents visited me in Hollywood I wanted to show off by taking them to one of our swankiest restaurants, Edna Earle's Fog Cutter on La Brea Avenue. It is no longer there, but this Tinseltown watering hole was known for its fabulous filet mignon and the place to be when the stars would come out to eat. I made early reservations because dinner was at 5 p.m. when I was growing up. My dad had a sense of promptness when it came time for dinner, or "supper" as it was known in Idaho. (I grew up thinking we had breakfast, dinner, and supper; not breakfast, lunch, and dinner.) Now it was my business to entertain clients in places like these, and as a Capitol Records promotion man at the time, it was important that I establish a relationship with the resident staff. Guess what entrée my dad ordered? A salisbury steak—better known as ground beef. Oh my, I was so embarrassed.

The next day I told them I'd take them sightseeing, and naturally my mom wanted to see the movie stars' homes in Beverly Hills. She insisted we buy one of those tacky *Maps to the Stars' Homes* they sell on the busy corners of Sunset Boulevard. I informed her they were useless and didn't actually take you to where the stars lived. I did concede that maybe at one time the stars did live in the houses marked out on the maps, but for the most part it was a scam. She was undaunted, so I finally gave in and bought one of the maps. When she opened it her eyes lit up—my mom knew exactly where she wanted to go first. She pointed out that the map showed that Jack Benny and Lucille Ball lived right next to each other and that's where we should go. I relented but once again let her know it was a waste of time. Parents just don't get it that we know so much more than them!

We drove to the address on the map and I pulled up in my Cadillac (champagne convertible with the top down, of course) in front of the first house. A manicured walkway came straight down from the front door of this Beverly Hills mansion to the sidewalk on the street. As soon as we pulled up, a limousine pulled in behind us. Jack Benny, almost if on cue, opened the front door of the house the map said was his, walked down the sidewalk directly toward our car, waved at my mom, and then making a slight left turn got in the limo. Guess what we did for the rest of the day? We went to every house on that map.

I tell Connie of another time when I was on tour and I brought some of the Seekers (an Australian group who charted a few singles in the mid-'60s—"Georgy Girl," "I'll Never Find Another You," "World of Our Own"), to my parents' house. They had appeared the night before at Washington State University in the small town of Pullman, about thirty-five miles from Lewiston. We had a few hours to kill the next day and because we were so close to my home, I talked a couple of them into running down to the town where I was raised. They enjoyed this excursion because it gave them a slice of Americana. The Seekers were so kind, they raved over the home-cooked meal, and it made my folks feel better about what I was doing by being able to meet some very nice people who were famous. Dad especially loved listening to the Australian accents, something quite different from the way they talked down at the mill.

That day with the Seekers didn't end so well. After we drove back up to Pullman, we were supposed to be picked up by a plane at a small airport there and taken to Seattle for the next night's concert. The airport turned out to be a Quonset hut on the edge of a wheat field with a short asphalt runway. There was no waiting room, just a check-in counter inside the hut. We were told to stand outside on the edge of the runway and to climb aboard when the plane arrived.

The Seekers dressed properly at all times and the garb they wore was very European. Keith Potger, one of the members, was tall and handsome. I can still picture him standing out in the middle of nowhere in his starched white shirt, long suit jacket, and waistcoat with one foot up on his guitar case, silhouetted against the long rows of luggage and equipment lining the runway as he looked out across the fields. He was in that very stance when the person in the Quonset hut came out and informed us our scheduled plane would not be landing there that day. The cabs had already left and we were three hundred miles from Seattle with some pretty heavy touring commitments in the metropolitan area.

The Seekers' road manager was an unusual Ichobod Crane sort of guy, both in appearance and nature. I never knew his real name—he was known to us all simply as "Dr. Doom." He was, shall we say, a rather focused person. He immediately went into crisis mode and ordered us not to move from where we were. His presentation of this instruction was so authoritative that we froze in our stances, dutifully standing by while he entered the Quonset hut to discuss the matter with the young gentleman inside. About ninety minutes later a plane appeared on the horizon and landed on the strip. It was a commercial airliner, not one of those puddle jumpers. Somehow Dr. Doom pulled it out of the sky to make a special stop at our little wheat field.

Ron Carey was our opening act on the tour, a comedian who later became famous as Officer Carl Levitt on ABC's *Barney Miller*. Ron hated to fly. These little planes that ushered us about the northwest were a little shaky and we hit some major thunderstorms along the way. Ask anyone who has toured in the entertainment business and they will agree it is great to have a comedian as part of the show for the levity they interject into an often-tiresome travel schedule. But for Ron, these flights were no laughing matter. One of the storms we encountered was particularly brutal and he went ballistic. Ron went crazy with fear, screaming at the top of his lungs the whole time during the turbulence. In his fright he managed to rip out all the little window curtains in his immediate area. When things settled down he announced that his portion of the tour had just come to an end. He got off the plane in Eugene, Oregon. Turned out he was a man of his word. We never saw him again.

※ ※ ※

I am rambling now, and before I can start another even less-interesting story Connie stops me—she knows something is on my mind and that I am having a hard time sorting through the mechanics of telling her what I think our next move should be. I make a couple of false starts in trying to approach the content of what I want to say, but she holds tight to her intuition and finally asks for it straight up—less fertilizer and more harvest.

"I think this trip is over except for one more stop, and I think it would be best if I did it alone."

The details and reasoning now come easy once the situation has been simply defined.

What I have in mind is that in the morning I will catch the first flight out of Lewiston and connect to a flight in Seattle or Portland. I will go to London, to 3 Savile Row, and see if I can get on the roof where I'd seen the Beatles perform their last live concert, and take one last look. I feel if I did this one last thing alone we could wrap this "experiment" up and go back home.

What happens next not only catches me off guard but brings me back to the reality that there are two people involved here. She totally agrees that there is a part of this excursion that should be done alone—actually two alones! She feels she needs space and time as much as I do. She says the inference that there will be a definite end to all this has solidified the deal for her. We figure I can go to London and back in two days. Once my flight schedule is worked out we make plans for her and Moses to join me in Portland. We map out a route for her from Lewiston to Portland that will be easy, scenic, and one that will give her a chance to sort out her feelings about what we have just experienced over the last few months.

I think one of my early attractions to Connie was that she can be a bit of a loner too. I think the idea of brief solitude made the decision easy for her. She will take me to the airport in the morning and then make her way leisurely from Lewiston to Portland, Oregon.

This is the first time during the entire trip with some form of definite planning involved. My emotional state is a little blurred—it isn't that going to London makes sense but now there are actual destinations and scheduling. The visits to her native Kentucky and my native Idaho had given our voyage a sense of significance and import. We both realized that touching upon these two hometowns together, in sequence, had united these places and us in some mystical way. It turns out traveling the long distance between the two had drawn us closer to each other.

Now as we finalize our itinerary we both start feeling really laid-back. I offer no explanation to this beyond the one a pastor once gave me about this earth we walk on. He said he firmly believed there was a spot, actually a whole area, that when we are standing in that place a part of us deep down inside resonates to that particular setting. I am a westerner and always felt a little disconnected in the South. As great as the music, the food, and the people are, I never had the feeling that I fit. Set me down anyplace west of the Rockies and I am at peace. Connie is lucky in that she feels a connection to both places. If she had planned the world, though, she would have put the Pacific Ocean in Tennessee.

We go to bed early and sleep well, and in the morning I am on my way. The small airstrip borders the same fields and canyons as the graveyard we visited the day before. I always seem to be peering from some edge. As the plane takes off for Portland that edge softens as it fades into the distance. We hit turbulence and it is then I notice someone has torn away the small window curtains by my seat.

MILE MARKER # 10
ACROSS THE POND

WHO WERE THOSE GUYS?

As the plane prepares to make its approach into London, I think back on the four guys that first brought me here. I might be somewhat different than most when it comes to the Beatles. I was never really "into" their music when I was working with them. I had no idea how legendary and historical this band and those times were going to be. As I look down on their town, I remember them as individuals and not as superstars.

Paul was the energetic one. He would have been the popular kid in high school, the one with whom you would cruise Main Street with your arms hanging over the car door edge, pressing tight to make your muscles look bigger. He would wave at the girls and slow down so they could jump in the back. It didn't feel like I had to figure out who he was or where he was coming from. He was the person who presented the next project or place to go. It was the sheer impetus of purpose that put things in motion so what you saw was an idea and a goal, and none of it needed complicated examination. When Paul said, "Here's what we are about to do," that was exactly what we were about to do.

From my standpoint, Paul was the unabashed leader of the group, the hard-charging one with the ideas and the one who on the surface seemed to be less troubled about things in general. He was like a hyperkinetic kid who never slowed down—the difference being that he was able to harness this energy into his God-given musical talent and just let 'er rip. In all honesty, he wore me out. It was fun, the times I got to hang or work with him, but his tempo was maddening and his energy pool bottomless. I did have an underlying pressure as the U.S. manager of their company, so I couldn't just totally go with the flow and hang out and party. My responsibilities were always looming in the back of my mind. If we had been high school buddies and there had been no fame, I think Paul would be the person who would be great to hook up with at class reunions. It would always be good to see him again. He, like the other Beatles, had an admirable sense of loyalty to their old mates. I was with Paul when he brought Ivan Vaughn, an old friend from his Liverpool school days, to LA with him as a traveling companion. Ivan was just an old friend hanging out with a mate who just happened to be the "cute Beatle."

George was the one you would have seen in the cafeteria keeping to himself. But he would also be the one to move things aside in order to make room for you when you sat down in the seat next to him. He would welcome the company and share in the moment in an easy manner. He was the kind of guy with whom a slow, easy friendship would develop over time. George would have probably been the perfect college roommate. He was so gentle and easy to be with. There was a thoughtfulness in his responses whether it was the conversation or the next move. He was at peace with what was going on inside and his serenity spilled out into his surroundings. I could talk with him about simple things and was able to forget the Apple stuff because I could tell that the world didn't begin and end with that for him. He was more concerned about *how* I was doing rather than *what* I was doing. We shared some very personal times together because we were young, happening dudes with new wives who liked each other. I was the LA guy with him during his frequent and extended stays. Just because we were in Hollywood didn't mean we had to be crazy. It was simple and easy being with George—we'd go buy jeans together or sit around the house late at night and not say much.

John was the different one. He was the kid who would probably be standing up, leaning against the soda machine, looking out across the lunchroom like it was another planet. There was always this sense that he was a bit unapproachable and would be the one to do the approaching if anything was going to come down on a personal level. I spent less time with him than the others, the main difference being I never had that alone time with him away from the band or Yoko—except for the day over at Ringo's LA house in 1976. That particular event was an accidental encounter and definitely not a bonding moment. I wrote about this day in *The White Book*.

I wrote a lot about John in *The White Book*, and it surprised me how many pages I spent on him after having had so little contact. I believe it was because of the complexity of his nature that it took more words to describe him. He was a brooder. There seemed a distance in place that made me always wonder how our exchanges were being digested and assimilated. I found in time this had more to do with my insecurities than his inaccessibility. He was very focused and intent at times and didn't have time for niceties. When I finally understood him better I found this to be because he was very straight ahead and honest when it was one-on-one time. John cared about issues of importance and would get very frustrated when he couldn't make matters better. He was like many of the great artists I worked with who had the odd ability to be in the extreme corners of life, jumping back and forth from altruism to self-centered madness without ever spending much time in the middle. Gee, I wonder why he was the one everyone was so fascinated with?

Ringo was the long-term guy. He's the one you would meet the first day at school and just because you ended up in the cloak room at the same time going for the same coat hook, you became friends for the rest of your school years and never really thought much about why. He was the most natural, most accessible, and most down to earth. When I was in London it was his house I was invited to for a holiday feast. When we were in LA it was gatherings at our homes that were of the norm. We shared a lot of our lives over the years, and it is usually the simple things that stand out when I think back. He was the one I got to know best and the easiest to understand. I never liked the fact that he was relegated to the fourth man down on their totem pole when it came to the band's pecking order. Besides being the best absolute drummer they could have chosen, he is an exceptional actor in my opinion. It is hard to find someone sharper or funnier in head-to-head dialogue. He brought "Starr" power to the band.

* * *

My thoughts are broken up by the overhead announcement indicating that it is time to put the tray tables back, bring the seats forward, and prepare for landing. I am on the aisle so I can't look out this time.

The Beatles were London to me. It was really the only reason I have been there. The last time was in early 1986 when Ron Kass and I were there for meetings concerning putting Apple back together. Connie has seen more of England during one visit with her mom on a vacation trip. She went all over the place, country and city. I have always flown in; gone to the hotel, Apple offices, clubs, and restaurants with one of the Apple gang; and then after a few days returned to California. This time is different and I honestly haven't thought through it too much—I just know that I am to go to the roof. The reason will come to me later.

I know I am not here for the weather.

Two of Four for Fore

It is amazing how one thing can be home, prison, fantasyland, the most exciting as well as most claustrophobic place in your life at any given time—or all these at the same time. I am talking about this strange phenomenon known as being "on the road" and how it has a chameleon character about it.

It would happen often, especially when I was with Capitol. I would be on the road and calls from the Tower executive offices came pouring in, telling me that there was a problem or situation I needed to attend to in some other city. The calls had to do with artist relations, concerts, radio stations, field staff—you name it. I'd leave for a three-day trip and come home three weeks later.

After a while the hotel rooms, airport waiting areas, the nightclubs and even the fine restaurants became claustrophobic. It got to the point where being "out there" became confining because I felt trapped and couldn't move. Not only did I miss out on a home life, but I also missed out on some primo experiences that were the perks of my job. As an example I will never forgive myself for not making the historic Woodstock concert a priority—I just couldn't get there from where I was and what I was committed to at the time. Another "so sorry I didn't go" was when I turned down John and Yoko for their infamous bed-in for peace in Toronto, Canada. That one had a lot to do with me just being too tired and too tied up with other matters.

One day I received a call from Ron Kass in London, who informed me that Ringo Starr and George Harrison were going to be in the San Francisco area for a few days of playtime. He told me I needed to accompany them as an official sidekick during this time. Mal Evans (the Beatles road manager) would be with them but they also wanted me, their guy in the U.S.A., to show the way. I was in Philadelphia and the request came in Thursday concerning the Fab Two's weekend plans. This was just too good to be true — to spend the weekend goofing off with a couple Beatles. Unfortunately, I just couldn't make it and was committed to another artist's tour. The logistics were rough and it would have been extremely difficult to get there when they wanted me.

As this unfolded, it turned out to be a blessing in disguise for Bud O'Shea. Bud was the top promotion man on my fifty-man national team and was based in San Francisco. I could always count on Bud to deliver the goods time after time in a tough market. In some ways I made Bud's life miserable because I called on him so often. As a result, he didn't get to spend enough time at home with his pretty new bride, Donna. He worked very hard, dedicated long hours during the week, and worked equally hard to keep his weekends as free as possible to help make up for being gone so much in the evenings.

I called Bud on Friday morning at the San Francisco Capitol office because I knew he would be preparing his routine reports regarding the previous week's activities, a requirement that each of the promotion men had to do on a weekly basis for my review.

Around this time I had hired a young lady from London named Carolyn Allmark, who would come in early each morning, summarize our national promotion team's accomplishments, and put the information on a separate phone line. Before heading out in the morning each promotion man would call this phone number and find out what was happening in other markets. This way they could go into their radio stations the next day and tell them where our records were breaking in other cities on a very up-to-date basis. This was powerful information because the local stations did monitor the activities of stations in other markets.

For the most part, the record companies relied on a weekly tip sheet by either Bill Gavin out of San Francisco, Kal Rudman in Philadelphia, Ted Randall in Hollywood, or wait for the Monday morning trade magazines — *Billboard*, *Cashbox*, and *Record World* — to retrieve this information. With our instant info system, as soon as my team would place a record on important playlists, it was easy to parlay this exposure across the country to the stations on a daily instead of a weekly basis, which was the basic time lag in gathering airplay action across the country up to this time. By getting in early with our info we often snagged the week's few available record spots before the other promotion teams could make their pitch.

It wasn't long before Capitol had the top promotion team in the nation—we were adding more new records to the major stations each week than any other company. The field promo guys loved it not only because of the advantage this system gave them but because they fell in love with Carolyn's sweet, sexy English accent.

When Carolyn came from England to join the team, she stayed in a hotel close to the Tower for the first week while she looked for an apartment. Her first night in America she called down to the front desk to leave a morning wake-up call, and as was customary in England hotels in those days, she also ordered a pack of cigarettes to be sent up to the room at the same time. This all sounds normal, but there was a translational problem despite the fact we do operate from the same basic language. Her request to the front desk went something like this: "Would you send some fags up in the morning and knock me up at six a.m.?" (*Fags*=cigarettes and *knock me up*=wake-up call in her homeland.) Needless to say, she came in pretty flustered and red-faced on her first day on the job.

Back to Bud O'Shea, my top marketing man.

I immediately got Bud on the phone and naturally he was guarded. He knew my reason for calling just before a weekend probably meant more work for him. He was particularly nonplussed when I told him I needed a big favor and that I considered it necessary for him to work some more overtime for me. I told Bud I needed him to baby sit a couple of our artists for the weekend. He respectfully explained to me that he had family plans and it would be very inconvenient to change them. I think his exact phrase was "Donna will kill me!"

"Bud, I really need you to do this for me and I am sorry that I have put you on the spot. Tell Donna that I will make it up to you guys in another way. I am hung up out here on the road; I, too, am away from my family so

I know how you feel. Just tell me you will do it so I can rest easy and I'll fill you in on the details," I pleaded.

"All right," he said with certain lack of enthusiasm. "Who are they and what does it entail?"

I told him Ringo Starr and George Harrison were checking into one of the grandest hotels on the West Coast, the Hotel Del Monte in Pebble Beach. I informed him they wanted someone to hang with them and show them around. I know he didn't hang up but the phone seemed to have gone dead for quite a while.

"You've got to be joking," he said in an almost whisper.

I replied I wasn't joking and that he had an unlimited expense account to live it up. This was at the height of the Beatles' stratospheric fame and popularity. Just to be in the same town with any of the Beatles in those days (1968) was exciting, but this?

He caught a commercial puddle jumper to the Monterey airport. From there he took a cab to Pebble Beach and the hotel where he hooked up with Ringo, George, and Mal. (George's and Ringo's wives, Pattie Harrison and Maureen Starkey, also accompanied their husbands on this trip).

Bud said the next two days was like living in a movie—A *Hard Day's Night* to be exact. They wanted to go into the city and hang out in places like North Beach and just dig the local scene. Easier said than done. Bud tried to talk them out of it because he knew how crazy things would get but they were insistent. He played the whole San Francisco thing down, telling them it was all just a big tourist trap, but they wanted to go anyway. How could *he* tell a Beatle no?

Getting around was easy because they had a private plane with a big green Apple painted on it. They just hopped aboard and went into the city. When they walked the streets; almost everyone did a double take. And when they would turn around and stare, George and Ringo waved at them and smiled. I knew the routine because Paul and I walked to lunch through the midday crowds in London and it would catch people off guard in the same way.

The next day Ringo and George wanted to play golf on one of the most prestigious courses in the world. The fact that George and Ringo weren't golfers was of no matter. It turned out that the back nine holes had to be closed down because of their presence. The whole thing was just bizarre—they were hitting golf balls all over the place. They'd drive from one tee and their balls landed on another fairway. The main thing they were into was commandeering the golf cart—pushing each other away so that they could drive it. Picture this: two Beatles going all over the place like kids in a bumper car. They were having a ball.

Bud, like me, never carried a camera when working with artists. However, this situation was different. He didn't know how to use an Instamatic let alone a professional camera, but he borrowed a friend's and took one with him anyway—he forgot about it until they were at the golf course. He asked Mal if he knew how to operate the fancy camera. Mal said he wasn't sure but gave it a shot. Bud said he was very nervous when he took the film in later for development. Luckily, he ended up with some great pics of him and his new friends from Britannia. When he picked up his photos, the clerk looked at him like he was a very major dude. As the photos exchanged hands, the clerk flat out asked Bud—"Who *are* you?"

Back at the hotel, the two Beatles insisted on eating in the hotel dining room. Once again, Bud was unable to convince them otherwise. It didn't take long before the word spread around. The hotel was inundated with hordes of people and bedlam was breaking out. The hotel brass actually suggested that the pair leave even though they weren't doing anything wrong. It was a very formal and stodgy place, and things were getting a little too frenetic for their taste and clientele. George and Ringo were eventually moved to a private house on the Del Monte grounds.

Bud said the coolest part was his return to San Francisco. He was trying to figure out how to get back and they simply gave him their plane. It was just he and the pilot going home after a weekend of working overtime for his *favorite* boss.

Bud and I talked not long ago and he told me that weekend was his most precious memory from his record-company days.

This Bud—was for you.

BACK TO THE ROOF

For the first time I can see clearly from where I stand, not only physically but also spiritually. I find myself transfixed looking out over a vaguely familiar portion of an unchanging London skyline.

I am on the roof of the old Apple building at 3 Savile Row in London's financial district. I am a scant distance up and away from King's Road and Carnaby Street where I bought my hip English duds in the '60s. It's just an illusionary inch away from Piccadilly Circus and the clubs, the posh hotels, the four Beatles, and the people inhabiting their world. A spatial Rolling Stone's throw from all those moves and all these bits and pieces that had so much to do with the shaping of my life later on. Good things, bad things, senseless things, important things—"things" being the operative word here. I have returned to this spot as the concluding stopover on my search. After all the miles seeking resolution, I now realize I never expected to find enlightenment in any of the places I kept returning to. I had been mistakenly looking for the answers in the mechanics of the search and the return visits—not from the perspective of the final destination.

The time is one o'clock in the afternoon, the same time of day I gathered here with an incredibly bizarre flock of four unruly angels four decades ago.

I am stopped in my tracks by the sudden realization that I have journeyed so far zeroing in on this singular moment. Like Moses, after years of wandering in a desert, I have been brought to the top of the mountain to hear from my Father God—just the two of us. It is time to stop having conversations and to be still and listen. He has filled my collection plate with sweet offerings of wisdom from His faithful servants—the passionate, generous pastors of my past who placed golden contributions into my outstretched soul. After many years of pressing into God's heart, I sense there is something timeless in the wind that is blowing up from the historical street below.

In my mind's heart, God starts our communion by letting me know the only reason I needed to come here was to find out that I didn't need to come here.

It is just a building, this is just a town, that was just an event, and unfortunately, in some ways, I have returned to this place just a little less confused as I was then. I was dealing with the shallow importance of worldly things in those heady days, and the dilemmas I've experienced since were always about not letting go of those same old terrestrial considerations. For decades a part of me has refused to change. The realization that I had developed a sophisticated lack of trust in God's ability to do a better job with my life brought about a peculiar sense of awkwardness to this moment.

I was ready to run from what was beginning to unfold on this roof, but I was aware within a matter of a few feet I would become airborne if I did! I just needed to make all this stuff less a part of me. That's what it was all about. It was not about the trials, the pain, the disappointments, the failures, or the downward slide. It definitely was not about the hit records, the fame, the money, the stars, the exciting tours, or even the immutably appointed or pointless times in my life. No, it has always been about the other part, the new part, the part that leaves the old part behind, the part that has a fresh beginning, the part that is about Him and not me.

The din from the street below roars up into my awareness and startles me into the realization I am the only one standing in this place right now—a lonely, misguided soul. How could I even imagine recouping anything out of this moment or any other moment or place with the ground rules I had established? My thoughts are rushing now—they begin crowding the strained edges of my mind as the law of emotional centrifugal force gains momentum and memorial speed—stirred-up debris from my past wildly scraping against the edge of a thrashed consciousness.

I was so surprised I had been able to walk in the downstairs door of this historic place, which is currently boarded up—a sad contrast to the glory of the Apple days. I heard hammering and because of an unconcerned main-tenance crew I proceeded unchallenged up the surprisingly familiar stairs and out onto the roof. When I opened the door leading out to that gritty vista, I got an overwhelming sense that not only was I feeling a rush of cold air but I would be hit flat in the face with warm memories, echoes of solid rim shots, and the strains of "Get Back."

I expected Paul to turn around and smile at me through that beard I never liked—nodding his head to the side as if to say, "Hey, great, look, we're all here. It's just us and it still feels good."

I picture John staring into space, leaning into the microphone with his long hair flowing from the rooftop winds.

I can still see Ringo looking out and beyond the backs of his mates appearing almost alone in the backline of the band, very noticeable in his shiny red coat.

And George—bent over his guitar checking on his frozen fingers to make sure that they were in the right place.

On that day, January 30, 1969, four idealistic long-time friends had no idea they were saying good-bye to a monumental era in musical history, as well as the end of a bond and friendship that would never have the same boyhood street passion that had anointed their music for so many years. The last song of the set on the roof that day, "Get Back," proclaimed the end of a beginning no one was really ready to accept. The local Londoners heard it on the streets below but were unaware of a reverberation that would never die. An eerie echo wafted out and over the rooftop railings that incredible day and still resonates in the hearts of those who remember.

I know now how monumental that day was in my life, and because of such incredible successes and events at such a young age, I know I peaked too high and too soon. A pinnacle of that magnitude happening so early in my unsaved life dominated everything that followed. A milestone became a millstone. It became a shifty idol that I worshiped without realizing and became a point that I have been unable to go beyond.

I am not diminishing the recent stops on this long trek, nor am I sug-gesting the incredible reflections I experienced on the way were not immensely important. What I am saying is because I was not a believer in those fabulous days I had no armor to protect me from gathering the ill arrows of worldly thinking and ambition.

This roof is a critical spot—the top of a long, steep climb. You only spend a minute there—at the very top of the world's world. Most of your time is spent going up and down the mountain, and that is the part I needed to focus on. Even after being saved, those arrows that penetrated my being in the "before Him" years are still hanging from my hide.

Finally one day I did accept salvation and in doing so became a new person. The problem is that I never totally let go of my old wounds, and in the spirit, I probably looked like a brand-new Jaguar towing an old Dempsey Dumpster.

I look out and see everything for the first time. I soared through this period in my life picking up worldly possessions and lifelong impressions. Then one day everything seemed to fall apart and I had to get rid of "stuff" in order to move on. The homes, furniture, and cars were the easy things to lose. It is the baggage I had unknowingly gathered along the darkened way that has clung to my walk like grass stains. It wasn't the things that were the problem—it was the nothings. I had passed through my whole life collecting worthless junk while leaving very little of permanent value behind.

I look out from this place and I can see forever. Forever—that is the where, why, what, and mainly "Who" it is eventually all about. Forever evolves into eternity and I know the journey has ended here.

That cold January day had always been the biggest day in my life. As I look around I discover—it is just a roof. I look away from the roof and there is forever. I look back at the roof and it looks even smaller than it did a few moments ago. It looks a hundred times smaller than it did yesterday when I boarded a plane in Lewiston, Idaho, to come here. Standing frozen in place by these cold facts, I realize these reflections and a warm jacket are already more than I am going to leave this life with.

I can actually sense God smiling up at me from the street below, laughing across the ledges of the surrounding buildings, in rhythm with the banging door I left open behind me when I came out into this moment. I can tell He is thrilled that I finally get it. He laughs in celestial disbelief that it took me so long. I don't need to "Get Back"—I need to get going. It is all so very simple—it's just so hard to be simple.

I walk down and out of the building just as unnoticed as I walked in—out and away from that man-made structure onto a street of gold. I finally became a man today because I realized it is all about just being His child. I know now this journey actually started long before I set out and will end in eternity with Him.

I move off the curb into the edge of traffic and hold out my hand for a cab to take me to the airport. I came straight to the roof from Heathrow and am going to return as simply as I came. There is no need to see one more time some of the places from that time period. I feel emptied out and filled up at the same time. The mountain of words I have poured forth on these pages and in this journey become a heap of torn clippings blowing away in the wind. Solomon nailed it when he said our vain efforts are of no import now. I had no bags when I left on this leg of the trip and in returning I have ended up with even less baggage. I am going to board a plane and fly to Portland where Connie and Moses will meet me at the airport.

We will take Highway 1 down the Oregon and California coast to Bodega Bay—to get back homeward.

MILE MARKER # 11
THE HOME STRETCH

In Plane English

We have cleared the runway at Heathrow and before I drop my seat back to get some rest I peer out of the window to see London, probably for the last time. Once again I feel like the young naive man who sat glued to that small oval pane in amazement at what lay below—decades ago.

The difference now is in the direction I am headed.

As I fly away from London and the roof, my understanding of what I learned there expands into an astounding postscript of insight. I realize the gentle turmoil leading up to my decision to embark on this flower-child endeavor to "find myself" was not defined by recent periods of mulling things over. Instead, it is the result of a decades-old four-way conversation. That is why this whole crossing has been so confusing.

What I have just learned is that I was four people when this all started: 1) the young innocent fellow of my growing-up, high school, and college years; 2) the selfishly ambitious person of my successful career years; 3) the beaten-down victim of my failure years; and 4) the brand-new being I became as a Christian. Each of these entities had been vying for space and the "me" in all this was being jerked around like a rag doll. I essentially became new wine poured like a bedraggled brew into old wine skins. It is no wonder that, emotionally and spiritually, I started leaking out all over the place.

In the middle of this revelation I recall a story I was told many years ago that speaks very clearly to this situation. There was an old Native American who, a few months after his conversion to Christianity, came back to his pastor and said, "I feel like I have two big dogs constantly fighting inside of me. One dog represents my old nature that wants me to do bad things and return to the ways of my past, while the other dog represents my new nature that wants me to do right and be at peace with being a new creature in

Christ." The pastor asked, "Which one of them is winning?" After thinking about it, the old Indian replied, "I guess the one I feed the most."

I can identify with that old Indian except I have been hosting not just two dogs but an entire wolf pack. My mind races through the myriad of instances that define each of these four aspects of my makeup. I begin to understand how they had come into play individually and in their generalities in my life over the years. I now find elements from my past that made up my old nature were in a fierce battle with my new nature, my Christ nature. I had bought the lie that the battle and the collateral damage to my soul were totally a result of my doing. I never grasped the understanding that this is the way the devil operates when we are born again. The devil had his way with me for a long time and he wasn't about to give me up without a fight. I needed to tell him a long time ago to go to hell where he belongs.

The biggest revelation was in uncovering the devil's ace card in all this—a hole card that he used over and over again throughout the years. He deceived me into letting one event in my life define me more than anything else. It had to do with the roof I just left. It was the pinnacle experience of being one of the few people who were there the day the Beatles played in concert together for the last time. Now, don't bow out on me here because I admit that I am pinning a million moments of complicated existence on to one shallow event, but I believe this whole dilemma has been about an event that simple and unimportant. I let that moment and accomplishment define me. It was my Olympic Gold Medal, my Super Bowl ring, and my Medal of Honor all wrapped up into one. When I stood once again on that dirty old roof and looked up into the clear eyes of perfection watching over me, I finally saw the difference. Here is what I discovered and want you to understand: the problem was not with the people, places, and past occurrences—it was my prioritizing of these things. I had become a grown man hanging on to this Britannia-based "blanky" instead of moving out and beyond that space in time.

God reminded me that when I became a Christian I understood the concept of the Holy Trinity from day one. I understood it completely and never doubted it or became confused with its meaning. I had won when I found the One. The problem was that by the time I had come to Him I had already become a four in one. God told me that, yes, all these people and the events that created their persona were a part of me, but they were the other parts, not the part that was me today. They were like old files that needed to be deleted because they have nothing to do with what's going on now.

My head is hurting from trying to think this through, but my heart is finally at peace. I am weary and lay my head back to rest. I am floating on air and fall asleep on the wings of the snow-white dove that is taking me home.

Suddenly something bumps and I turn and look out the window. I have conked out for several hours. I am in Portland and can sense Connie waiting for me at the curb with Moses and the motor running.

It is good to be home.

If it looks like I have become smaller, it's because He is loving.

PRECIOUS MEMORIES

From the time my airplane landed to when Moses cleared the final outskirts of the Portland metropolitan confines, less than an hour has passed. When I tell Connie my thoughts about what happened in London, she nods knowingly. We agree in the silence that there is now a sense of resolution to this curious quest.

We glide through greenery resting in the serene awareness the journey has come to its final stage. Music from Connie's iPod is playing softly in the background. I hear something melodically familiar and reach over to turn up the volume. The song playing is "Precious Memories." I have no idea who is singing but the words engulf me and bring a sense of summary to our travels.

Precious memories, unseen angels
Sent from somewhere to my soul
How they linger ever near me
And the sacred past unfold

Precious father, loving mother
Fly across the lonely years
And old home scenes of my childhood
In fond memory appear

As I travel on life's pathway
Know not what the years may hold
As I ponder, hope grows fonder
Precious memories flood my soul

Precious Memories, how they linger
How they ever flood my soul
In the stillness of the midnight
Precious sacred scenes unfold

I recorded this song two different times over the years as a producer. The first time was in a continually stoned state with Waylon for his *Are You Ready for the Country* album. The song just happened late one night at the end of a session. It was as if Waylon drifted back to his childhood for a few minutes. We had finished recording another song for the album and the master tape was still running when he started strumming his guitar softly with the opening chords of this plaintive standard. I learned to watch Waylon for inspired moments like these. The engineer had also been instructed that during Waylon Jennings sessions I was the one who said when the tape was to be stopped.

Through the darkened studio glass I saw Waylon lower his head. I knew something special was about to happen. This wasn't the first time I had experienced this with him. Most times it was just a magic moment that was shared by the few who happened to be in the vicinity. This time, though, we captured the moment on tape and it became part of the album. As the crowd the Outlaws appealed to was not typically made up of nuns and baptists, I found irony in that we were now interjecting a bit of country-gospel music in this particular album, considered to be one of his most rebellious.

The second time I produced this song was under much different circumstances. Instead of stone being the operative word, I would have to say it would be Rock—*the* Rock. Not the rock of our age but the Rock of Ages rock. The second time was for the Gaither Vocal Band's historic *Homecoming* album. It, along with the Imperials' *Big God* album, was one of my last projects after all those years of producing records.

Darrell Harris, president of Star Song Records, one of the era's leading and most cutting-edge record companies in the Christian contemporary music field, had been working out a concept for a gospel album for some time. He was a fan of the classic 1972 album *Will the Circle Be Unbroken* by the Nitty Gritty Dirt Band. That album was a collaboration project recorded with traditional country artists such as Mother Maybelle Carter, Earl Scruggs, Doc Watson, Roy Acuff, Merle Watson, Jimmy Martin, Junior Huskey, Norman Blake, Pete Oswald Kirby, and Vassar Clements. Darrell wanted to do a gospel version of this album featuring that genre's legendary artists before they began passing away. Darrell decided it was finally time to act on this idea when Rusty Goodman, a member of the Happy Goodman Family, one of gospel music's most famous quartets, died in November 1990. He knew if he waited any longer it could be too late because it was only a matter of time before more of these legends would follow Rusty.

He described his idea to Star Song artist Bill Gaither, who was immediately intrigued because he, too, was a fan of the *Circle* album. Darrell knew that Gaither was one of the few people in the business who could pull this off. Gaither's songs were in hymnals and he had industry respect as well as the professional clout needed to gather such a group together. Once this seed was planted Darrell called me to see if I would be interested in producing the album.

His reason for choosing me was simple in that he knew the project needed a seasoned producer (a nice way of saying older) who had worked with established artists. He knew because of my background these gospel legends would most likely feel comfortable with me. I wouldn't show favoritism since I didn't know any of the artists nor had I worked with any of them or their managers, record labels, agencies, etc. In fact, I had never produced a gospel album before other than the one I did with Jessi Colter in 1976 for Capitol's pop division.

A lot of ironies and supernatural happenings unfolded once the project progressed. Bill Gaither had previously decided this would be the last album with his Gaither Vocal Band before retiring the group. He didn't realize what his gathering of old friends would lead to. He put together the all-time super-group of gospel: the Speer Family, Jake Hess, Hovie Lister, Howard and Vestal Goodman, George Younce, Glen Payne, James Blackwood, Eva Mae LeFevre, Buck Rambo, J. D. Sumner, the Stamps (Jim Hill and Daryl Williams), plus Rudy and Larry Gatlin of the Gatlin Brothers. Darrell had wanted to do the whole album with this select group but Bill shaped it into being a Gaither Vocal Band album with a one-song guest appearance featuring these artists.

It took us about a month to record the album, which at that point was still untitled. Once we had finished recording the Gaither Vocal Band portion, we set up the studio for the taping of one classic gospel song with Bill's guests. He had chosen "Where Could I Go but to the Lord?" as the song to sing with the group. I recorded all of the instrumental tracks with the tracking musicians beforehand while keeping enough tracks open for overdubs so I would be ready for whatever might happen once they started singing.

Connie lent a hand by taking care of all the logistical moves. She helped coordinate everything from booking studio time, hotels, and travel, to having food on the table in the green room when they arrived.

We recorded the project at Mabel Birdsong's His Master's Touch Studio in the Berry Hill section of Nashville. We were blessed this facility had a very large space that allowed for a two-foot-high stage to be set up at the far end of the studio. We arranged microphones in a performance manner so everyone could be heard and also feel comfortable creating a concert atmosphere. After the performers were gathered at the studio, had eaten some food, and caught up on old times (it had the feel of a summer church picnic), we moved them into the recording area and onto the stage. It was a joyful time, and the one song they had come together to sing came out great. What happened next was clearly unexpected and out of the blue. (I like that phrase because I recently learned that it originated in reference to something that came from heaven).

The guests were gathered around the piano for a few candid photos before saying good-bye, maybe for the last time. Larry Gatlin urged Eva Mae LeFevre to "play something." Eva Mae, the matriarch of the gospel-singing LeFevre family, began playing a familiar tune on the studio piano. Someone began singing the lead melody, then feet started to tap, hands began to clap, and voices split into four-part harmony. Soon the group began singing from their souls and the building became alive with reverberations akin to a heavenly choir. The next two hours were magical. They traded places at the piano and sang their favorite songs. There were no arrangements except those written on their hearts after decades of singing these gospel classics separately and together. What a thrill it was to see legends singing these great songs together, harmonizing, weeping—embracing. The Spirit of God was definitely present. Bill Gaither, watching from the sidelines, motioned for the video photographer, who had been brought in to shoot footage for a short promotional video of "Where Could I Go but to the Lord," to keep the videotape rolling. Something wonderful was unfolding and he wanted to preserve the memory. It wasn't long before Bill was at the piano singing with his head tossed back and his eyes closed as he led his old friends in this holy hootenanny.

The extended session was to yield much more than memories for its participants. The album containing "Where Could I Go but to the Lord" earned a Grammy and a Dove Award. More importantly the raw film footage was edited and polished into a fifty-eight-minute package and launched a multimillion-dollar business. It also sparked a rebirth of interest in southern gospel music and rekindled the careers of the veterans who sang on the album and appeared in the video.

After these sessions Darrell Harris suggested to Bill Gaither the album title should be *Homecoming*. The video, also called *Homecoming*, debuted on *The 700 Club* in 1992 with a toll-free number for ordering. The response was so astounding the show was repeated during "sweeps week" as a ratings booster. For all of its technical shortcomings, it struck a chord with viewers, who begged for more. The by-product of those sessions has been years of sold-out gatherings in major arenas and stadiums featuring various versions of this incredible event that took place in a quaint recording studio in Nashville, Tennessee.

These guys were old-timers in matters of divine occasions, but I was a newcomer to such moments. I felt like a child spun out into space—a glimpse of heaven in a way. Looking back on this experience from the dimmed interior of the van, I now recognize that day was a time of forgiveness and grace.

The lessons I have been searching for on this road trip appear to have already been revealed to me in the past—in moments like these. God had been laying out the answers all along my old highways but I was not paying attention to the signposts. These people led hard lives on the road and in the spotlight. They knew fame and failure, exultation and disappointment. They had been carried and dropped, delivered and dumped, praised and condemned, honored and betrayed. They had experienced the heights and depths of being rich and poor. They shared victories and defeats and faced cross-purposes with one another, but on that sweet day they stood in one place with the song of songs on their lips. The group melded together in one spirit with one purpose, which was to the glory of God. They, like me, lived exaggerated lives and it is not unusual to become confused in the process of being blessed at what they were gifted to do.

During the *Homecoming* sessions I witnessed a tender mixture of soft-ened hearts and gentle grace. Some of them had run aground with each other over the years, and in some cases there had been unresolved resent-ment and bad feelings. But they came one by one, entering into this special place as if called by a vision that eventually bound them together by the anointing that unexpectedly fell over the room. As they gathered around to sing "Precious Memories" and other old favorites, they were united in pur-pose and soon arms, hands, and hearts touched. With eyes closed and tears flowing, these weary travelers down glory road came to rest in the Spirit that day. All the unresolved disparities were washed away as forgiveness and grace took its rightful place in the hearts of its champions. As complicated as the events were that brought this situation about, it was the simplicity in the Word of their loving heavenly Father that melded everything into sweet-ness and serenity.

▨ ▨ ▨

Just as these people became a unique congregation that day, and just as their differences were resolved, I realize now as Connie, Moses, and I clear a mountain crest and encounter a stunning Pacific Ocean sunset on the hori-zon, I am acutely aware that the four people I have been carrying around inside myself for so long could do the same thing. We could resolve our differences and become one as God intended. One of the problems with a jagged history is when someone does overcome their past through the grace and forgiveness of God so many times people from the "old days" refuse to accept that change. They insist on keeping the old sinner person alive in their minds.

Moses' worn tires cling to the edge of the narrow Highway One along the Oregon coast while Connie and I cling to each other in spirit as we let go of what we just left behind.

The first step in forgiveness is to forgive ourselves.

The good thing about our past is that it has passed.

BETWEEN DUSK AND DAWN

Author's Conclusion

I seem to be working
and thinking
But I am really running
through a meadow.

I seem to be a canyon with love
and happiness filling me
But I am really a mountain
reaching up for more.

I seem to be a sparkling smooth running brook
cool and refreshing
But I'm really dawn and dusk joined together
to make the stars come out.

I seem to be like the moon
floating along lazy like.
But really I am a cricket
trying not to be eaten tonight.

We began the journey with this pensive native poem. I now understand the writings of that young Navajo lad for the first time: *I am the cricket in his poem.*

Over the spatial span of my wanderings I have seen and sensed the beauties and the bestials of life and was never sure where I was positioned in the ether between them. Looking back, it is apparent I was always running from something I thought was going to destroy me—or searching for something that I believed could save me. Maybe the reason I was so confused was because I was doing both. I would bounce between the country church upbringing of my youth and the sophistry I had been force-fed by the devil during my later years. For long periods of time I lived a life of elusion until I found myself doubting I could ever attain a truth of any substance. I never knew for sure if I would make it to the very end without being devoured by the impossibility of it all. I *was* just a cricket trying not to be eaten on any given night.

That worn scrap of paper I carried around my entire life has now revealed to me that God had His hand on me the whole time. He wanted to give me something I could hang on to—something that had been with me every step of the way. It was what launched me on my search, but as I stare at it now, I see it as something beyond a paper presence in my pocket. It has become a crumpled scroll of ancient wisdom. He had me cut it out of a magazine, knowing it would someday become physical testimony to my searching soul. It is a clear confirmation of His promise that He has always been with me on what seemed a purposeless and disjointed pilgrimage.

In times of crisis I am left with fewer options as a Christian than I had as an unbeliever. I now have only two: trust God or don't trust God. Like Jonah fleeing Ninevah, running away only got me in a whale of trouble. When I first set out from Bodega Bay on this journey, crutches were torn away. My travels into the places of my past became more like careening down a road to nowhere, but in the process of getting lost in familiar territory I found my way home—home to a heavenly Father.

It has been slightly less than three months instead of a year as planned since we set out with Moses. Today, after hours of silent driving, we pull up in front of our house. The need to venture forth in discovery was so intense that we are not sure we even locked the doors or turned off the lights when we left. What was once landscaping has become "weedscaping" that surrounds this almost unfamiliar place. We remain in the van staring up at the house—still not speaking. It is almost as if we can't move because there is so much memory to download from our long excursion. I finally get out and walk around to the front of the van and lean on Moses' bumper. This pitted chrome pew had become my mercy seat along the way whenever I needed to think things through. Once again, I find cold comfort before its bug-stained reflection.

I've spent a lot of time saying to myself that I was going to trust God before I got to the point where I actually started trusting Him. The transition from trying to apply one's faith to having it actually kick in is like sipping sweet well water for the first time. The process begins with this great thirst and then after what seems like forever—aahh, righteous refreshment!

Incredible calm and beauty overtake this moment.

How delicious it is when I know in my heart God is all I truly need. It is like a spiritual house cleaning where there is a wonderful sense of accomplishment in knowing a lifetime of junk and clutter is cleared away. It feels like a cool breeze on a warm day when I realize the empty chamber inside can now become filled completely with His love and His promises. Worldly weights fall away leaving in their place all that really counts—His mercy and grace and unfailing love.

I can now press on to win the race He has set before me and I don't have to drive somewhere to do it.

It's getting dark outside and it is very quiet on our street. I look up at the house and then turn around and go back to the side door of the van. I climb in that kindly carriage, and for what I know will be the last time—I crawl into its bunk with Connie.

We have come home and I know now that we've gone far enough.

Maintenance Record

Marshall Terrill

If Moses were a horse instead of a van we would have needed a *blacksmith* along the way, but *Between Wyomings* was about a vision. Fortunately Marshall immediately understood the depth of its complexity and became a trusted literary companion as well as a needed *wordsmith* to the excursion. He is the master mechanic that enhanced the telling of these tales—some that would have never made it to the pages if it wasn't for his encouragement and nurturing. Thanks, pal, for helping me keep the words and wheels "on the road."

Bucky Rosenbaum

I am blessed among men to have a personal *"3-in-One Oil"* that keeps my creative engine running smooth. Bucky is my literary agent, my inspirational compass, and most of all, my dearest friend. Our earthen frames may be dusty and rattling from the rocky road we have shared, but I have always known where we're headed because his headlights are locked on high beam and focused on eternity.

Connie

You came into my life when I was stumbling somewhere *between* heaven and hell. I was completely lost until that sweet day you grabbed me by the heart and pointed me in the right direction. Because of your love . . . now I am found.

Thomas Nelson Team

You know you have a great editor when you can't wait for her to get her hands on your manuscript—once again that would be Kristen Parrish who always makes it better. I live on the road but have found a home with the greatest group of executives in the publishing arena. Gifted to the core and good people all—thank you for joining me in the voyage—Joel Miller, David Schroeder, Gabe Wicks, Heather Skelton, Jennifer Womble, Kristen Vasgaard, Heidi Segal, Betty Woodmancy, and Wayne Hastings.

NANCY ALCORN

As always, a tithe from my books will go to your vision and the wonderful girls of Mercy Ministries. You are the ace in Grace.

APPENDIX

OUTLAW/MANSFIELD DISCOGRAPHY

WAYLON JENNINGS
March 1973
(Honky Tonk Heroes)
We Had It All
When She Cries (Unreleased?)
(Also two other songs from that
    four-song session—titles forgotten)

September 1974
(The Ramblin' Man)
Amanda
It'll Be Her

June 1976
(Are You Ready for the Country)
Are You Ready for the Country
Them Old Love Songs
So Good Woman
Jack-A-Diamonds
Can't You See
MacArthur Park (Revisited)
I'll Go Back to Her
A Couple More Years
Old Friend
Precious Memories
Texas Sand (Unreleased?)

June 1977
Brand new Tennessee waltz
    (Unreleased?)

January 1978
(Waylon And Willie)
A Couple More Years

September 1978
(I've Always Been Crazy)
I Walk the Line

April 1979
(Waylon's Greatest Hits)
Amanda

TOMPALL GLASER
1973
(Charlie)
Cowboys and Daddies

1977
(Tompall Glaser and His Outlaw Band)
You Can Have Her
Release Me (And Let Me Love Again)
Tennessee Blues
Come Back Shane
It'll Be Her
Look What Thoughts Will Do/Pretty
    Words/It Ain't Fair
Sweethearts or Strangers
Let My Fingers Do the Walking (Late
    Night Show)
I Just Want to Hear the Music

WILLIE NELSON
1978
(Waylon And Willie)
A Couple More Years

JESSI COLTER
1975
(I'M JESSI COLTER)
Is There Any Way (You'd Stay Forever)
I Hear a Song
Come On
You Ain't Never Been Loved (Like I'm
    Gonna Love You)
Love's the Only Chain
I'm Not Lisa
For the First Time
Who Walks Thru Your Memory (Billy Jo)
What's Happened to Blue Eyes
Storms Never Last

1976
(JESSI)
Hand That Rocks the Cradle
One Woman Man
It's Morning
Rounder
Here I Am
Without You
Darlin' It's Yours
Would You Walk With Me
All My Life, I've Been Your Lady
I See Your Face

(DIAMOND IN THE ROUGH)
Diamond in the Rough
Get Back
Would You Leave Now
Hey Jude
Oh Will (Who Made It Rain Last
    Night)
I Thought I Heard You Calling My
    Name
Ain't No Way
You Hung the Moon (Didn't You
    Waylon)
Woman's Heart Is a Handy Place to Be
Oh Will

1977
(MIRIAM)
For Mama
Put Your Arms Around Me
I Belong to Him
God If I Only Could Write Your Love
    Song
Consider Me
There Ain't No Rain
God I Love You
Let It Go
Master Master
New Wine

OUTLAW/MANSFIELD NATIONAL CHARTS

SINGLES

WAYLON JENNINGS
"Amanda" (#1)
"I'll Go Back to Her" (#4)
"Can't You See" (#4)
"Are You Ready for the Country"(#7)
"So Good Woman" (#7)
"We Had It All" (#28)

JESSI COLTER
I'm Not Lisa (#1)
What's Happened to Blue Eyes (#5)
It's Morning and I Still Love You (#11)
I Thought I Heard You Calling My
    Name (#29)
I Belong to Him (With Roy Orbison and
    Waylon Jennings)

ALBUMS

WAYLON JENNINGS
Are You Ready For the Country (#1)
I've Always Been Crazy (#1)
The Ramblin' Man (#3)
Honky Tonk Heroes (#14)

TOMPALL GLASER
Tompall Glaser And His Outlaw Band
    (#38)

JESSI COLTER
I'm Jessi Colter (#3)
Jessi (#4)
Diamond in the Rough (#1)
Miriam (#29)

**WAYLON JENNINGS AND
    WILLIE NELSON**
Waylon & Willie (#1)

ADDITIONAL ALBUM DISCOGRAPHY

DEEP SIX
Deep Six
Liberty Records
1965

LARRY MURRAY
Sweet Country Suite
MGM/Verve Records
1970

SWAMPWATER
Swampwater
RCA Records
1971

DOYLE HOLLY
Doyle Holly
Barnaby Records
1973

CLAUDINE LONGET
Let's Spend The Night Together
Barnaby Records
1973

MARTY COOPER
A Minute Of Your Time
Barnaby Records
1973

SAND
Sand
Barnaby Records
1973

CONNY VAN DYKE
Conny Van Dyke
Barnaby Records
1973

THE HAGERS
Music On The Countryside
Barnaby Records
1973

RICK CUNHA
Songs
GRC Records
1974

DON HO
Home In The Country
Mega Records
1974

DUSTY DRAPES AND THE DUSTERS
Dusty Drapes And The Dusters
Columbia Records
1974

DOYLE HOLLY
Just Another Cowboy Song
Barnaby Records
1974

ROBB STRANDLUND
Robb Strandlund
Polydor Records
1975

GARY HILL BAND
Mountain Man
Capitol Records
1975

CM LORD
CM Lord
Capitol Records
1976

GARY HILL BAND
Booga Billy
Capitol Records
1976

**BYRON BERLINE AND
    SUNDANCE**
Byron Berline And Sundance
MCA Records
1976

CONNIE EATON
Connie Eaton
GRC Records
1977

CARTER ROBERTSON
Shoot The Moon
ABC Records
1978

SOUNDTRACK
Van Nuys Blvd
Mercury Records
1979

DAVID CASSIDY
Best Of David Cassidy
Curb Records (Japan)
1979/1991

LA COSTA
Changin' All The Time
Capitol Records
1980

NICK GILDER
Rock America
Casablanca Records
1980

RICK CUNHA
Moving Pictures
CBS Records
1980

OXO
OXO
Geffen Records
1982

JUDY FIELDS
Halfway to Paradise
Victory Records
1985

DAVID FRIZZELL
David Sings Lefty
Playback Records
1987

GAITHER VOCAL BAND
Homecoming
Star Song Records
1991

THE IMPERIALS
Big God
Star Song Records
1991

FLYING BURRITO BROS
Eye of the Hurricane
Sundown Records
1993

KEN MANSFIELD
MAGICAL MINISTRY TOURS

Ken's exciting outreach event gave us our biggest Saturday night attendance ever. We seat 2200 and packed it out!

Pastor Lincoln Brewster
Bayside Community Church
Sacramento CA

Ken Mansfield inspired our people. The story of his transformed life spoke to the entire congregation. I know he will be a blessing to your church."

Dr. David Jeremiah *(Turning Point)*
Shadow Mountain Church
El Cajon CA

God spoke to Parkside Church vicariously through the life of someone else. He sent in a prophet. The entire evening was a blessing.

Pastor Alistair Begg *(Truth for Life)*
Parkside Church
Cleveland OH

With his stories filled with pathos and contemporary applications, Ken delivers a powerful message of Christ's grace for our day.

Pastor Paul Sartarelli
The Chapel on Fir Hill
Akron OH

Ken knocked it out of the park at the Magnification event at Saddleback. A great time was had by all!

Pastor Rick Warren
Bucky Rosenbaum (*CEO Purpose Driven Ministries*)
Saddleback Church
Orange County CA

Ken is a velvet hammer; he is gentle and kind as can be, but pulls no punches when he talks about how he could never find the satisfaction he sought until he met Jesus. I recommend his ministry highly!

Pastor Bill Ritchie
Crossroads Community Church
Vancouver WA

We recently invited Ken to our mid week service—the attendance was spectacular and the ministry powerful. We were so excited about Ken that we brought him out to our Calvary Chapel Northwest Pastors Conference and, again, he was a huge hit with the six hundred pastors that were in attendance. This is a home run event!

Pastors Wayne Taylor/Brett William
Calvary Fellowship
Mt. Lake Terrace WA

For information on Ken's unique outreach ministry go to:
www.aubaycom.com

THE WHITE BOOK

Through exclusive photographs and uniquely crafted personal stories, former U.S. manager of Apple Records and Grammy Award-winning producer Ken Mansfield invites readers to know the characters of the Beatles and the musicians of their time-the bands that moved an industry and a culture to a whole new rhythm.

This engaging and unusual account spans some of the most fertile and intense decades in music history, including insight into celebrities such as Brian Wilson, Dolly Parton, Roy Orbison, Waylon Jennings, David Cassidy, and James Taylor. As the man who helped shape much of the music of the sixties and seventies, Ken Mansfield is in the rare position of observer, friend, and colleague of these sometimes quirky, sometimes ordinary, always talented individuals.

by Ken Mansfield

Ken Mansfield and I shared the experience of the famous Apple rooftop session. There is no one better equipped to tell the Beatles' story—factually, from the inside.

ALAN PARSONS
Alan Parsons Project Producer/Engineer to the Beatles/Pink Floyd

Ken was different, real California guy—the Beatles took to him straight away. He is one of the few insiders left that bore witness to the highs and lows of those insane days when we ruled the world.

JACK OLIVER
Former President of Apple Records International

I lived through the record industry's most exciting years with Ken. It is a pleasure to experience so much of it all again through the accuracy of his story telling and the clarity of his memory.

PETER ASHER
Peter & Gordon/A & R Chief Apple Records/Multi Platinum Producer

Ken has a unique gift. I respect the affection he has for our game, and what he brought to it, will get you.

ANDREW LOOG OLDHAM
Rolling Stones Manager and Producer

In his 'White Book" Ken Mansfield salutes The Beatles as only a true insider can. Ken's book is the time machine that can travel back to that age of innocence that truly changed the world.

ROBIN LEACH
Producer/Host, Lifestyles of the Rich & Famous

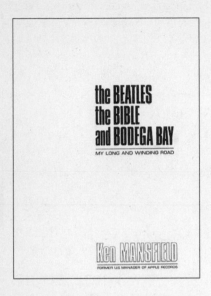

the BEATLES
the BIBLE
and BODEGA BAY

MY LONG AND WINDING ROAD

Ken MANSFIELD

FORMER U.S. MANAGER OF APPLE RECORDS

THE BEATLES
THE BIBLE
AND
BODEGA BAY

Ken Mansfield can write authoritatively about the music business of the sixties because he was there making it happen. As a young record label executive at Capitol Records, the Beatles were his clients, and they became his friends. Ken was handpicked by the Fab Four to be their first U.S. Manager of Apple Records and thrust into a world that would change his life forever.

Some thirty years later, Mansfield's spiritual memoirs are set against the backdrop of his personal and professional relationships with John, Paul, George and Ringo, offering an insider's view of the group collectively and individually. From his first meeting with the "lads", to rare glimpses of what it was like to be part of the Beatles inner sanctum, Mansfield offers a transparent and intimate look at the Beatles and the impact they had on his life. But that is only part of the story...

The Beatles, the Bible and Bodega Bay features never-before-seen photographs and memorabilia from Mansfield's personal collection and presents two portraits: the young man in London on top of the Apple building (and on top of the world!) as he watches the Beatles perform for the last time, and the older man on a remote Sonoma beach on his knees looking out to sea and into the heart of his Creator.

Amazon.com Rock Editor ranks The *Beatles the Bible and Bodega Bay* as one of the top two best Beatles books of all time second only to the Beatles' *Anthology*

To order or contact Ken directly visit:

www.aubaycom.com or
www.fabwhitebook.com